THE GERMAN COLONIAL EMPIRE

The German Colonial Empire

Woodruff D. Smith

THE UNIVERSITY OF NORTH CAROLINA PRESS
CHAPEL HILL

Copyright © 1978 by
The University of North Carolina Press
All rights reserved
Manufactured in the United States of America
ISBN 0-8078-1322-2
Library of Congress Catalog Card Number 77-18155

Library of Congress Cataloging in Publication Data

Smith, Woodruff D
    The German colonial empire.

    Bibliography: p.
    Includes index.
    1. Germany—Colonies—History.   2. Germany—
Politics and government—1871–1918. I.   Title.
JV2011.S63   325'.343   77-18155
ISBN 0-8078-1322-2

Contents

Preface

Germany acquired her overseas colonies during the period of massive European imperial expansion in the late nineteenth century, and she lost them less than a generation later during the First World War. Taken altogether, the German colonial empire was not inconsiderable. The most important German possessions were four African territories: Southwest Africa, Togo, Cameroon, and German East Africa. In addition, Germany controlled several territories in the Pacific: northeastern New Guinea, part of Samoa, the Bismarcks, the Marshalls, the Carolines, the Marianas, and Kiaochow on the Shantung Peninsula in China. On occasion the German colonies played an important part in the diplomatic history of the pre-1914 era and for brief periods were a major focus for political dispute within Germany. Yet by many obvious standards Germany's short colonial history was unimpressive. In comparison with the overseas possessions of Britain and France, Germany's colonies were small. Even more importantly, they were, with minor exceptions, economically unprofitable. Germany's trade with her colonies was an insignificant percentage of her total commerce, and by most material criteria of imperialist thinking, the German colonial empire was highly unsuccessful.

Nevertheless, the German overseas empire has historical importance. The German colonial expansion of the 1880s helped to set off the partition of Africa among the European powers, an event of obvious significance for African and European history.

The German interlude also played an important and complex role in the development of several African countries. This book, which is a summary history of the German colonial empire and of German colonialism, must consider these aspects of the subject, but they do not provide the continuous focus of the study.

This book will instead concentrate on the interaction between the German colonial empire and domestic German politics and, by extension, the connection between colonialism and major socioeconomic problems in Germany in the nineteenth and early twentieth centuries. Within the German political system the colonies created many issues for debate that surfaced during attempts to resolve much more fundamental domestic social disputes. Colonialism was one of the earliest and most important elements of German imperialism, which was itself a result of major social changes in Germany in the nineteenth century. The prime importance of the colonial empire to Germany lay neither with its negligible economic worth nor with its equally negligible strategic value but with its role as a source of political controversy and a means of building support in German politics.

Since German colonialism had at least as much to do with political realities in Germany as it did with the economic and administrative realities of the colonies, colonial policy tended to be framed in terms of German political conceptions and then imposed on colonial territories. This was true, for example, of the "period of reform" within the German colonial empire after 1906 and of the two quite separate, but equally inappropriate, policies that resulted in massive resistance in Southwest and East Africa in 1904 and 1905. In this way the domestic political aspect of German colonialism had a profound influence on the indigenous societies that made up the overseas empire.

The chapters that follow are intended to serve as a summary history of the German colonial empire and also to indicate some of the more important recent directions in German colonial historiography. The amount of work that has been done on aspects of German colonialism in the past fifteen years has been considerable.[1] It justifies the attempt to gather the various strands of research, including the author's own, into a single brief volume that will, it is hoped, be useful to students of German and African history and at the same time accessible to nonspecialists.

I should like to thank the following people for their advice and assistance at various stages in the preparation of this book: Roger Louis, Lewis Gann, and Sharon Turner, who read the text and offered suggestions; Ralph Austen, who has guided me throughout my studies of German colonialism; Veronica Ibarra and Sandra Rodriguez, who did the typing; H. Pogge von Strandmann and Henry Blair for permission to use their microfilms of *Kolonialamt* archives at the Hoover Institution; the staffs of the Hoover Institution and of the Frobenius-Institut of Frankfurt University; and my wife for her help and encouragement. Part of the research for this book was funded by a Summer Stipend from the National Endowment for the Humanities.

Abbreviations in Text

DHPG	*Deutsche Handels- und Plantagen-Gesellschaft*
DKGfSWA	*Deutsche Kolonialgesellschaft für Süd-West Afrika*
DOAG	*Deutsch-Ostafrikanische Gesellschaft* (German East Africa Company)
GfdK	*Gesellschaft für deutsche Kolonisation*
GSK	*Gesellschaft Süd-Kamerun*
KWK	*Kolonial-Wirtschaftliches Komitee* (Colonial Economic Committee of the German Colonial Society)
NGK	*Neu Guinea Kompagnie* (German New Guinea Company)
NWKG	*Nord West Kamerun Gesellschaft*
SPD	*Sozialdemokratische Partei Deutschlands* (Social Democratic party)

PART I

THE ORIGINS OF
GERMANY'S COLONIAL EMPIRE

1

Prelude to Empire

Bismarck's surprising acquisition of colonies between 1883 and 1885 was misinterpreted by contemporaries as the product of a brand-new colonialist movement. Actually, German colonialism was a result of social and political changes that had occurred over the course of the whole nineteenth century. Colonialism had been a subject of discussion in Germany since the beginning of the century, and distinct varieties of colonialist ideology had grown up by the 1870s as adjuncts to major trends in political thought. In this chapter we shall discuss first the political aspects of preacquisition German colonialism and then the socioeconomic factors that made colonialism a well-known, if minor, force in German political life.

The Political Background

The possibility of acquiring colonies was discussed at length at the Frankfurt National Assembly in 1848. The colonial proposals considered at Frankfurt, like most of those advanced in Germany in previous years, were tied to the problem of the *Aus-*

wanderung, the massive nineteenth-century emigration from Germany. They ranged from schemes for emigrant-protection societies to plans for outright German settlement colonies, usually in the United States.[1] The latter were based to some extent on actual attempts to establish settlements of Germans in North and South America, some of which had been reasonably successful. To the 1848 liberals the prime function of colonies was to receive the overflow of the German population that was represented by the *Auswanderung* and that was considered a severe problem in the southwestern German states. The liberals thought that colonies would also drain off lower-class people who had been displaced by changes in German agriculture; it was feared that these people would otherwise become a criminal, and possibly revolutionary, class.[2] The politicians of 1848 had just had some significant lessons in the revolutionary capabilities of an urban proletariat.

Some advocates of German colonization in 1848 also thought it essential that the new German state pursue an active foreign policy, including colonial expansion, as a method of uniting the sentiments of the nation. It is doubtful, however, whether colonialism in 1848 would have achieved this purpose. Its intellectual antecedents were concerned mainly with colonies in already established states overseas. As private concerns that did not challenge the sovereignty of the countries in which they existed, German colonies had functioned in Texas, Brazil, and other places.[3] The situation would have been totally different for colonies established by a German government, which would have desired a political relation with the territories that no foreign government would have tolerated. It was no accident that colonial proposals tended to be tied to the creation of a German navy that could be used to force foreign governments to accept the creation of colonies and regulation of emigration.

Even without the dissolution of the National Assembly, it is unlikely that any real action would have been taken to establish German colonies. Thinking on the subject was too vague to serve as the basis of consistent policy, and the majority of delegates apparently preferred legislation that attempted to improve traveling conditions for emigrants instead of schemes for colonization. Colonial advocates complained that this approach would do nothing about the loss of capital, manpower, and culture that the *Auswanderung* entailed. However, the general view was that of Assembly President Heinrich von Gagern (the son of an early colonial enthusiast) who believed that these arguments were meaningless except in terms of mobilizing public support for the new constitution.[4]

Perhaps most importantly, in 1848 no major interest groups, except a minority of western German liberals whose prominence in politics in 1848 was very temporary, supported colonial expansion. The state governments most in a position to effect a colonial policy—Prussia, Hamburg, and Bremen—were against the whole idea. Prussia, in which large-scale emigration was something new, had previously opposed efforts to do anything at all about the *Auswanderung*. In 1841 the ruling bodies of Hamburg had opposed a scheme put forward by one of the city's leading citizens, Karl Sieveking, for establishing both a colony in the Pacific and a united German navy.[5] As they continued to do through the 1880s, the elites of the Hanseatic cities believed that German colonial expansion would be perceived as a threat in England and would spoil their special relationship with Great Britain. Until the last quarter of the century, Hamburg and Bremen were basically entrepôts of trade between Britain and central Europe. Since their businessmen traded heavily with Britain and in areas in which they were protected by the British navy, Hanseatic politicians were sensitive about their dependency. The same desire to keep its position as middleman in the British–central European trade lay behind Hamburg's refusal for many years to join the *Zollverein*.

Also absent in 1848 were the great economic-interest organizations that later were major factors in the process of decision-making in Germany. Early industrialists such as Camphausen, Hansemann, and Mevissen were very active in liberal politics, but they did not form industrial pressure groups until later. Nor, for that matter, were the industrialists particularly interested in colonies. Most people perceived colonialism in 1848 as a solution to the problem of emigration. Colonialism was not yet popularly related to the needs of German industry, which was only beginning to emerge.

However, colonialism as a political idea did not die out after 1848. It remained a minor element of liberal nationalist political thought and retained its focus on the *Auswanderung*. Yet certain newer varieties of colonialism, linking the concept of overseas colonies with the new industrial sector of the German economy, did come to public attention after 1848. This was not originally a major trend, but it was occasionally found as a subsidiary aspect of colonial writings that followed the dominant line of emigrationist colonialism.

In the 1860s colonialism again became a public issue during the events in which Prussia unified Germany. Proposals that Germany acquire overseas colonies appeared in a number of places, apparently as a result of rekindled thinking about the possible consequences of a unified Germany and also as part of a campaign orchestrated by procolonial elements close to Bismarck—particularly Lothar Bucher, one of the chancellor's leading idea men in the Foreign Ministry, a former 1848 Liberal, and a colonialist. Bismarck himself remained publicly opposed to overseas colonies until the 1880s, but he was apparently willing to allow his assistants and some of his mouthpiece newspapers to appeal to sentiment in favor of colonies in order to rally support for unification in western Germany. In 1867 the *Norddeutsche Allgemeine Zeitung*, a newspaper under Bismarck's control, published a series of articles advocating vigorous overseas colonization by the North German Confederation.[6] The *Norddeutsche* essentially followed the traditional emigrationist view, even to the extent of suggesting settlement colonies in other sovereign countries. Probably inspired by Bucher, the articles were written not as much to advance colonialism as to direct colonialist sentiment toward the support of Bismarck. Bucher's own view of the reasons for acquiring colonies did not actually correspond to that set out in the articles; he was more interested in colonies as aids to industrial development than he was in emigration.[7]

Members of the Prussian military establishment also debated the question of colonial acquisition during and after the Franco-Prussian War. The leaders of the tiny Prussian navy suggested that Germany pick up French colonies—possibly including Indochina—as economic dependencies and as naval bases.[8] The implication for the navy was obvious: in order to protect the colonies, Germany would have to build a larger navy. Despite support for this position from some civilian publicists, neither Bismarck nor the leadership of the army was particularly impressed. The naval argument for colonies had little force in Germany until the 1890s.

With unification, colonialism took on a new aspect in German politics. Even before 1871 it had been argued that German economic integration through the *Zollverein* would eventually force Germany to seek her own overseas colonies.[9] It was thought that the *Zollverein* might come to be considered by Britain and other countries as an economic rival against whom informal sanctions, and possibly tariffs, would have to be levied. An adverse British reaction might exclude German merchants from trade with the British Empire and might create problems for Germany in areas of indirect British influence. Under these circumstances overseas colonies would become a necessity, at least as a guarantee of sources of raw materials that could not be acquired in trade with central Europe. Moreover, the economic area defined by the *Zollverein* eventually might not be large enough to support continuous industrial growth and might require expansion of markets overseas, perhaps through colonies.

These considerations became more urgent after 1871. The presence of a strong and united Germany in the middle of Europe had an extremely unsettling effect on international relations, which Bismarck spent the rest of his career attempting to counteract. The effect of German unification, especially when combined with intense international economic competition following the crash of 1873, was to give an unwonted importance to German colonialism and to relate colonialism to the interests of significant economic groups within Germany for almost the first time.

Two major, related sets of interest groups propagandized for German acquisition of economic colonies from the mid-1870s. In one category were organizations representing certain areas of commerce and industry, and in the other were Hanseatic tropical trading interests. The concerns of the two groups did not always correspond exactly. Most business interests did, however, share a basic desire for government protection in the face of the post-1873 depression and the threat of foreign competition.

Led by the Hamburg merchant Adolf Woermann, the tropical traders sought to stabilize trading conditions in West Africa and the South Pacific and to prevent the monopoly of their trading areas by the British and French. The trading interest put direct pressure on the government to declare protectorates in those areas and also to grant economic support to failing commerical firms.

Hanseatic tropical trading influence was generally exerted through the Foreign Office. The leaders of some of the major enterprises, including Woermann himself, were closely connected by friendship, business and political ties, and family relationships to key officials. They attempted to use these ties to promote an active colonial policy after 1879.[10] Their main contact was Heinrich von Kusserow, a Foreign Office counselor whom Bismarck put in charge of colonial affairs after his own conversion to colonialism. Kusserow was probably chosen for this role, not because Bismarck listened to his advice, but because he wanted to use Kusserow's business connections. When colonial acquisition did occur after 1883, the locations of Hanseatic trading interests often provided guides to the territories to be claimed. Colonialist thinking had in the past been directed toward various areas of the world, but most particularly toward South America. Primarily due to the influence of Woermann and his allies, German colonialism focused on areas of Africa and the South Pacific with potential for trade in tropical agricultural products but with little likelihood of supporting the kind of European settlement that many German colonialists sought.

Despite their political connections, however, the role of the Hanseatic merchants in creating the German overseas empire was severely circumscribed. Many of the tropical trading houses of Hamburg and Bremen, including Woermann's, were comparatively small and unprofitable in the 1870s. One of the largest, the Godeffroy firm, was approaching bankruptcy.[11] Hamburg did only a small amount of its total trade with the areas of future colonization. Furthermore, the tropical trading interest usually had little political clout, and most Hanseatic leaders still opposed colonies. Woermann's influence apparently counted for more in Berlin than in Hamburg, and even there Bismarck was under no obligation to respond to it.

The other major colonial interest group consisted of a number of organizations of businessmen and industrialists, many with financial interests in overseas trade and export-oriented manufacturing. Some companies had direct reasons for supporting colonialism. For example, the Bleichröder investment bank was one of Woermann's financial backers. Several other financial houses were apparently interested in safe (and possibly government-subsidized) investments in tropical areas; a few of them actually invested in colonial enterprises in the late 1880s, but not very many did and they did not invest extensively.[12] Part of the influence that the tropical trading interest exerted on the government was directed through big-business spokesmen with governmental connections. Nevertheless, the direct financial involvement of industry in tropical enterprises was limited. The major concerns of the chambers of commerce and other business interest groups that adhered to the colonial movement in the early 1880s were related to the general set of imperialist ideas of which colonialism was a part and to the role of those ideas in German politics rather than to the specific interests of German businessmen in particular areas.

Socioeconomic Change and Colonialist Ideology

Although industrialization was the major event of German economic history in the nineteenth century and a prime influence on German colonialism, it was not the only one. The emergence

of colonialism in the *Vormärz* period, both as a political movement and as a set of ideologies, resulted from economic and
social changes that preceded industrialization. In particular, the
restructuring of agriculture in many areas of Germany, which
caused massive cycles of emigration throughout the nineteenth
century, also helped to create a colonialist theory that looked to
overseas colonies as a solution to the problems of emigration.[13]
The initial agricultural restructuring in southwestern Germany
was interpreted by observers as overpopulation. It was believed
that rural society had simply produced too many people for the
economy to support and that some of the excess had to leave the
country. From a more modern standpoint we can perceive that
emigration was the product, not of absolute overpopulation, but
of the development of German agriculture toward larger-scale
capitalistic forms under severe economic pressure, compounded
by a gradual reduction in the size of independent farms through
their division among the sons of farmers.

Changes in the rural economy affected not only farmers but
also members of various occupational groups that existed on the
periphery of rural enterprise: retail shopkeepers, artisans, and
small-scale dealers in agricultural products. Together with farmers and farm laborers, these groups made up the bulk of *Aus-
wanderer*. The *Auswanderung*, accentuated by dislocations due to
industrialization after 1850, continued to occur in cycles throughout the century. After a period of intense emigration in the 1890s,
the *Auswanderung* declined precipitously as the German industrial economy reached maturity and became an importer of labor.

As we have seen, most early versions of German colonialism
concentrated on the utility of colonies as solutions to the problem of emigration. The connection between emigrationist colonialism and the *Auswanderung* was the main basis on which
middle-class support for colonialism rested. As a concept the
Auswanderung became an article of faith among the lower ranges
of the middle class, especially among the occupational groups
that supplied most of the emigrants. Freedom to emigrate if
conditions should become too unbearable was widely accepted

as the ultimate recourse of the lower orders of respectable society, and parties (such as the Progressive party in the 1860s) that emphasized continued freedom of emigration were supported by these groups. The same groups also tended to support emigrationist colonialism, since colonies offered an alternative to normal emigration that preserved both the German culture of the emigrants and their contributions to the German economy. Especially after 1871 and the growth of lower-middle-class nationalism, colonialism attained some popularity because it reconciled patriotism with freedom to desert Germany.

Another factor that affected the development of emigrationist colonialism was the social situation of its early liberal formulators. German liberalism, particularly in the *Vormärz* period, was notable for its exceedingly narrow base of support, largely limited to upper-middle-class groups whose status depended on traditional education: academics, lawyers, government officials, teachers, and so forth. The predominant connection between liberalism and significant business interests that existed in Britain and France was lacking in Germany until the mid-1840s. As a result, German liberalism developed a relatively conservative view of economic change and of industrialization. As representatives of a social order to whom economic development had no relevance and was possibly threatening, moderate German liberals were driven to be concerned with the social effects of industrialization even before it appeared on a large scale in Germany. Many of them expressed dismay at the effect of industrialization on German culture (over which their social type presided) and the relative valuation of classes.[14]

Partly an outgrowth of this uneasy attitude toward economic change, emigrationist colonialism was based to some extent on the liberals' concern for their social status but was given continuity and strength because of the responsive chord it struck among various sections of the lower middle class that were also threatened by economic change. To the moderate liberals settlement colonies appeared not only to be palliative measures applied to the general problem of emigration but also places where traditional life-styles and virtues could be maintained in the face of economic change.[15] They helped counteract the inevitable effects of industrialization.

The coming of large-scale industrialization created the economic and social basis for a whole range of political concepts, of which a new kind of colonialism was a part. Classical concepts of free trade and free enterprise had never been greatly favored by even the liberal sector of business leadership in Germany. The nature and timing of German industrialization were such that industrialist thinking tended to favor state action to construct transportation facilities, widen markets, remove restrictions on investment and industrial concentration, and protect German manufacturing against foreign competition. The Prussian, and after 1871 the Reich, government's policy of free trade was not entirely accepted by big business, and it was continued primarily because of agrarian producers' interest in free access to British markets before the mid-1870s. Business sentiment in favor of protection and concentration was advocated by proliferating chambers of commerce, export societies, and the like and by the *Centralverband deutscher Industrieller* (Central Association of German Industrailists) after 1876.[16] This process of interest-group formation took place throughout German manufacturing and finance as business attempted to control competition, present a united front to labor unions and socialist parties, and influence the making of political decisions.

The ideological prophet of many of these organizations of the 1860s and 1870s was Friedrich List, an economist who had committed suicide in 1847 but whose writings remained the cornerstone of a long line of proindustrial, protectionist economic thinking encompassing the idea of a central European customs union. During the First World War, List was considered a precursor of the idea of *Mitteleuropa* by its liberal imperialist supporters; in the 1860s his was the primary theoretical voice of industrial progress, protection, and the direct attachment of an industrial Germany to her own exclusive markets and sources of raw materials. His views were repeated by the spokesmen of many business organizations and by independent industrial protectionists such as Lothar Bucher.

The development of industry and industrial thinking gave rise to a new form of colonialism. This new form, first stated in detail in Germany by List himself, presented colonies, not as settlement areas, but as means of protecting Germany's markets and sources of raw materials from possible retaliation by foreign competitors against the import tariffs that List recommended for Germany. Of course, "economic" colonialism had many intellectual predecessors, but it entered German thinking with List and the beginnings of German industrialization.[17]

However, neither rapid industrialization nor the boom years immediately following the establishment of the German Empire in 1871 made colonialism, whether in its emigrationist or its economic form, a real force in politics; rather the depression that followed the worldwide financial crash of 1873 gave colonialism a political voice.[18] The depression—characterized by falling profits, increased costs of production, sluggish demand, and heightened international competition—led German industry to call much more vigorously for tariff protection and for a government drive to create new markets, in part to counteract the effects of protection. The depression also encouraged the concentration of German industry into large, multiunit conglomerations, closely connected with the major organs of German finance. Efforts to reduce competition, allocate markets and raw materials, and acquire state protection were accompanied in Germany by massive reinvestment in physical plants, introduction of technological innovations, and a major restructuring of industrial organization. In the long run the latter efforts were the basis of Germany's rapid overtaking of Britain as an economic power at the end of the century.

From the standpoint of colonialism, the most important result of the depression for industry was the redoubled effort by commercial interest groups to obtain generalized government support—which caused a focusing of industrial, protectionist attitudes into a formalized ideology that heavily emphasized economic colonies.[19] Industrial propagandists put forward for adoption by Germany an integrated set of proposals that included protective tariffs on manufactured imports, state action to restrict labor unions and to hold down wages, and an overseas "export offensive" to increase the size of markets. Within a system created by the acceptance of such proposals, colonies would perform two major functions: they would protect existing overseas markets and sources of raw materials from British retaliation, and they would increase effective German markets by organizing underdeveloped areas for trade and keeping foreign investment out. In a very real sense the colonialist aspect of the industrialist depression ideology was an intellectual necessity rather than a sign of actual interest in specific colonies. A colonial policy was needed to complete the logic of the protectionist system and to make it appear reasonable to public opinion. This was where the Hanseatic trading interests converged with industrial interests over the adoption of a joint depression ideology and mode of approach. Colonial acquisition, which nevertheless continued to be regarded as vital by the tropical trading interest, was to depression-plagued industry one part of a more general set of aims; it was important for political purposes but not really vital. And industry's view eventually got across to the government.

The type of colony envisioned by the economic colonialists of the 1870s was the classical trading colony—in which European merchants, protected by a minimal governmental presence, would trade with indigenous societies or develop extractive industries.[20] With a few exceptions large European settlements were not included within the general scheme of economic colonialism, which in its socioeconomic origins and internal logic radically diverged from the emigrationist colonial line.

Yet the depression affected many groups besides the leaders of German industry, and the reactions of some of those other groups transformed German colonialism from a set of concepts into political reality. For example, the protectionist movement would certainly not have succeeded if the depression and American agricultural competition had not also undermined the economic position of the Prussian landowning class, changing the influential Junkers into supporters of agricultural tariffs that would protect their domestic grain market. The stage was therefore set for an alliance between big industry and big Prussian agriculture to establish a comprehensive system of tariffs. This alliance was manifested politically by the "league of rye and iron": the formal recognition of joint interests by the large organizations of industry and those of Prussian agriculture and the establishment of an arrangement between part of the National Liberal and Conservative parties in the Reichstag.[21] The alliance both strengthened Bismarck's hand and required of him a new political course.

The new course was made public in 1879 when Bismarck changed his economic stance; repudiated the past policies of the free-trader commerce minister, Rudolf von Delbrück, who had resigned in 1876; and established a schedule of protective tariffs for both manufactured goods and agricultural products. The tariff policy of 1879 is usually taken as the key element in the process that led to overseas empire because of the connection in industrial ideology between protection and the abstract concept of trading colonies and because, for the first time in German history, a powerful alliance of interests that supported colonial acquisition existed. It should be noted that in industrial-protectionist thinking colonies were to be only one part of a more general attempt to widen markets, especially in central Europe. The connection between economic colonialism and economic imperialism in *Mitteleuropa* continued to be important well into the twentieth century.

Of course, the depression also affected the tropical trading interests of Hamburg and Bremen, causing the actual or near failure of a number of companies. The companies trading in West Africa were especially conscious of their vulnerability to changes in the attitude of the British government toward German commerce because of the informal British paramountcy in the area.[22] Given Germany's turn to protection, it was conceivable that the British government might intervene to destroy German trade in West Africa, either by occupying part of the coast or by pressuring West African states not to trade with the Germans. Some British companies, such as Goldie's Niger conglomerate, would presumably have liked nothing better than to see their competition reduced. Furthermore, both Britain and France might have reacted to German protectionism in concert, with the West African coast offering an ideal location for joint action against German economic interests.

Both the Hamburg trading group led by Woermann and their sympathizers in the Foreign Office were afraid of exactly this sort of Anglo-French action and tended to read into any hint of agreement between Britain and France over African issues a threat to German commercial interests.[23] The exaggerated fears of the Hanseatic tropical traders were one of the prime elements in the situation that resulted in the declaration of German protectorates in Togo and Cameroon in 1883 and 1884.

The Great Depression of 1873–96 also impinged on the larger groups in German society. Although it affected the industrial working class, the depression in the long run saw increasing real wages and standards of living for labor. This was not the case with the lower middle class (small-scale shopkeepers, white-collar employees, farmers, and skilled workers in the traditional areas of manufacturing), who were among the hardest hit by the depression. Falling profit margins struck them directly, and for the most part they could not respond, either by massive reinvestment or by influencing the government through pressure organizations. The only political party that came close to representing their interests, the Progressive party, was comparatively weak and perpetually opposed to Bismarck.

The Progressives saw themselves as the spokesmen of classical liberalism, with its emphasis on free enterprise, individual freedom, and limited governmental regulation of the economy.[24] This approach was never without adherents in Germany, but in order to make itself effective in politics, the party had to retain the support of either a numerous group of people or a significant one. The traditional supporters of the Progressives were the broad lower middle classes, to whom the party's left-liberal ideology had originally appealed. During the long economic crisis that began in 1873, lower-middle-class faith in the efficacy of liberalism was severely strained, and the Progressives were slow to change their thinking to respond to the new situation. Although the Progressives retained their popularity into the 1880s, there existed a strong doubt among their supporters concerning the effectiveness of the Progressive ideology; this doubt could be exploited by Bismarck and by the right in order to weaken the Progressives' sources of strength.

The depression was also one of the reasons that the lower middle class, many of whose members considered themselves to be threatened with loss of income and social standing through further industrialization, became increasingly a base of support for new antiliberal, antiindustrial, radically conservative movements.[25] The experiences of the *Mittelstand* during the depression helped to radicalize part of that class, opening it to political manipulation by interest groups willing to capitalize on growing antiindustrial feeling.

Lower-middle-class reaction to the depression provided one of the forces that led Germany to acquire colonies. The depression discredited liberal economic thinking among part of the *Mittelstand* and installed the general ideology of protection—domestic and foreign—as the dominant middle-class economic attitude. However, much more important was the impetus given to the spread and acceptance of emigrationist colonialism.

By striking hard at the traditional middle classes' modes of living, the depression both accelerated the decline of preindustrial social forms and encouraged a renewed spurt of emigration, especially among lower-middle-class occupational groups. Emigrationist colonialism was an existing set of concepts that suddenly took on new apparent meaning in a major socioeconomic crisis because it appealed to middle-class discontent with industrialism and provided discrete proposals for action to ameliorate problems of social decline. Emigrationist colonialism was explicitly dissociated from the ideologies that emphasized large-scale industrial development. It combined a positive view of the advantages to Germany of emigration and the need to keep the option of emigration open—always a popular view among the lower middle class and especially so in times of economic distress—with an appeal to German nationalism, which was increasingly felt by the same class. Not only were colonies believed to be a necessary symbol of any nation's strength, but they also offered a haven against the social effects of industrialization. According to colonial publicists, Germany's strength depended on the traditional virtues of her ordinary people (i.e. preindustrial middle-class people). If, for the moment, these virtues were threatened with extinction through the destruction of the modes of social existence that nurtured and maintained them, the solution was to establish overseas colonies for German settlers where preindustrial forms of social and economic activity could be pursued.[26] Emigrationist colonialism, then, although originally a theory developed by liberal intellectuals as a response to emigration, became politically effective in the 1870s and 1880s as an expression of lower-middle-class discontent with current conditions. In the process it lost most of its connection with liberalism and provided Bismarck an opportunity to separate the left liberals from their electoral support by backing colonial acquisition.

To be sure, many of those who supported emigrationist colonialism clearly did so, not because of concern for the lower middle class or because they wanted to attack any particular political party, but because they desired the establishment of colonies for personal and financial reasons. In recognition of the new potential of emigrationist colonialism, many of the interest groups favoring tropical trading colonies began in the early 1880s to include emigrationist arguments in their propaganda. Industrial and commercial interests, in other words, used the popularity of a moderately antiindustrial form of colonialism in order to benefit themselves.

Nevertheless, it would be incorrect to assume that the prime supporters of emigrationist colonialism during the period of colonial enthusiasm in the late 1870s and 1880s were cynical propagandists of industry's point of view. This is evident from a close examination of the writings of leading colonial publicists such as Friedrich Fabri and Wilhelm Hübbe-Schleiden and from an investigation of their careers in the later colonial movement. As we shall see, these men clearly took the emigrationist ideology seriously and advocated colonial policies that were quite different from those that business spokesmen favored.[27]

As we have seen, the ideological aspect of colonialism is of paramount importance in understanding the process of German overseas expansion, since ideologies involving colonies translated group reactions to social phenomena into prescriptions for political action. We have discerned the creation of two distinct trends in German colonialist ideology during the nineteenth century. One of these, which we have called the "emigrationist" or "settlement" ideology, grew out of early concern for the problems of emigration and proposed a view of colonies as areas for white farming settlement. The alternative view looked upon colonies as trading areas and adjuncts to the German economy, hence the term used in the following chapters: "economic" colonialism. The difference between these two points of view makes them important terms of reference for explaining colonial politics in Germany both before and after the period of acquisition.[28]

2

The Seizure of the Colonies

Germany acquired colonies between 1883 and 1885 as the result of a sudden diplomatic gambit that Bismarck carried through with characteristic surprise and thoroughness. Many political circumstances, including the formation of an organized colonial movement between 1879 and 1884, impelled Bismarck to this action.

Origins of the German Colonial Movement

In the 1860s and 1870s several organizations that had the acquisition of colonies among their aims were founded. Of these perhaps the best known was the *Central-Verein für Handels-Geographie und deutsche Interesse in Ausland*, formed in 1868 by overseas trading interests that included Adolf Woermann and several of his Hamburg associates. This organization and the similar *Verein für Handels-Geographie* of Leipzig were concerned primarily with the development of new markets for German manufactured goods and related geographical research, as the title of the *Central-Verein's* magazine—*Der Export*—attests. These and similar groups established during the 1870s were the vanguard of the movement calling for an "export offensive," a deliberate government-sponsored policy of economic expansion and imperialism in competition with Britain.[1] They were the ancestors of the *Kolonialverein* of the 1880s and its successor, the German Colonial Society (*Deutsche Kolonialgesellschaft*).

However, the real growth of organized colonialism did not occur until the depression of the late 1870s, when Germany's switch to protection called forth attempts to create new, active colonial organizations. Typical of these was the *Westdeutsch Verein für Kolonisation und Export*, founded in 1880 by Friedrich Fabri, the inspector of the Barmen Rhine Mission in Southwest Africa.[2] Fabri attempted to bring together into one society not only spokesmen of commercial and missionary interests who had been involved in some of the older organizations but also people without direct interests in establishing German hegemony over particular areas—people who largely thought of colonies in terms of the emigrationist model. Most of the new organizations followed the emigrationist line as a means of engaging public support among the middle classes. The potential political importance of the new colonialist organizations was not lost on Bismarck and his associates, nor did it escape the attention of business interests anxious to have the government support their enterprises abroad. Therefore, both convinced emigrationists and many to whom emigration was relatively unimportant combined to support organizations that put forward essentially emigrationist colonial propaganda, among other things.

There was also, however, colonialist propaganda based on economic and commercial assumptions. Regardless of the formal statements of colonialist organizations, the really telling arguments to the government and to business were those that showed the necessity of trading colonies to protect German investments and to expand German markets.[3] At the same time many of the supporters of economic colonialism were also interested in rallying public opinion to encourage government action in the world economy. Emigrationist colonialism, as a moderately popular and familiar ideology, could be used for this purpose, since it seemed to justify a colonial expansion that could in turn justify a large number of economically expansionary policies. As far as plans for acquiring specific areas were concerned, however, theories more directly attuned to the specific interests of the groups actually engaged in tropical trade were applied. This naturally resulted in the seizure of territories that were of use primarily as trading colonies and not as settlement areas for emigrants.

The leaders of the German colonial movement, sensing a favorable climate of public opinion after 1880, concluded that their case could be advanced if they combined into one great colonial organization. Colonialists of all stripes supported the idea— although some of the more radically nationalist and conservative feared that the union would be unduly controlled by particular economic interests, especially traders. Despite these misgivings the *Kolonialverein* was formed in December 1882, and almost immediately commenced to propagandize for colonies and to lobby for them with the Reichstag and the major parties.[4] The *Kolonialverein* participated in an attack on the Progressive party and the Center party for spearheading the Reichstag's refusal to pass subsidies for a Samoan steamship line—a budgetary item sponsored by Bismarck that the colonialists rightly saw as a sign that the government would support colonial expansion.

The formation of a large, national colonialist organization did not mean that all the colonialists automatically assembled under the same roof. During the critical years in which the overseas empire was established, Carl Peters and a number of other colonial enthusiasts remained aloof from the *Kolonialverein* and formed their own establishment, the *Gesellschaft für deutsche Kolonisation* (GfdK), which actually claimed territory in East Africa and became involved in trade.[5] Despite its commercial activities, however, the GfdK emphasized emigrationism and settlement in its propaganda, and it opposed the influence of established commercial interests in the colonialist organizations.

The *Kolonialverein* was replaced in 1887 by a new organization, the German Colonial Society (*Deutsche Kolonialgesellschaft*), which was formed from the *Kolonialverein* and the GfdK.[6] The Colonial

Society remained the main independent colonial organization throughout the period of the overseas empire and after 1918.

The colonialist organizations not only propagandized for German colonial expansion but also created in the public mind the images of colonialism and the value of overseas possessions that characterized a significant segment of colonialist opinion for many years. Three of the major formulators of the ideas put forward by the colonialist organizations from 1879 to 1884 were Friedrich Fabri, Wilhelm Hübbe-Schleiden, and Carl Peters.

Fabri, a missionary and one of the best-known German colonial activists, published in 1879 his most famous book, *Bedarf Deutschland der Colonien?* (*Does Germany Need Colonies?*). The book initially centered on consequences of the world economic crisis for all aspects of European society. If Germany were to survive in a highly competitive world, it had to secure its material base by developing economic areas overseas that were bound to the fatherland. Having introduced his subject according to the economic analysis favored by big business, Fabri immediately dropped that line of discussion and adopted the accepted emigrationist version of colonialism,[7] which held that colonies should be settlements of German farmers and small bourgeois located in temperate countries with an agricultural economy and a traditional middle-class society. The population overflow caused by the natural vigor of the German race could be directed to the colonies, which would save the emigrants' capabilities for Germany and would prevent their de-Germanization. Fabri clearly implied that Germany's competitive strength lay, not with industry and manufacturing, but with the virtues of the German people themselves—middle-class virtues that had to be protected by the creation of colonies. Fabri's thinking was in fact so traditional that he repeated the old concept of a German colony in the midst of another sovereign state. His favorite location for colonies was in the temperate region of South America, and he implied that German military power should be used to create them.

Fabri was unquestionably sincere in his advocacy of settlement colonialism, unlike some other colonialists who used it to cover personal commercial interests. At the founding meeting of the *Kolonialverein*, Fabri strongly defended the settlement conception of colonies and the connection among colonial acquisition, emigration, and overpopulation from attack by people who thought that colonies should follow only the trading model.[8] To the end of his life, he continued to inveigh against what he believed to be Bismarck's "misdirection" of German colonialism into purely commercial channels. In his very last speech, in 1891, Fabri called once again for German settlements in South America.[9]

Hübbe-Schleiden, whose ideas were similar to Fabri's, if more violently expressed, was a Hamburg lawyer, explorer, and nationalist politician. He possessed financial interests in a number of tropical trading concerns and was a political ally of Woermann. Hübbe-Schleiden's commercial motives did not, however, appear very often in his colonialist writings, which were devoted to downplaying the commercial and industrial sides of German life and to emphasizing the heroic, cultural, and agricultural aspects.[10] Industry was an evil, necessary because it was a constituent of power but something to be held carefully in check because of its potential for social and cultural damage. To Hübbe-Schleiden there existed a permanent state of war among the nations and races of the earth. England was Germany's main enemy, and inevitably only one could survive the struggle between them. Hübbe-Schleiden's attitude toward England verged on paranoia, and even his friends obliquely indicated that he was probably a little mad.[11] Nevertheless he enjoyed a brief period of popularity as a colonial publicist and as one of the first prominent German radical nationalists.

Hübbe-Schleiden's version of emigrationist colonialism was not original, but he clearly stated many of the implications of the theory. Colonies were necessary to prevent the degeneration of the German people through industrialization and the sapping of Germany's strength through emigration. Rather than following the example of England, where the typical person had become a crass materialist and a cog in an industrial machine, Germany should establish colonies that would, he thought, maintain German culture and prevent its decline.

Hübbe-Schleiden clarified the meaning of *cultural loss* through *Auswanderung*, one of the main props of the emigrationist theory. To Hübbe-Schleiden *culture* as intellectual activity and as a collection of social traits directly depended on *culture* in the sense of agriculture. The most basic and important parts of human society, the most necessary economic activities, were agriculture and the occupations that supported it. It followed that the human traits, social organizations, and ideas most essential to the health and power of the nation were those directly related to a traditional agrarian economy. The threat to German culture posed by the *Auswanderung* was not just the loss of individual national identity or numbers of Germans but also the loss of the *kind* of people who were the products of a traditional agrarian society. The virtues of this social type were lost with the people, and the increasingly materialistic and commercial society of Germany could not replace them. Hübbe-Schleiden believed that colonies would permit the maintenance of this most valuable social type in a nonindustrial setting. The "heroic" German with his agrarian culture would prosper in the colonies, and Germany would be able to continue on its road to greatness and dominance. Colonialism was, of course, not the only answer, but it was a convenient starting point. Trading colonies, which were useless for this purpose, should be only a minor concern of national policy.

The most famous colonial publicist of all was Carl Peters. In the early 1880s Peters was a young man with a brand-new doctorate and connections with overseas trading companies. Having absorbed some of the more radical strains of British colonial ideology during a stay in England, Peters received the writings of Fabri and Hübbe-Schleiden with a passion and returned to Germany to find a widespread colonial enthusiasm in full swing. He contributed a number of forceful, if somewhat simplistic, articles to the corpus of colonialist propaganda, and finding the *Kolonialverein* too much devoted to words rather than deeds, he established his own organization, the *Gesellschaft für deutsche Kolonisation*. Peters is a difficult character to assess. He was genuinely interested in advancing Germany's position in the world and seemed sincerely to have believed in settlement colonialism, but he was also out to make a fortune. His actions in East Africa were intended to ensure not only that Germany would have a colonial empire but also that he would get his cut.

Despite Peters's obvious personal interest in colonial acquisition, he became the leading exponent of colonialism as a personal sacrifice for the national good. In Peters's formulation the need for colonies was a simple matter of physics: people naturally moved from areas of high to areas of low population density.[12] Germans living in overpopulated Germany had to move somewhere, and if Germany were to retain the productive power of the emigrants and protect their culture, colonies were a necessity. Although Peters and his associates did establish colonial trading enterprises, the propaganda that they issued was couched in terms of large-scale agricultural settlement.[13]

Therefore, during the period of intensified colonialist propaganda in the early 1880s, the majority of the statements made by colonialists to elicit public (i.e. middle-class) support followed the settlement colonialist line. However, the amount of actual influence that settlement colonialism had on Bismarck, on the German government, and on business interests that supported colonial acquisition was probably quite limited. Among these people the economic view of colonies was more popular. Envisioned as reserved trading areas that would protect German markets, ensure access to raw materials, and serve as new outlets for German manufactured goods, economic colonies in theory required little expense and risk to the government. Profitability, again in theory, was to be the criterion for colonial success.[14] As we have seen, economic colonialism was linked to a more extensive economic imperialist ideology that in turn represented the desires of exporting industries for generalized governmental support. Economic colonialism was a relatively minor aspect of the larger ideology and was of direct concern mainly to the tropical trading interests. Since more public support obviously existed for settlement colonialism, economic colonialism's adherents benefited by playing down their differences with the emigrationists and by making it appear that trading colonies would satisfy the emigrationists' requirements. The lack of distinction between the two views in the early 1880s allowed the business interests and Bismarck simultaneously to achieve the kind of colonial policy they wanted and to elicit emigrationist support.[15]

Others, such as missionaries and explorers, had their own vested interests in supporting colonial expansion, but by and large their influence was small. German missionaries were not an organized force and traditionally worked closely with foreign missionary societies. The major exception was Fabri, whose Barmen Rhine Mission had campaigned for a protectorate in Southwest Africa since the 1860s. But Fabri was influential as a publicist, not as a mission inspector, and his avid support of settlement colonialism was not typical of missionary opinion.[16] Explorers like Ernst von Weber and Gustav Nachtigal joined general-interest organizations like the *Kolonialverein* rather than forming narrow exploration societies.

By 1883 the colonial movement was an organized and vocal force in German politics. By itself, however, it could not have caused Germany to claim an overseas empire. Rather, it created a situation in which it appeared advantageous for Bismarck to drop his former opposition to German protectorates in Africa and the Pacific. Bismarck's motives were extremely complex, and they were of great importance in determining the direction of German colonialism even after the period of acquisition.

Bismarck and Overseas Expansion

Bismarck's reasons for claiming a colonial empire have been debated for many years, but general agreement about them among historians has not appeared. It is unlikely, in fact, that Bismarck himself would have been able to explain them in a completely consistent manner. Nevertheless, over the years has emerged a series of parallel interpretations, some combination of which probably constitutes the best approximation to Bismarck's motivation that can be produced.

One interpretation sees Germany's grab for colonies as a diplomatic move on Bismarck's part to secure Germany's international position by embroiling Britain and France in a colonial scramble, or alternatively to protect Germany against a possible Anglo-French alliance against German interests.[17] There is considerable evidence that Bismarck, a trained diplomat who tended to visualize political questions in international terms, perceived in German colonial expansion an opportunity to maintain the level of tension between France and Britain created by Britain's occupation of Egypt in 1882, thereby preventing an Anglo-French accord without much danger of war between them. It is, however, unlikely that Bismarck would have changed his previously negative view of colonies and would have committed the German government to unpredictable administrative expenses and diplomatic adventures without simultaneously, and even primarily, expecting domestic political advantages. Other less expensive means existed of creating a moderate amount of discord between Britain and France.

A second major approach to Bismarck's motives takes at face value the claim that Bismarck thought the seizure of colonies necessary to protect German mercantile interests. There were many attempts to influence Bismarck and some of his advisors by companies and individuals with financial interests in tropical trade.[18] Woermann, a member of the Reichstag, corresponded with Bismarck, and Kusserow communicated some trading influence from Hamburg. One of the events that apparently set off the actual declaration of protectorates was an exchange of correspondence between Bismarck and Adolf Lüderitz, a tobacco merchant with interests in Southwest Africa. Bismarck's advocacy of a subsidy for a Samoan steamship company in the early 1880s was partly intended to assist the Godeffroy trading house, just as the declaration of a protectorate over northeastern New Guinea in 1883 was occasioned by the interests of the banker Adolf von Hansemann in the area. Except for Hansemann, however, these were tiny and politically weak interests.[19] Woermann's influence in Hamburg, for example, was not extensive, and he was certainly not a mover and shaker of Reichstag politics. At most, the trading interest managed to convince Bismarck that, contrary to his previous opinion, formal colonies would benefit at least some segments of the economy, however minor, and would not necessarily involve much government expense. If the extent of German colonial involvement were kept strictly limited, the trading companies themselves could conduct most governmental functions at their own expense. The traders and Kusserow also convinced Bismarck that Anglo-French agreements concerning spheres of influence in West Africa were the first steps toward formal colonization, which would eventually lead to the squeezing out of German merchants from markets in West Africa.[20] Such an occurrence would not have been disastrous for Germany, but it would have been at least annoying.

Another related interpretation emphasizes the role of overseas colonies in the overall scheme of the nationalist, protectionist economic policy that Germany adopted in 1879. Bismarck's switch to protection was taken as a signal that a new idea of national economics, which included the concept of colonies, was installed in ruling circles. It took some time, however, before Bismarck himself concluded that colonies were a necessary part of the new policy. Although it has been argued that his conversion to colonialism may have occurred earlier, not until 1880 did he come out for an overseas economic policy (the sponsorship of the Samoan steamship subsidy) that could be identified as a first step toward colonialism.[21] The timing of Bismarck's actions seems to indicate that after he was sold on the advantages of protectionist economics, he adopted a colonial policy because the orthodox theory of industrial protectionism included colonies. The influence of business interests in convincing Bismarck of the need for protection and an export offensive therefore brought about colonial expansion. Once again, however, considering the minor role of colonialism within protectionist politics and Bismarck's essential opposition to colonies, it seems unlikely that this explanation is adequate by itself. It does, however, explain why Bismarck viewed colonies solely from an economic standpoint and opposed the establishment of settlement colonies.

Most of the recent scholarship on the origins of Germany's colonial empire has emphasized the domestic political aspect of Bismarck's action: it appears practically certain that any explanation must give to political motives a large, and probably dominant, part. In an extension of the last interpretation noted above, Hans-Ulrich Wehler has argued that colonial acquisition was one part of Bismarck's policy of "social imperialism," a bogus policy intended to solidify business and middle-class opinion behind Bismarck and the threatened conservative forces that he represented.[22] Wehler argues that Bismarck took advantage of the protectionist ideology created by business propagandists in the late 1870s and through gestures such as claiming colonies that fit protectionist requirements but also seemed to offer little likelihood of government expense, Bismarck tried to show that business and middle-class interests were well served by a conservative, Junker-oriented government. This interpretation probably does relate Bismarck's colonial policy to one of his long-range political aims, but it does not account for the role of the specifically colonialist organizations (especially the *Kolonial-verein*) in colonial expansion, nor does it explain the significance of emigrationist colonialism. The continued importance of emigrationist colonialism even after acquisition, despite its weak basis in economic reality, is a problem that will recur throughout this study.

A different line of approach can be taken through examining the specific political circumstances surrounding colonial expansion. Bismarck himself wrote in 1885 that "because of domestic policy the colonial question is a vital problem for us." He continued, "public opinion in Germany so strongly emphasizes colonial policy that the position of the German government essentially depends on its success."[23] If the statement can be taken at face value, it indicates that Bismarck's policy was merely a response to public pressure in favor of colonies. However, the situation was not that simple. The number of actual colonial enthusiasts who joined or supported organizations was fairly small, and colonial enthusiasm was apparently limited to certain sections of the middle class.[24] Bismarck, who had taken on the entire Catholic church in the previous decade, could surely have found the resources to ignore the colonialists. Also, it is quite clear that Bismarck actually encouraged the efforts of "respectable" organizations like the *Kolonialverein*. Bismarck was manipulating as well as responding.

The objective behind his manipulation can be seen in Bismarck's attempts to get the Reichstag to provide financial backing for a Samoan steamship company as a step in German economic penetration of the South Seas. The attempt was beaten back by the opposition of the Center, the Progressives, and the Social Democrats, but the opposition was led by the left-liberal Progressives (*Freisinnige Partei*).[25] Bismarck regarded the Samoan subsidy as a means of obtaining Reichstag approval of his new policy of trade expansion and commercial protection, and he clearly believed that the still-powerful Progressives could do his administration great damage by attacking his policy. The subsidy was attacked by the Progressives on two grounds: it was too expensive, and it worked to the advantage of narrow business interests, not those of the whole nation. Against the threat of this kind of attack, the accuracy of which Bismarck was all too aware, he apparently shifted to full-fledged support of colonialism. In it he saw a way, not only of passing the Samoan subsidy, but also of doing permanent damage to the Progressives by using the colonial movement to detach the Progressives from their popular support.

The appeal of the Progressives rested on their adherence to classical liberal ideology, which gave them and their leader, Eugen Richter, a highly effective base from which to attack Bismarck's policies. But the Progressives depended heavily on voting support from the middle and lower ranges of the German bourgeoisie: from the groups, in other words, hardest hit by the economic depression and with the strongest vested interest in *Auswanderung*.[26] To this group the propagandists of emigrationist colonialism appealed, just at a time when the validity of the Progressives' ideology was open to sharp questioning by

their supporters; this questioning shortly led to the decline of
the party as a political force. By encouraging the hopes of the
organized colonialist movement that was mostly committed to
settlement colonies and by actually moving to acquire colonies,
Bismarck placed the Progressives in a dilemma that he hoped
would accelerate their decline. Although their longtime advocacy of free emigration had always gained them middle-class
support, their orthodox liberal opposition to colonies lost them
votes, since the colonial movement under Bismarck portrayed
them as opponents of the best and most patriotic solution to the
emigration problem. However, in order to use the colonial movement, Bismarck had in fact to establish some colonies. He did so
by accepting the advice of the tropical trading interests concerning the best locations for protectorates in West Africa and
their assurances that the new colonies would cost Germany practically nothing.

Bismarck's political motives can be seen in his actions concerning the one colonial enterprise that he had not planned—
Carl Peters's declaration of a protectorate over the coast of East
Africa (present-day Tanzania). Peters had broached his plan to
Bismarck and the Foreign Office. The reaction had been ambivalent at best, but Peters had received a tentative go-ahead.[27]
While Peters was preparing to set off from Zanzibar in 1884 to
obtain recognition from mainland chiefs of the German emper-
or's sovereignty, he received a cable from Bismarck ordering
him to call off the expedition. Peters ignored the cable, went
ahead with his project, and proclaimed a German protectorate.
Bismarck was then faced with the dilemma of whether or not to
recognize the claims made by Peters. Bismarck did not want to
get involved in the complicated politics of East Africa or to challenge the British in an area that had previously been regarded as
a clear British sphere of influence. He also predicted that the
German presence would involve much greater expense than he
was willing to endure.[28] The precedent existed for repudiating
or ignoring Peters, as Bismarck had done in the case of Fabri's
claims in Southwest Africa in 1868, but Bismarck went along
with Peters—with great misgivings that were fully justified by

later events—because of Peters's status as the new hero of the German colonial movement. Bismarck, moreover, could not repudiate the East African claim as unsuitable for the kind of colony he had in mind because it would have made clear something that he preferred to leave obscure: Germany's new colonies were not compatible with the popular settlement colonialist image, and the chancellor had no intention of picking up additional territories that were compatible. Bismarck's motives in acquiring colonies were complex and varied, but it appears from the available evidence that the basic impetus to expansion is to be found in domestic politics and Bismarck's attempt to manipulate them.

Bismarck's conception of an ideal German colony, to which he held under great pressures for change after 1885, was essentially the classical trading colony. He had been persuaded that such a colony could be operated at minimum expense: it would be a reserved trading area in which German commercial interests already existed and in which the government would merely maintain internal peace and prevent other European powers from taking over. Bismarck hoped that recourse to force would be infrequent. Since the direct beneficiaries of the declaration of German protectorates would be the trading companies doing business there, the companies would take responsibility for government and development.[29] Colonial rule would normally involve the enforcement of German sovereignty over a pre-existing and self-regulating system of trading relations. By implication, heavy reliance would be placed on native political and economic structures. In places such as Southwest Africa, where the development of mining was expected or where native social structures were inadequate for German purposes, single companies could be given exclusive rights to develop and govern large areas at their own expense.

The actual pattern varied. In Togo and Cameroon, the two West African protectorates, long-standing European trading arrangements existed, and Bismarck expected that a consortium of the trading companies could perform most governmental functions. In Southwest Africa, Bismarck granted concessionary rights to Adolf Lüderitz for the development of part of the area. In East Africa, Bismarck initially granted a concession to the GfdK, although in 1887 the concession was transferred to a more substantial company. In northeast New Guinea and adjacent islands, which were declared a protectorate at the request of Adolf von Hansemann of the *Diskonto-Gesellschaft*, a concession was granted to the German New Guinea Company, a new organization founded partly with Hansemann money.[30]

Bismarck selected areas for colonization and developed his theory of limited colonial administration partly because he wanted to avoid costs but partly also because he accepted economic colonialism as a segment of economic imperialist ideology. As we have seen, his conceptions did not correspond to the emigrationist colonialism of most colonial publicists and of procolonial opinion, and the colonies that he claimed were clearly not suitable for large-scale German settlement, except perhaps for Southwest Africa. Bismarck simply excluded settlement colonialism from practical consideration.

Fabri and the other advocates of settlement colonialism went along with Bismarck's moves since they could hardly oppose government action to accomplish some of the things for which the colonial movement had been campaigning for years. They hoped, however, that the momentum achieved by the initial spurt of colonial acquisition would lead also to the occupation of areas that were suitable for settlement. The emigrationist colonial theory did not, after all, exclude trading colonies; it merely considered them to be secondary. After a few years, when it became clear that Bismarck had no intention of supporting massive colonial settlement, Fabri attacked government policy publicly for disappointing the expectations of the colonial movement.[31] This posed a political problem for Bismarck since it threatened him with the choice of extending Germany's colonial endeavors, to which he was opposed for good financial reasons, or courting the opposition of the colonialists. Bismarck was not the last German chancellor to use popular imperialist sentiment for limited purposes and then to be trapped by the consequences of its use.

The Establishment of Empire

Bismarck's first overt effort at colonial expansion took place in 1883, when an agent of Adolf Lüderitz signed a treaty with a Hottentot chief in Southwest Africa that recognized Lüderitz's control over much of the area's southern coast.[32] In September the German government formally inquired whether Britain, which had maintained informal suzerainty in Southwest Africa, claimed any territorial rights there. This placed the British government in a dilemma, since a positive reply would be interpreted in Britain and Europe as an announcement of an active imperialist policy in Africa and a disavowal of British rights would be seen as a free hand for Bismarck. In the end the British government informed Germany that it claimed no rights in Southwest Africa other than Walvis Bay, which had been declared a protectorate in 1880, and a group of islands near what was later called Lüderitz Bay. The precedent was also set for establishing protectorates in other areas of Africa in which Germans were active but that had previously been considered British spheres of influence.

In a telegram of 24 April 1884 to the German consul in Cape Town, Bismarck officially declared that the areas reserved to Lüderitz under his treaties with local chiefs were under the "protection" of the German Empire. In April 1885 Lüderitz founded the *Deutsche Kolonialgesellschaft für Südwestafrika* to assemble development capital for his concession, handle administrative functions, and negotiate with local peoples. Shortly thereafter Lüderitz launched a series of expeditions to discover mineral resources; on one of them he was accidentally drowned in 1886.[33]

The establishment of German protectorates in West Africa took place on Bismarck's instructions in the summer of 1884. Dr. Gustav Nachtigal, a well-known explorer, geographer, and anthropologist and a former German consul in Tunis, was dispatched in the gunboat *Möwe* to sign treaties of protection on the coasts of what later were called Togo and Cameroon.[34] Nachtigal used threats of bombardment and exploited local political disputes to encourage signatures, in most cases to the advantage of German merchant interests that determined exactly where the colonies would be. The treaties on the Togo coast were signed 4–6 July 1884, and those with the Duala of Cameroon on 14 July. The treaties were followed by formal declarations of protectorates by the German government.

The West African protectorates were declared in areas in which German merchant and missionary interests had been active since the 1840s. By the mid-1880s the German commercial presence in Cameroon was slightly larger than the British, although neither was particularly great. The Woermann Company was by far the largest trading concern in Cameroon, and both Woermann and the Duala chiefs sought loose, official German protection to forestall possible action by the British Royal Niger Company to establish a monopoly and to bypass the Duala in interior trade. Even so, German trade with the rest of the West African coast was, and for years remained, larger than with the German protectorates, and a very large segment of the trade of both Togo and Cameroon continued to be in British hands.[35] Under the circumstances it was not really to the advantage of the German trading companies to press the government to exclude British interests, since a reciprocal policy could be expected on the part of the British.

The unique manner in which Germany acquired East Africa has already been mentioned. Peters's "treaties" with the chiefs of many areas on the East African coast were accepted with reluctance by Bismarck, and in 1885 the German government dispatched warships to enforce Germany's claim to a sphere of influence on the coast and free passage into the interior.[36] On subsequent missions Peters and his associates signed more treaties that, backed by the insistence of the German government, had the effect of depriving the sultan of Zanzibar of his continental possessions. However, Bismarck was not willing to allow a free hand to the GfdK, an organization closely connected to the Conservative and Free Conservative parties. Although he could not afford to alienate public opinion by repudiating Peters and his works, he could impose his ideas of colonial government on the GfdK and some controls on Peters's activities.

In 1887, while Peters was in the interior signing treaties, Bismarck created the German East Africa Company (DOAG) as the concession company for Germany's East African claims. DOAG was supposed to prevent Peters from starting an armed confrontation with Britain, to develop East African commerce, and to take over the government of areas that it was necessary to administer directly. Bismarck hoped that DOAG would exercise more restraint in its relations with indigenous political authorities than had Peters, whose methods were violent at best.

Peters and his associates became shareholders and agents of DOAG, but they lost control of it as soon as a few large business interests, including the Krupp concern, bought in.[37] As we shall see, however, the establishment of DOAG did not solve all of Bismarck's problems in his largely unwanted colony. Peters was restrained to a certain extent, but his participation in the 1887 Emin Pasha expedition led to a further extension of territorial claims in rivalry with Britain, which Bismarck had sought to avoid. Also, actual investment in DOAG was woefully inadequate, especially after full-scale war with a series of African states began in 1888. Bismarck's misgivings about East Africa were quickly borne out.

The rest of Germany's new colonial empire was picked up in the Pacific. German interests had long been important in the South Pacific, and German explorers and missionaries had been active there, as elsewhere. One of the major areas of German commercial concern was Samoa, where an indirect German influence was considered to be adequate for purposes of commercial protection. Until 1889 Germany exercised no formal authority, but German interests were economically dominant and German representatives in essence controlled the government.[38] When the Germans deposed a Samoan chief in 1889 and sought to extend special privileges for German traders, the British and American governments intervened. A tripartite administration over the islands was established; it later caused several international incidents.

Bismarck did not establish formal protectorates in Germany's main Pacific and Asian trading areas but rather in northeastern New Guinea (Kaiser Wilhelmsland), the Bismarck Archipelago, Palau, and the Marshall Islands. German economic involvement in these areas was quite small. The establishment of a colony in New Guinea and the Bismarck Archipelago was undertaken at the behest of Adolf von Hansemann, who thought that the totally virgin territory could be profitably developed, although there was really very little evidence for supposing that it could be. The smaller islands appeared to be better bets, on the basis of experience in other Pacific areas. Northeastern New Guinea was claimed in 1883, mainly because Bismarck thought it likely that the British and the Dutch would soon declare their own protectorates. New Guinea, an area of which only the coastline had been explored and whose economic potential was highly doubtful, was therefore partitioned before Africa, although none of the parties involved was particularly bellicose about it. Both German and British agents (the German agent was the explorer Otto Finsch) operated from Australian ports, and on-site agreements over practical boundaries were fairly easily made. New Guinea did not produce its Carl Peters. Hansemann's German New Guinea Company (NGK) was set up as concessionaire in New Guinea and the Bismarck Archipelago. The company functioned with a great deal of publicity and comparatively large capital backing, but its economic results were meagre.[39] The other islands were governed by other concession companies, the most important of which was the Jaluit Company. Perhaps because these companies had no grandiose plans for development and were content simply to make a profit from the trade in copra that already existed, they were rather more successful than the NGK. However, except for Samoa and the base at Kiaochow, which we shall discuss later, the activities of the Germans in their formal Pacific territories were quite negligible in their impact on Germany.

By 1885, therefore, Bismarck had staked out an empire for Germany. It was not as large as the empires of Britain and France, nor did it contain many areas of proven economic worth, but it set off a round of territorial annexations in Africa and in the Pacific that ushered in a new era of imperialism and a new set of international political tensions. In response to the German moves in Africa and to the situation created by Britain's occupation of Egypt in 1882, France and Britain claimed for themselves territories in various parts of Africa, partially in competition with Germany but even more in competition with each other.[40] However, since most of the areas occupied were of relatively little value and since no major power was willing to go to war over them, there existed a strong tendency from the beginning to settle disputes through compromise. In Germany, Bismarck worked to restrain people like Peters from confrontations with the British, and he also sponsored the Berlin West Africa Conference in 1884 and 1885.

The Berlin Conference, which was attended by the major imperialist powers, was a major success for Bismarck.[41] It enhanced his political image at home and abroad, and it also regularized the procedures for colonial occupation in Africa, thereby reducing the risks of international colonial conflict that the chancellor so feared. By giving the Congo Basin to King Leopold, it removed a potential source of trouble among the powers. By establishing a free-trade area in Central Africa, it assuaged many of the fears of European trading companies that colonial markets would be limited to each home country's producers. On the other hand, the criterion set up for official recognition of a country's colonial claims—that of *effective occupation* —required a formal governmental presence in all areas of each colony. Effective occupation meant a much heavier colonial involvement than Bismarck had ever intended for Germany, with attendant expenses that threatened his entire colonial scheme.[42]

3

Colonialism in the Postacquisition Years

The fever pitch of popular, middle-class colonialism did not last much longer than 1885, although colonialism was by no means dormant after the initial phase of expansion. The colonialist organizations remained a factor in politics, and with the formation of the German Colonial Society (*Deutsche Kolonialgesellschaft*) in 1887, popular colonialism in Germany acquired a permanent institutional form that survived the actual colonial empire.

The German Colonial Society

The Colonial Society was one of the better known of the many nationalist organizations that were characteristic of Wilhelmian Germany. It was never as large and powerful as the Navy League, but its influence lasted longer. Although the Pan-German League was somewhat disreputable, the Colonial Society remained eminently respectable—an association to which the best people could belong. Because of limited funding the official colonial administration was often forced to rely on the Colonial Society for assistance in development projects. Even when the society criticized government policy, its leadership was still regularly consulted by the Colonial Department.[1]

When the Colonial Society was founded in 1887 as an amalgamation of the *Kolonialverein* and the *Gesellschaft für deutsche Kolonisation*, its prospectus represented it as the spokesman for all varieties of colonial opinion. The society was intended to influence the making of colonial policy, to carry out actual projects in the colonies, "to exert its influence on the *Auswanderung* question in a 'national' sense, and to work against the increasingly dangerous strengthening of other nationalities in world trade at the cost of German capital and German labor."[2]

The society's stated goals indicated one of its major problems. In ideological terms its aim of holding together all colonial interests meant coordinating the economic imperialists' view of colonial enterprise and that of the settlement colonialists. This could be done in propaganda but not when major disputes arose between the adherents of the different views within the Colonial Society, as was the case during the debate over colonial concession companies around 1900. Often, the society just remained neutral and carried the opposing views in its newspaper, the *Kolonialzeitung*.[3]

Within the Colonial Society ideological splits were institutionalized. Although the society as a whole publicly tended to favor the development of settlement colonies as solutions to the emigration problem, its Colonial Economic Committee (KWK) concerned itself mostly with agricultural development and took a severely economic view.[4] The KWK, which originated in a separate economic colonialist organization, became associated with the society in the 1890s and sponsored technical research on a separate budget. It exerted great influence on the colonial administration.

The division within the Colonial Society between settlement and economic colonialists represented a difference between those interested in colonialism as a rallying force for the political right and those who had direct economic interests in the colonies or envisioned them as adjuncts to German industry. The split became acute in the 1890s during the national dispute over German economic policy between agrarian and industrial interests. Besides the main ideological groupings the society also contained contingents of settlers, administrators, and other specific interests.

Throughout its existence the Colonial Society tried, with difficulty, to combine the roles of pressure group and government supporter. The society's membership was decidedly upper middle class, but it was fairly small (17,483 in 1893; 40,000 in 1910), so the society's political effectiveness depended on rallying broad middle-class support. This led to a heavy emphasis on nationalist rhetoric and on emigrationist colonialism.[5] At the insistence of its local branches, the society pushed for the development of Southwest Africa as a settlement colony and the revision of the emigration laws long after emigration ceased to be a real problem. Although the society usually took an ultranationalist stance on foreign policy, it tried not to jeopardize its good relations with the government and therefore avoided the extremism of the Pan-German League. Carl Peters, a prominent early member of both the Colonial Society and the Pan-German League, was much more at home in the latter. Although Peters was Germany's best-known colonialist, he was not chosen as the society's permanent president. The job went to the Prince zu Hohenlohe-Langenburg, a conservative nobleman and traveler, rather than to the popular but unreliable Peters because the society wanted to demonstrate its acceptability to the government and to the upper classes.[6] Despite the continuing divisions among colonialists, however, the Colonial Society maintained an outward show of unity against leftist attacks on the colonial empire in the Reichstag. And despite the society's desire to get along with the government, it joined in the general colonialist attack on Bismarck between 1887 and 1890.

The Collapse of Bismarck's Colonial Policy, 1885–1890

The linchpin of Bismarck's scheme for colonial administration was the idea that the trading or concession companies in each of the protectorates would handle governmental functions themselves. The German government was to provide only a few officials and occasionally some warships to back up the companies.[7] Behind this concept were not only Bismarck's basic reservations about colonies but also some very real constitutional restrictions on the government's actions. There was no provision for a colonial empire in the Imperial Constitution, which meant that the empire had to be organized by expedient. Moreover, the same tenuous financial system that applied to all imperial departments had to apply also to the colonial administration. Since the imperial government could not levy direct taxes, its finances were always in a precarious condition.[8] Without a major revision of funding priorities, Bismarck believed that he could not afford to spend much on luxuries like colonies. He kept the colonial administration within the Foreign Office partly in order to control expenses. The unclear constitutional status of the colonies and their lack of designated funding, moreover, meant that if Bismarck had wanted to spend more money on the colonies, he would have been forced to go to the Reichstag, to open his government to criticism by the political parties, and to bargain for approval of his budget by horse trading with the parties. Bismarck clearly believed that an extension of the colonial administration would not have been worth the effort.

The only trouble was that the trading companies were unwilling or unable to do the job of governing. The Woermann and Jantzen & Thormälen concerns never had any intention of governing Cameroon, and the New Guinea Company had insufficient resources to rule.[9] The companies had accepted political responsibilities as part of a bargain with Bismarck in order to obtain protection and support through an active colonial policy. Almost immediately they began to complain of the intolerable burden that administrative expenses placed on their profit rates and capital reserves. Although Carl Peters originally appreciated the free hand that Bismarck's limited system gave him, DOAG fell into line with the other companies as soon as it began experiencing heavy losses through indigenous resistance in East Africa.[10]

After 1885 other elements of the colonial movement were also becoming restive with the direction of policy. The leaders of the colonial movement, especially those who wanted Germany to create settlement colonies, increasingly realized that Germany's colonies were inadequate for their purposes and that Bismarck had no intention of allowing either settlement or expansion. Within a short while after the establishment of the Colonial Society, prominent colonialists began a campaign to change Bismarck's policy.[11] The attack was led by Fabri, who criticized the government for not establishing a regular administration in the colonies, for failing to invest in development, and especially for not acquiring areas suitable for German farming settlement. Fabri was seconded by several colonial publicists, especially Carl Peters, who in his "search" for Emin Pasha was actively expanding the area in East Africa that could be claimed by Germany. The colonialist movement rapidly began to turn away from Bismarck, and it remained in opposition to him until he fell from power in 1890.

This presented Bismarck with a problem, since he needed continuing support from nationalist sentiment and conservative political groups—the Cartel of 1887—as he prepared for a final showdown with the socialists.[12] Yet in order to keep the support of the colonial movement, it was necessary to extend the scope of his colonial policy, and by 1887 he was even less willing to do so than previously. Extension of colonial administration would have required considerably greater expense than Bismarck was willing to bear. A settlement policy, which implied military expeditions to pacify or displace indigenous peoples and an expansion of existing colonies in the face of foreign opposition, was even less desirable.

Bismarck ultimately refused to bend to pressure from the colonialists except on a few points. He did agree to a more regular establishment of German political control in some of the colonies and to other limited changes, but they did not satisfy any portion of the colonial movement.[13] While many colonialists called for more annexations and while Carl Peters continued to sign treaties to use as vehicles for expansion into Kenya and Uganda, Bismarck maintained his posture of comparative restraint, working for negotiated settlements of boundary disputes with Britain through compensation. For this he lost colonialist support, which was one of many factors contributing to the disintegration of Bismarck's cartel after 1887 and, in a minor way, to his fall from power in 1890.

The Colonial Department

Bismarck did eventually realize that the colonial empire required greater central control than he had expected, but only after his dismissal in March 1890 did his successors institute major changes in the central administration.[14]

Originally, colonial affairs were handled within the Foreign Office by a single counselor, Heinrich Kusserow, who advised Bismarck on colonial matters and issued orders to lower officials but who had to refer to Bismarck on questions of policy. However, Kusserow was removed in 1885 for lackluster performance, and no single designated colonial counselor was appointed until Dr. Heinrich Krauel, a relatively obscure official, took over Kusserow's old job in 1889. In the interim, colonial affairs were channeled through various departments on a case-by-case basis. This low-level pattern obviously conformed to Bismarck's notions of colonial administration, but it was impossible to maintain when actual German presence in the colonies increased in scope.

Krauel was in office in March 1890, when Bismarck was dismissed, and he was named *Kolonialdirigent* a few weeks later when a central colonial administration was finally set up as the fourth department of the Foreign Office. Although the repercussions of this change were felt in many of the colonies almost immediately, it did not go far enough to satisfy the leadership of the Colonial Society, which had been pushing for a separate colonial ministry. The major reason for the reorganization was the desire of the leaders of several of the Reichstag parties to have a responsible official, with his own budget, who could be questioned on colonial matters—which was exactly what Bismarck had tried to avoid.

The colonial administration was transformed again in July 1890 into the *Kolonialabteilung* (Colonial Department) of the Foreign Office and was given a new director, Dr. Paul Kayser. Kayser was an extremely ambitious official who had been active in supporting the emperor in his overthrow of Bismarck; he received his reward.[15] The status of his new department was unusual. For most normal purposes, such as personnel matters, the Colonial Department was an integral part of the Foreign Office. It remained so until 1907. In the early years assignments in the Colonial Department and in the colonies were taken by regular Foreign Office officials as part of their career patterns, although such assignments were not considered desirable. In routine matters the director of the Colonial Department reported to the foreign secretary. Uniquely among officials at his level, however, the colonial director reported directly to the chancellor on matters of any importance, bypassing his nominal superior in the Foreign Office. This was essentially a compromise between those like Bismarck's successor, Leo von Caprivi, who wanted to limit the scope of the colonial administration and the proponents of an independent Colonial Office. It became customary for the colonial director, rather than the chancellor or foreign secretary, to defend the colonial budget before the Reichstag Budget Commission.[16]

In reality the Foreign Office retained a good deal of control over the Colonial Department because in the early years many of the department's senior personnel had to anticipate extradepartmental review for promotion. Initially there was little sense within the colonial administration of an individual corporate existence. Nevertheless, the Colonial Department possessed greater independence than almost any other component of an imperial ministry. This was due partly to its separate budgetary function and its official relation to the chancellor and partly to the fact that it dealt with matters of little interest to the rest of the Foreign Office. In the 1890s the Colonial Department was criticized for harboring an easygoing attitude and a lack of attention to work, but a low profile was clearly to its advantage, given the restricted financial conditions under which it operated.

In 1891 Kayser established the *Kolonialrat* (Colonial Council), an advisory body that expressed opinions on matters of colonial policy presented to it by the colonial director.[17] Its members were appointed from colonial businesses and interest groups, and it was intended both to assemble expertise for solving policy problems and to allow the department to manipulate and reconcile differences among colonial interests. In 1894 Kayser's title was changed to *Kolonialdirektor*, which was supposed to emphasize the independence of his department from the rest of the Foreign Office. The official administrations in the colonies were also expanded in the 1890s, and a professional colonial service was developed in a small way.[18]

Although a regular and theoretically centralized structure of governance was established for the overseas empire after 1890, the role of the colonial administration, and thus the scope of colonial policy, continued for years to be extremely limited. Within the Colonial Department the empire was regarded as an enterprise for the benefit of the German economy, as represented by those who invested in the colonies.[19] Budgetary restrictions imposed by the Reichstag together with the conception of their own function held by most colonial officials severely circumscribed the range of action open to the colonial administration in Berlin and to individual colonial governments. In the colonies many local factors also limited policy initiatives. The impatience of the colonial movement with the Reichstag for not establishing expensive schemes for colonial development was also partly directed against the Colonial Department because of the department's consciousness of its own limitations. In the 1890s the Colonial Department remained wedded to the concept of private colonial development and reduced government involvement. This attitude eventually changed, although not completely.[20]

PART II

THE COLONIES, 1885–1907

4

Southwest Africa, 1885–1907: White Man's Country and the Roots of Genocide

The Early Period of German Rule: Intentions and Realities

Southwest Africa was the largest of the German colonies in area and, from quite early in the colony's history, in the size of its German population. In 1901, for example, the white population was 3,743. In 1912 it was 14,816 as compared to 4,886 for East Africa, 1,537 for Cameroon, and 345 for Togo.[1] This in itself would have made the German colonial experience in Southwest Africa markedly different from that in the other colonies even if the social and geographical environment had not also worked to make it so. Southwest Africa was the only one of Germany's colonies that could reasonably be considered a potential settlement colony, although such potential was highly limited. The Colonial Society and other nationalist organizations had therefore a special interest in Southwest Africa and an ideological commitment to a settlement policy that had a decisive, and dev-

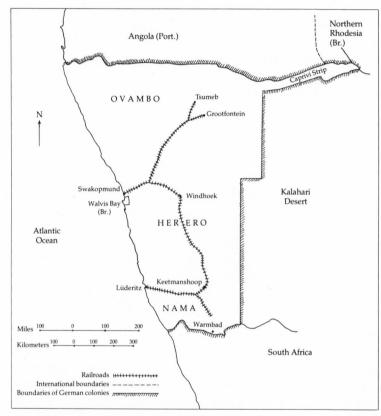

German Southwest Africa, 1914

astating, effect on the history of the colony. Among other things, it contributed to events that culminated in the Herero and Nama war of 1904–1907, which was a full-scale attempt to obliterate the political structures of the major African peoples of the colony and exterminate an entire segment of the indigenous population.

As in all other colonies, the direction of German policy was dictated to a considerable extent by political and ecological conditions. Southwest Africa (or Namibia) is a vast subtropical region of grassy hills and plains that are suited for grazing but not intensive cultivation. Ranges of mountains run through the middle of the country, and to the east the land merges with the Kalihari Desert. Although ranching is important today, the territory's major economic resources are mineral. Southwest Africa's mines make it far more valuable now than it ever was under German rule.

When the German protectorate was declared in 1884, the majority of the country was inhabited by cattle-raising, semi-nomadic peoples, the largest of whom had developed national state structures and had maintained political relations with Europeans in their midst and in South Africa for many years.[2] The Herero, who occupied Damaraland in the central part of the country, were a numerous Bantu-speaking people who had lived in Southwest Africa for over a century and who had attained a high degree of national consciousness as a result of their wars against another major people, the Nama, who lived in the south. The resumption of these hostilities in the 1880s caused both the Nama and the Herero to appeal to British South Africa and Germany for support or mediation and caused the Herero leader Maherero to sign a treaty of protection with the German Imperial Commissioner Heinrich Goering in 1885. The chief of the Nama, Hendrik Witbooi, refused to sign a similar treaty until 1894. The third important population group of Southwest Africa, the Ovambo, were a sedentary agricultural people who lived in the far north. They were essentially left alone by the Germans until after 1907, which is probably the reason that they are today the largest and most important African people in the country.

By 1884 the Germans, who had been active in Southwest Africa for many years, were the most important European cultural and economic influence there. The interior of the territory had been explored by Germans in the employ of English missionary societies. German missionaries had operated in both Herero country and Namaland from the 1830s, setting up a permanent interior station at Windhoek that later became the capital of the colony.[3] German societies had taken over British missionary operations in most of the country in the 1860s, and German traders had supported the Herero against the Nama. Consequently when the protectorate was established, Germans were deeply involved in the relation between the two major indigenous political units, which they had already exploited for their own benefit. The pattern for German native policy in Southwest Africa for almost the next two decades was already set: maintaining the formal peace between the Herero and the Nama while preserving a level of tension between them that would uphold German authority at minimal German expense.

This was clearly the policy that Lüderitz and Bismarck had in mind in 1885, and while Goering, the official representative, was trying to establish an armed peace between the Herero and Nama presided over by Germany, Lüderitz searched for minerals in the interior. Although Lüderitz was drowned in 1886, the arrangement between his company, the *Deutsche Kolonialgesellschaft für Süd-West Afrika* (DKGfSWA), and the government continued to be essential to German policymaking. According to Bismarck's scheme, the DKGfSWA was to pay all development costs and to provide all necessary capital equipment; the government would temporarily provide an imperial commissioner paid by subvention.[4] After the impracticality of Bismarck's system was demonstrated and government involvement was increased, official policy still held that the government's main function was to create, at minimal cost, conditions under which the DKGfSWA and other companies could make a profit. Policy is one thing, however, and political reality is another. The official line did not take into account the problems of economic development in Southwest Africa, the difficulties of relations with indigenous states, and the establishment of a small white settler population.

Soon after the establishment of the German protectorate, it was discovered that maintaining the imperial presence in Southwest Africa would be much more expensive than had been anticipated and that private investment in the chartered concession company could hardly bear the expense of adequate economic exploitation, much less the cost of government and defense. Formally, the subscription capital of the *Deutsche Kolonialgesellschaft für Süd-West Afrika* was two million marks, in itself too small a figure to support a major prospecting and trade-development effort and much too small to allow the company to fulfill its obligation to build roads and port facilities. In addition, only part of the capital was actually invested in the colony. It was suggested that the company was most interested in allowing the value of its land concessions to increase. By 1905 neither the DKGfSWA nor any of the other concession companies chartered in the 1890s had paid a dividend, nor had their profits been sufficient for the government to derive much of its own income from them.[5] The companies had many problems. Expeditions looking for minerals were simply unlucky in not finding them. More importantly, however, even those economic resources that were known to exist (such as copper) could not be properly exploited because of lack of capital and scarcity of labor. The fact that many of the people of Southwest Africa had had little involvement in trade with Europeans and that there were few locally produced agricultural products that could find an overseas market meant that consistent profits could not be made by extending the scope of commerce with the indigenous peoples. The trade in hides that developed in the 1890s was of very minor proportions. Through the 1880s and 1890s the economic development of the colony, which was supposed to proceed under the protection of the German government and its native policy, remained essentially stagnant, and the government attempted to rule at its own expense.

The problem facing the colonial administration in Southwest Africa, meanwhile, grew over the course of time. Contrary to expectations, the policy of threatening violence and playing the Herero off against the Nama did not adequately protect German interests or prevent opposition to German rule. Although the Herero remained quiescent and their leadership cooperated with the German authorities, their enemies the Nama naturally did not. The Nama carried on a continuous guerilla war against the Germans and their allies in the early 1890s, requiring constant punitive expeditions and lengthy campaigns into the southern interior. These doubled as exploratory expeditions. Only in 1894, when a compromise peace was made with the Nama, did Hendrik Witbooi sign a treaty recognizing the German protectorate.[6]

The lack of economic success in the colony and the unexpected military difficulties encountered there changed the nature of the German official presence. Goering, essentially a diplomat with few military and legal resources at his disposal, was replaced as imperial commissioner in 1890 by First Lieutenant (later Major) Curt von François, an army officer who was also appointed commander of a small force of soldiers (the *Schutztruppe* or Defense Force).[7] In addition to a permanent military structure, a tiny civil establishment was also set up to handle native relations, to supervise economic development, and later to exercise control over German settlers. As in other colonies at about the same time, the creation of a civil administration and a military force changed the complexion of overseas German colonialism. Among other things, it greatly increased governmental costs. In 1890 these changes were regarded as experiments. Chancellor Caprivi—whose name is perpetuated on the map of Southwest Africa in the Caprivi Strip—believed that the government should set up conditions conducive to economic development for a year or two and if no profits were forthcoming in that time, it should abandon Southwest Africa.[8] He failed to realize that his own decision to strengthen the administration of the colony would involve Germany more deeply in local affairs, and he also reckoned without the German colonial movement, which made it impossible to give up the colony.

A new, very significant factor entered into the situation in Southwest Africa in the 1890s: the colony began to attract settlers. Some of the settlement was the result of deliberate efforts by the Colonial Society and, more reluctantly, by the Colonial Department to settle Germans as farmers in Southwest Africa.[9] Such settlement, obviously required for political purposes, was in keeping with the concept of colonization favored by the largest segment of colonialist opinion. Of the German colonies, Southwest Africa appeared to be the most promising for settlement, although it was only minimally promising.

Other more local factors also contributed to white settlement. Small numbers of traders in hides began to buy cattle from the Herero and to establish their own ranches, as did some company employees and soldiers. A small "urban" population appeared at the towns of Windhoek and Lüderitz. The first large groups of white settlers to enter Southwest Africa with the intention of breaking new ground were not Germans at all but rather families of South African Boers trekking across land to maintain their pastoral way of life. François, after investigating the situation, recommended that the Boers be allowed to stay, but only in conjunction with a large-scale policy of recruiting German farmers.[10] François suggested that the example of the indigenous population and the Boers be followed and that Southwest Africa be developed as a cattle-raising economy. This would require fairly substantial white settlement, although not nearly as much as emigrationist colonial imaginations envisioned. It would also require government action to procure cattle and labor from the Herero and Nama. The idea seemed reasonable in view of the geography of Southwest Africa, and besides, it seemed to be a way of reconciling economic rationality with the demands of the colonial movement for white settlement colonies. The Colonial Department was reluctant to commit itself to an all-out settlement policy, although it was not able to oppose settlement directly. Yet despite the department's continued commitment to development by concession companies, a movement of Germans to Southwest Africa to establish ranches and livestock farms did commence on a small scale. Although emigration to Southwest Africa remained small during the 1890s, it built up considerable momentum by the end of the decade and increased rapidly after 1900.[11]

Although experiments were made with many different forms of agriculture in Southwest Africa, the only consistently successful form was cattle raising on extensive ranches. European ranchers, since they maintained small, stationary herds, were not immediately competitive with the seminomadic Herero, but by the late 1890s many sources of friction existed. There was conflict over the best highland grazing land, which settlers naturally appropriated. Since most of the early settlers had little capital and small herds, many attempted to supplement their incomes through trade with the Herero and sought government assistance in collecting bad debts. The entry of settlers and the eventual building of railways placed severe strains on the pattern of African social and economic life. Since most of the cattle used to start European herds were purchased from Africans, new European settlers created an increasing drain on the supply of livestock after the mid-1890s.[12] Settlers pressured the government to take over Herero herds as a response to resulting high prices. The building of the Southwest African railways and the growth of European ranches also created a demand for African labor. Over the course of time, this tended to pull Africans out of their traditional economic patterns and to threaten the stability of African social and political systems. Until after 1900 government policy advocated maintaining the political structures of at least the major tribes, which meant that an organization existed for eventual resistance to these tendencies. The pressure for change was felt most strongly by the Herero, into whose lands the German settlers made their first inroads, but the Nama were not immune. The potential for a major clash was therefore building up in the 1890s, although the conflict itself did not come until 1904, when official government policy in Germany had become more favorable to settlement and German settlers had begun arriving in much larger numbers than before.

Other factors acted more slowly to alter the German presence in Southwest Africa. As it began to appear that the DKGfSWA was undercapitalized and relatively inactive, other concessions were issued by the government, in accordance with the Colonial Department's policy and because of considerable pressure from potential colonial investors who wanted to tap new sources of capital. One of the key figures in bringing this pressure to bear was Dr. Julius Scharlach, a prominent colonialist and a member of the *Kolonialrat* in the 1890s. Scharlach convinced the Colonial Department that Southwest Africa required very large inputs of capital and that therefore new concessions that would be attractive to major German investment houses and would also bring in British capital had to be granted.[13] Scharlach was himself a business associate of Cecil Rhodes.

Most new concessions of the 1890s entailed grants of land and mineral rights but also included obligations to build transportation facilities and to pay a proportion of profits into the German treasury. The DKGfSWA was soon overtaken in scope of operations. Of the eight concession companies in Southwest Africa in 1905, it was the second smallest in amount of operating capital —the smallest being the *Siedlungsgesellschaft für Südwestafrika*, a company founded largely at the behest of the Colonial Society to encourage German farming settlement in the colony and approved by the Colonial Department as a gesture toward settlement colonial opinion.[14] The two largest and most important companies were incorporated in Britain: The Southwest Africa Company Ltd., a Rhodes-dominated establishment, and South African Territories Ltd., founded by Scharlach and later a subsidiary of the Southwest Africa Company. Both were essentially mining concerns. The other companies were primarily German. One, the *Otavi Minen- und Eisenbahngesellschaft*, was capitalized by a number of prominent German financial interests and was intended to develop mines in the Otavi region and to build a system of railways out of its profits. Until the opening of new copper deposits in 1907 and the discovery of diamonds in 1908, however, none of these companies showed a profit or paid a dividend. Not until 1912 did Southwest Africa possess a favorable balance of trade.

The concession-company policy in Southwest Africa was heavily debated among colonialists in the late 1890s and after 1900. This dispute was actually part of much wider debate over national policy, but it affected some aspects of the political situation in Southwest Africa. In particular, with the growth of a settler population, the colonial administration's lack of sympathy with settlement colonialism became readily apparent. Even when the administration in Southwest Africa was forced to enunciate a formal settlement policy in 1903, it did so unwillingly. When a special settlement commission was appointed from Berlin in 1903, it met with hostility from the administration, but the settler population looked upon it as a first step toward self-government.[15] Settler self-consciousness and organization constantly increased, partly in anticipation of coming racial struggle and partly because leaders of the settlers discovered that they could obtain right-wing political support in Germany by employing the emigrationist colonial ideology. One matter of dispute between the administration and the supporters of the settlers, which became more explicit after 1907, was the form in which capital inflow into Southwest Africa should be directed. Although government policy was to limit state input and to emphasize private investment through the concession companies, the settler argument, largely lifted from German conservative colonialist writings, was that the government should assemble investment capital itself and apportion it in loans to German farmers in Southwest Africa.[16] The argument contributed to a growing sense of conflict between the colonial administration in Southwest Africa and the agrarian segment of the white population there.

The Origins of the Herero War, 1897–1904

Despite the standing policy of limiting state involvement in Southwest Africa, the government's role and outlook gradually changed, reflecting new circumstances. Southwest Africa became the first of the German colonies to undertake an extensive program of railway building, needed because of the size of the country. Originally it had been intended that the concession companies pay for the railroads, but in the end the Reichstag had to be asked for subventions and loan guarantees. The building of the railroads accelerated the process of dispossessing the Herero and changing official native policy.

From 1894 to 1905, the administration was headed by an army officer, Theodor Leutwein. Leutwein was originally appointed as *Landeshauptmann*, a title that implied a more permanent administrative presence than had that of imperial commissioner but also indicated that Germany was not yet committed to an outright colonial administration. However, as the number of Germans and German interests in Southwest Africa increased, the administration took on all the appearances of a full-scale colonial government. This change was recognized in 1898 when Leutwein was made governor. Leutwein's own theory of colonial government originally corresponded to the outlines previously described. He attempted to operate through agreements with the major Herero and Nama chiefs on trade, peace keeping, and designated territories in which the concession companies could operate. He continued to play groups off against each other so that all parties would have to have recourse to the German authorities for arbitration. This was done quite deliberately, and it was justified in that it constituted the cheapest means of government available that was consistent with the understood aims of German official colonial policy.

Leutwein blamed the eventual failure of this type of government on lack of cooperation by white settler groups, who disregarded official native policy.[17] This was, indeed, one of the immediate causes of the eventual conflict, but it is likely that Leutwein's own policy would have eventually led to the same result, since in the long run he anticipated having to destroy the existing indigenous social and political systems to facilitate economic development.[18] In any event, with the discovery of diamonds and copper, an economic structure would have been imposed that would have affected African society as greatly as the advent of white agriculture and that could not have been easily reconciled with African political and social organization. Even in places like Cameroon, where preexisting patterns of native production, trade, and government were better attuned to European exploitation, the entry of large-scale capitalism led to conflict. In Southwest Africa the local population was simply not organized for sudden entry into a European economy.

Leutwein's criticism of the settlers was somewhat disingenuous, but he was correct about the immediate cause of conflict. The settlers, an economic element in the colony that could not be accommodated within the political system established by the authorities, brought the clash between Europeans and Africans to a head before Leutwein predicted and before he thought it necessary for economic reasons. It had been expected that in the normal course of things the imposition of a capitalist economic system would be sufficiently gradual that attrition from the traditional African structure would minimize the degree of ultimate conflict, which would arise only when the colony was sufficiently profitable to pay for it and sufficiently valuable that the advantages of retaining control would be obvious in Germany. The appearance of the settler-based economic system before Southwest Africa had become self-supporting and before its possession had been justified upset Leutwein's timetable. This was the basis of the crisis over the Herero War that arose in Germany after 1904.

There were other related reasons for conflict. In 1897 an epidemic struck the Herero cattle, killing over half of them.[19] This, at least for a few years, ruined the basis of Herero economic life at the same time that European demand for African cattle and labor was increasing. It also made the possibility of employment on European farms more attractive to some Herero, thereby accelerating the process of social change. At the same time the colonial administration began to alter its policy toward settlers —under strong pressure from Berlin. The Colonial Department, with the cooperation of the Colonial Society, began more actively to encourage German settlement in Southwest Africa, at first through the *Siedlungsgesellschaft* and later through the Settlement Commission.[20] When several groups in the Reichstag insisted on a more vigorous settlement policy in Southwest Africa, the Colonial Department was forced to respond, although basic official distrust of settlement remained. The new settlement policy did not become integrated with the overall colonial development policy until after 1904; it was instead allowed to exist, as it were, alongside the latter.

The most obvious manifestation of the new settlement policy was the removal, by treaty and by force, of the Herero to reservations in 1897.[21] The move was advertised as a response to the epidemic, but the actual intent was to open up new grazing lands to Europeans and make it easier to appropriate Herero cattle. This was soon perceived by the Herero, many of whom had been relegated to permanent poverty or starvation on the reservations. It was probably only because the Herero leadership was so closely identified with the German colonial administration and so willing to accept the official German view of things that war was delayed until 1904. The inevitability of the conflict could have been predicted from the reservation policy of the United States government in the American West. When the struggle came in 1904, however, it apparently caught the German authorities by surprise.

War and the Attempt to Exterminate the Herero, 1904–1907

The Herero rising finally commenced in January 1904.[22] It was a coordinated attack led by Samuel Maherero, the leading chief of the Herero, whose father had signed the original treaty with the Germans, and it resulted immediately in the killing of over a hundred Europeans, mostly German farmers. To a considerable extent, as we have seen, the Herero were driven to this action by threats of social and economic extinction. It is fairly clear that official policy was not deliberately designed to provoke a major war, which did not benefit those in authority. Leutwein was soon removed and after a time was replaced by Friedrich Lindequist. Although the official establishment was obviously surprised by the revolt, many German colonialists were quite willing to employ the opportunity presented by the war to destroy once and for all the indigenous political structure of the country in order to establish a firm and secure settlement colony there. These people eventually got the upper hand in setting policy in Southwest Africa and conducting operations against the Herero. Lindequist himself was one of them; so, to some extent, was the newly appointed commander of the *Schutztruppe* and of the expeditionary force sent to Southwest Africa, General Lothar von Trotha.

Trotha was an officer unusually experienced in colonial wars; he was also an unusually repulsive example of a person to whom military considerations were an end in themselves. For the previous decade Trotha had made a very successful career outside of Germany—first as commander of the *Schutztruppe* in East Africa in a series of small, brutal campaigns to extend German authority and then as general commanding a German force sent to China to help quell the Boxer Rebellion.[23] Encouraged by the kaiser to behave ruthlessly in China, Trotha did exactly that, leaving behind fierce hatred for Germany and setting an example for German colonial warfare that was much remarked in other countries. He also achieved a wide reputation in Germany, and when he arrived in Southwest Africa, he set about living up to it.

After their initial success the Herero met unmitigated disaster in the campaign that followed. Although hard pressed, the colonists began a campaign of extermination against them that Trotha and his specially recruited troops followed up with great vigor when they arrived. The main Herero force was defeated, was surrounded on a mountain called the Waterberg, and was driven into the desert where most of its members died. Smaller-scale guerilla action continued without leadership after Samuel Maherero fled the country. The Germans initiated an orgy of killing following the defeat of the main Herero army. Trotha himself actively sought to wipe out the Herero by refusing to negotiate with them, authorizing his troops to kill Herero on sight, and issuing a notorious extermination order to shoot or exile every Herero man, woman, and child. He came close to succeeding. By 1906, of the eighty thousand Herero who had lived in Southwest Africa before the war, less than twenty thousand remained; most of these were confined in concentration camps at the coast to be used for cheap labor. Trotha's activities were too much even for colonialist sentiment: he was recalled in 1905 after criticism in the Reichstag. Lindequist himself, although committed to a prosettler policy and to punishing the Herero severely, saw that Trotha's actions amounted to senseless slaughter and that they threatened the future labor supply of the colony. After Trotha's departure Lindequist cancelled the extermination order. The Herero, although drastically reduced in numbers, were saved from extinction.

The Herero had not revolted alone. The Nama, who had never been as close to the German establishment as the Herero had, saw that their turn was soon to follow and went to war later in 1904 under old Hendrik Witbooi. Their military operations were more effective than those of the Herero, and their leadership remained more intact; it took until 1907 to "pacify" them. They were led first by Witbooi, who was eventually killed, and then by a number of chiefs, including Jacob Morenga—a chief who, having risen to paramountcy on his own merits, was unusually conscious of the political situation in which he was operating.[24] Clear perceptions and good leadership were not enough, however, for the Nama were also defeated. By 1907 Southwest Africa had entered into a new phase of its colonial history after having contributed through its wars to a major crisis of the entire German colonial empire in 1906 and 1907 and having presaged the genocidal policies of a later era in German history.[25]

5

Togo:
The "Model Colony"

As in other colonies the economic and social structures previously existing in Togo and the nature of prior European involvement strongly influenced the pattern of early German rule. Unlike other German colonies, however, Togo essentially retained the outlines of its early economic and political patterns until the Germans lost the territory in the First World War.[1] This happened partly because the precolonial economy provided a basis for profitable commerce and cheap government and partly because an unusually competent administration quickly recognized the failure of schemes to alter the existing system.

Togo came to be known as Germany's *Musterkolonie*, or "model colony," primarily because it was the only one of Germany's African territories that consistently showed a trade surplus and more government revenue than expenditures, therefore not requiring imperial subventions. Small military expeditions, when needed, were paid for from local taxes and duties. Despite the small volume of its trade, Togo was a profitable undertaking, and colonial propagandists played this fact for all it was worth. Togo, therefore, came as close as a German colony ever did to

Bismarck's ideal but not entirely by means of which Bismarck would have approved. The Germans did make maximum use of indigenous social structures, but instead of allowing free European enterprise to dominate economic and political life, the colonial administration very early took a preeminent role in directing development. In this sense Togo became a model for the other German colonies, in which the government did not perform a similar function until well after 1900.[2]

However, the enthusiasm of Togo's supporters was not shared by all German colonialists. Many believed Togo to be no more than a sideshow because its tropical climate was clearly not suited for mass European settlement.[3] Togo was a model colony only from the standpoint of economic colonialism—as a market and source of raw materials—but it was at best a miniature model. It added very little to German commerce, and in the event of an economic war that excluded British and French trade, Togo would no longer have been solvent.[4]

Moreover, neither the economic nor the native policy pursued in Togo was as uniformly successful as German colonial propagandists indicated. The maintenance of existing "peasant" forms of production, which was the cornerstone of Togo's economic profitability, and the protection that the government afforded small producers against large European enterprises may also have reduced the ability of the Togolese economy to accumulate capital. Although German policy limited the violence of cultural change, it may also have restricted Togo's potential for economic growth. Government capital investment went primarily into transportation facilities, but because expenses for these had to be covered from local revenues, the amount of construction was small and the quality of material was frequently poor. The vast preponderance of imports into Togo were consumables useful in trade—cloth, beer, brandy, etc.—as opposed to capital goods. In 1900, for example, the value of machinery imported into Togo was 2.5 percent of the value of beer, wine, and spirits.[5] In addition, Togo's heavy reliance on exports of palm oil and other tropical products increasingly drew it into the fluctuations and long-term decline of the worldwide primary-goods market. Although peasant cocoa farming managed to develop into a prosperous industry under similar circumstances in the neighboring Gold Coast, Togo's size and geography left little scope for expansion, especially since the government decided to leave the northern half of the colony essentially alone. This is not so much an indictment of German rule as an indication of the dilemmas facing policymakers in all of the colonial empires.

Togo also gained a reputation for humanitarian colonialism and effective government, especially under its most famous governor, Julius Graf Zech (1903–10).[6] Much of this reputation was deserved, but it should not obscure the fact that like other colonies Togo was an arena for forcible exploitation in which the European position was maintained through violence, real or threatened. Togo was occupied by force, and military campaigns were mounted in the early years to pacify the interior. Even Zech, a self-conceived humanitarian, created concentration camps for political prisoners and developed means of assembling forced labor—although under more carefully regulated conditions than in other German colonies.[7] It is true that abuses of the administrative system and outright atrocities were less frequent in Togo than elsewhere, but this was partly because the white population of the colony was very small, not over 500 at the height of German rule. Only a few acts of brutality there, most notably Governor Horn's whipping of an African to death in 1902, became publicized in Germany.[8] Togo was unquestionably the most successful of Germany's African colonies, but it was not unique, and its size made it economically insignificant.

The Early Years of German Rule and the Development of the Political Administration

We have already seen how Nachtigal took advantage of internal political dissension in Anecho to declare the Togo coast a protectorate in 1884. German missionary and trading interests were comparatively strong there, but the desire of at least the missionary societies for German protection was far from overwhelming.[9] The German action appears to have been occasioned in part by the fear that the British occupation of Keta, the chief town of the eastern Ewe-speaking region, would lead to an attempt by British companies to oust German companies from the rest of the coast. The fear was not entirely unfounded, but it never became a reality. Even the actual partition of the 1880s and 1890s did not cause the wholesale removal of German interests from British areas or vice versa. The coastal areas were so closely interconnected and the movement of goods and labor was so essential to the economies of all of the colonies, British, German or French, that to interfere with foreign businesses would have been madness. Continual difficulty did arise over tariffs, since Togo's tariffs were higher than those of the Gold Coast and that led to smuggling. The tariffs were, however, mainly intended to produce revenue rather than to restrict trade, and the tariff problem was solved in a series of Anglo-German agreements in the 1890s.[10]

Originally German policymakers envisioned Togo as a base for developing a trade route into the interior of West Africa, crossing the Niger. This motive was the most important factor in official policy during the first ten years of German occupation, as expeditions were sent inland and treaties were signed with interior states in competition with the British and French.[11] The Germans, however, started with a number of handicaps. The effort that the German government and private organizations were willing to expend on the race was minimal, and established routes of advance lay in areas more amenable to French and British control. The Germans were cut off. In the end Germany was left with a small, rectangular area hemmed in by other countries' colonies, an area with a developed coastal economy that had little to do with the interior. Most trade in the interior moved northeast and northwest rather than south. From the early 1890s German efforts perforce had to concentrate on the coast.

In the first years the German administration contented itself with maintaining preexisting patterns of trade and government. Once the colony had to fall back on itself, however, attempts were made to extend uniform political control over the coastal region and to increase the area's productivity. With comparatively little effort the existing system was capable of producing revenues through import and export duties to finance a limited push to the interior. Increases in trade meant increases in revenue, and originally that was the limit of the administration's interest in expanding the scope of the coastal economy.[12] During the first years of the colony, the government encouraged the exploitation of local production by small companies already in business, and in the late 1890s it cooperated with the KWK in developing new products and methods. Before 1900 no large development company dominated the economy of Togo, nor did a very large European population appear there. At the end of 1895, for example, the total white population of Togo was ninety-six people, of whom eighty-one were Germans.[13] These people were fairly evenly distributed among official occupations, missionaries, and merchants. There were a very few planters. In 1892 a total of forty-eight commercial "stations" were operating in Togo as agencies of European firms (only a few actually run by Europeans).[14] Of these, twenty-three were German stations and fourteen were British. The situation on the British Gold Coast was similar, with fifty-one stations in operation—twenty-eight British and eleven German. Among the German firms in Togo and on the adjacent coasts, the most important were those of J. K. Vietor, F. Oloff, C. Goedelt, the *Bremer Faktorei*, and the *Norddeutsche Missionsgesellschaft*. The last entry represents a pattern inherited from precolonial times, in which missionary establishments acted also as trading companies.

The list also provides part of the background for the political disputes that arose over German policy in Togo in the late 1890s. The leaders of the "humanitarian" defense of policy in Togo against those who suggested development through concession companies were J. K. von Vietor, a missionary supporter and head of a Hamburg trading house, and the directors of the Protestant missionary societies in Togo, all of whom had a considerable stake in current policy.[15] The issues in dispute were therefore not just theoretical but also severely practical.

The turning of German attention toward the coast in the late 1890s resulted in two new developments: the establishment of a more or less complete colonial administration in the coastal region and the assumption by the government of direct responsibility for economic development. A hierarchy of officials, including a governor and a small support staff, was formed at Lome, the new capital, and the coastal region was divided into districts (*Bezirke*) headed by district officers. Beneath this structure the Germans relied almost entirely on local chiefs whom they confirmed in authority.[16] Much of the success that the administration had in governing cheaply and peacefully depended on the prior existence of a functioning indigenous system of local government in the colony. The success of the administration's economic policy also depended on an indigenous structure that existed prior to colonization and that linked the colony to an international market.

The Foundations of Economic Solvency

The coast of Togo had been involved since the seventeenth century in trade with Europeans—at first in the slave trade and then in the nineteenth century in the palm-oil trade, which grew up through accentuating normal peasant production of a tropical product.[17] Although the peoples of coastal Togo were related by language and economic ties to the other Ewe- and Aja-speaking peoples to the west and east of them, they were not absorbed into the Asante and Dahomean empires in the eighteenth century. They remained politically divided into small states in which the Atlantic trade was the paramount activity. Economic relations between the coast and the peoples of the hinterland existed but were never very extensive. The advent of the palm-oil trade in the nineteenth century increased the prosperity of the coast and, since palm oil was produced at the coast, reduced relations with the interior still further.

By the second half of the nineteenth century, coastal Togo had developed an economic system based on palm oil that continued to serve as the foundation of the German colonial economy. Palm oil in Togo was produced from palm kernels by small family units using crude, traditional techniques.[18] Palm kernels and processed palm oil were then assembled by the agents of European companies, who had frequently advanced credit to the producers. The palm oil and other products were gathered on the beach and were transported to ships lying off the coastal sandbar. These agents were occasionally Europeans but more often were indigenous businessmen operating under contract with the companies. Enterprise tended to be controlled by influential African or mulatto families such as the Lawsons and the Olympios, who were important in coastal politics and were the first people within coastal society to adopt Western customs and to send their children to missionary schools. They, together with the chiefly families of many of the coastal states, acted as intermediaries between European and African societies long before colonization, and they provided the Germans with an exceptionally useful basis for political and economic control.

Although there was considerable discussion within colonialist circles about developing Togo through large concession companies, it was decided in the late 1890s for practical and "humanitarian" reasons to build on the existing social and economic structure. From quite early in the 1890s, attempts had been made to introduce Togo to new forms of production, especially cocoa growing. These experiments were only marginally successful, but they demonstrated the willingness of the government to support economic development and to prevent the establishment of a monoculture in Togo. The government also established experimental stations on a small scale in the 1890s in an attempt to develop more efficient modes of production.[19] Rather more successful was an extensive educational project undertaken with missionary assistance, which resulted in a comparatively high African literacy rate and the spread of skilled trades.

In the period after 1900, the most ambitious attempt was one sponsored by the government and the KWK to develop a cotton culture in Togo.[20] This project, which attracted national attention and occasioned the expenditure of a considerable amount of money, will be discussed in a later chapter. In the end, despite intelligent planning and the assistance of black American farm experts from Tuskegee Institute, the scheme failed, although for a while cotton became an important export of Togo. Right up to 1914 palm products remained Togo's most significant economic commodity.

The administration concentrated most of its attention on the construction of transportation facilities to support trade. Lome became the center of a network of railways extending from the large wharf built there in 1904 to Anecho, Palime, and eventually Atakpame, to which a system of bicycle paths was added. The transportation program also demonstrated some of the less attractive aspects of the German colonial presence. The longest of the railroads, the line from Lome to Atakpame, was largely constructed with forced labor, and the pier at Lome, constructed cheaply and with long delays because of lack of capital, was falling apart after a few years.[21]

Many of the most successful aspects of German policy in Togo came to be associated with the name of Governor Zech, whose administration will be more thoroughly discussed in a later chapter. Zech was a prime example of the new generation of colonial officials with considerable prior experience (he had been in the Togo administration for eight years before becoming acting governor in 1903) who attained high colonial office after 1900. Zech was a leading advocate of government-directed scientific colonization, of indirect rule, and of a humanitarian native policy.[22] The respect that Zech was accorded in Germany, together with Togo's modest profitability and lack of political scandals after 1903, contributed to the building of Togo's reputation as Germany's "model colony."[23]

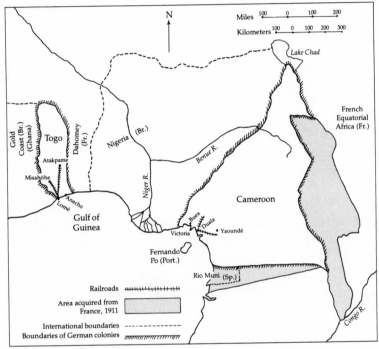

Togo and Cameroon, 1914

6

Cameroon:
Capitalism and Colonialism

Although Nachtigal's declaration of a protectorate in coastal Cameroon took place in 1884, German interests had been present in the area for some time. Both Nachtigal's treaties and the preceding commercial agreements arranged by C. Woermann and Co. were signed by the political leadership of the Duala, who had been involved in European trade for centuries and who were concerned about threats to their status as commercial middlemen. German and British missionary operations of long standing existed. The region's general orientation was toward Britain.[1] Britain had maintained loose official control over the entire Bight of Biafra since the 1840s through the British consulate on Fernando Po and the Courts of Equity of Duala and Victoria, which regulated the palm-oil trade. However, German merchant interests, especially the Woermann concern, had been expanding rapidly. In the early 1880s German trade with Cameroon had managed to draw barely ahead of the British, but in fact throughout the history of the German colony of *Kamerun*, British and German coastal trade kept pace fairly well. German colonialists argued that the division of the Guinea coast among the powers protected free trade and encouraged commercial expansion, and a British firm, John Holt and Company, eventually surpassed Woermann in Cameroon.

Conquest and Exploitation

The German traders in whose interests the German protectorate was declared were primarily concerned to prevent a monopoly by British companies over the Niger region rather than to exclude foreign competition from the Cameroon coast. Since the colonizing powers recognized the similarity of their economic interests, the boundaries of coastal Cameroon were worked out relatively quickly. Trade agreements followed, and although inland boundary confrontations occurred later, such disputes were always amicably settled.[2]

The German official presence was inserted into a coastal society that was highly commercialized and Europeanized but in which the European cultural component was largely English. The Duala themselves, although a small people, had a well-developed role as intermediaries in European trade with the interior and potentially constituted a base for the kind of colonial policy that Bismarck intended to follow. The European side of local administration was initially vested in courts made up of merchants and other resident Europeans, German and foreign. These were subordinated to an imperial commissioner, at first Max Buchner. As we have seen, however, this system quickly broke down when Woermann and his competitors complained of its costs. In 1885, therefore, a regular German colonial administration was established. It was headed by Governor Julius Freiherr von Soden, who was later a rather unsuccessful governor in East Africa. Many of the bureaucratic structures later employed in other colonies were tried out first in Cameroon, although the government there remained small for many years.[3]

Although Togo and Cameroon were occupied for similar reasons and were often classified together by colonialists, their colonial histories turned out to be quite different. Especially after the interior became better known, investment opportunities appeared to be much greater in Cameroon than in Togo. Although the existing middleman economic system based on the Duala and other coastal peoples continued to exist, it was paralleled by attempts to develop direct trade with the interior and by plantation enterprises run by European companies. The roots of future conflict with the Duala therefore existed right from the start.

The trading companies in Cameroon tended to be larger and more ambitious than in Togo. Woermann wanted to exploit the fertile coastal area and the land immediately behind it, especially the volcanic slopes of Mt. Cameroon, by establishing large, European-run plantations for producing palm oil, coconuts, and other tropical products requiring a heavy rainfall. Such plantations were first set up by trading companies and later by larger concerns, such as the Victoria Plantation Company, founded in 1897. Although the plantations were not spectacularly successful, they constituted an important component of the Cameroon economy.[4]

The European plantation economy in the coastal region was not large or well capitalized enough to supplant traditional native production or to threaten the trade of the Duala. The plantations did, however, have some impact. Their need for fertile land led to a policy that made it fairly simple for them to acquire "unused" land, which in Cameroon automatically belonged to the government. Since African land tenure and agricultural methods made it easy for land to be identified as unused, African populations soon became conscious that they were being exploited. The desire for land also led to military expeditions to establish German authority over higher land inland from the coast, especially around Buea. In addition, the plantations created a requirement for labor, both skilled and unskilled. The Duala and other coastal peoples among whom the Protestant Baseler, Catholic Pallotine, and American Presbyterian missions had worked supplied some skilled labor, and the government established state schools and training programs to produce more. As elsewhere, a major problem was unskilled manual labor. In the 1890s the government began to assemble forced labor for the plantations. Plantation labor in Cameroon probably did not have as disastrous a social effect as did white farming in Southwest Africa because of a heavier African population in Cameroon and because, in the 1890s at least, the African peoples involved were sufficiently commercialized to be able to respond to demand for labor without great social dislocation. It was not so much the coastal plantation economy as the attempt to establish direct inland trade and the creation of large concession companies in the late 1890s that seriously threatened many indigenous societies.[5]

The official formulator of German policy in Cameroon was Jesko von Puttkamer, governor from 1894 until 1906. Puttkamer has had a bad historical press, mainly because of heavy criticism of his administration after about 1900. Much of the criticism was deserved; Puttkamer was a thorough autocrat who carried out his duties with great brutality. On the other hand, he went to Cameroon in 1894 in the wake of a revolt by Dahomean soldiers against the sadistic Acting Governor Leist, and he removed some of the worst abuses of the early period of German rule. He was also a friend of Sir Roger Casement, which probably indicates that he had some redeeming features. It is clear that Puttkamer in making policy relied heavily on a number of able officials and business managers, especially *Schutztruppe* commander Hans Dominik and Eugen Zintgraff, founder of the Victoria Company. Under Puttkamer the government supported the plantation companies on land and labor matters to the best of its very limited ability.[6]

A major thrust of policy in Cameroon was the opening of the interior to German exploitation. Although the smaller coastal trading companies were originally content to build on coastal agriculture and limited, Duala-controlled traffic with the interior, the possibilities for rubber and mining behind the coastal rain forest attracted other, wealthier enterprises. Interior exploration by the government and by representatives of the larger trading companies commenced in the 1880s.[7] It soon became apparent that the trade monopoly of the coastal peoples would have to be broken and that areas of high economic potential occupied by people not amenable to concourse with the Germans would have to be conquered. The first goal could be achieved at the risk of friction with the Duala, which was partly averted through continued German reliance on them for skilled labor and local government. The second required constant military action to conquer and exploit the peoples of the interior.

The first thrust of German expansion was into the region west of Duala, which was suitable for plantations and a likely base for inland trade. The Germans met resistance with military expeditions, consisting originally of soldiers recruited in Dahomey. In the 1890s these expeditions grew larger and became a bone of contention in the Reichstag, which had to appropriate money for them. Cameroon produced the first significant German colonial military defeat. In late 1891 a force under Freiherr von Gravenreuth operating in the area of Mt. Cameroon was attacked near Buea and many of its members, including Gravenreuth, were killed.[8] This was used as an excuse for mounting a "punitive" expedition under Dominik, which in three years subdued Buea, subjected its people to forced labor, and opened up the country to plantation companies interested in cotton and rubber. The capital of the colony was moved to Buea for a time (1901–1909) because Puttkamer wanted to reduce German dependence on the Duala and to reduce the economic dominance of the coastal lowlands.[9]

The position of the Duala remained highly ambiguous. The Duala political leadership was in part responsible for the advent of German rule, but the same leadership had also attempted to play the Germans off against the British in 1884 and 1885.[10] German officials considered the Duala less than completely loyal, but at the same time they had to rely on the Duala as trading partners, skilled workers, and government and commercial employees. They were the most completely Europeanized group in the colony and they were essential to German political control, but they were not liked by senior officials. The Duala naturally opposed the policy of direct interior trade, and their considerable political sophistication, together with the assistance of the important Baseler Mission, allowed them to influence official native and labor policy, much to Puttkamer's annoyance.

Having to rely on an African people who could deal with them on their own terms produced in many Germans a predictable reaction. Puttkamer, never a gentle soul, echoed Buchner's earlier sentiments when he wrote the Duala were the "laziest, falsest, and meanest rabble on whom the sun ever shone, and it would certainly have been best when the country was conquered in 1884 if they had been, if not exterminated, at least expelled from the land."[11] Puttkamer blamed the missions for Germany's dependence on the Duala but also admitted the existence of that dependence.

In the end, as German rule was extended into the northern interior and as the attention of the administration turned inland, the situation of the Duala declined. Their trade domination and political independence were destroyed, and they were subjected to land expropriation and to increasingly heavy taxation. In 1907 the Duala appealed directly to the Reichstag for protection against the administration. Their timing was poor. A new colonial secretary, Bernhard Dernburg, enjoyed the support of the Reichstag majority, and he had already committed himself to a policy of economic development similar to that of the Cameroon government. Tensions increased after 1907 and culminated in attempts by the Duala to negotiate with the British and the hanging of a Duala chief in 1914.[12]

The German advance into the interior revolved around Yaounde, the eventual capital of the country, well inland from the coastal rain forest. The Germans found it easier to deal with the people of Yaounde and the surrounding territory than with most of the coastal peoples, partly because direct trade between the Europeans and the interior peoples appeared to benefit both sides, to the disadvantage of the middlemen. Yaounde became a kind of interior headquarters in 1894, from which the rest of northern and eastern Cameroon was reduced. The *Schutztrupper* —mostly Africans under German command—were led by Dominik and Zintgraff on a series of expeditions in which, by 1902, they reached Lake Chad, ending a period of boundary disputes with the British and French. The Germans also conquered the eastern part of Cameroon by force, but the major campaigns took place in the north against several Muslim states, especially the expanding Fulani principalities.[13] The Germans first defeated peoples under simultaneous attack by the Fulani and then forcibly established political hegemony over the Fulani themselves. Like the British in northern Nigeria, the Germans left existing northern political systems intact and ruled merely as overlords.

The indirect pattern of rule in northern Cameroon was the result of a number of factors: the practice of the British elsewhere, the favorable impression made by Western Sudanic state structures on European observers, and the absence of indigenous competition with German enterprises. Most importantly, northern Cameroon possessed much less economic appeal than did other parts of the country—which meant that, according to standard official colonial thinking, indirect rule was the only justifiable political regime because it was the cheapest. Formal German rule was needed in the north to keep the British and French out of an area that might become valuable in the future and to maintain order in a region of considerable population movement and political instability, which frequently affected the south. It was decided, therefore, to strengthen some of the existing states and to assist them in destroying their rivals. Additionally, Islamic law was maintained in force, and Christian missionaries were forbidden to work in the north.[14]

Official Policy and the Chartered Companies

Puttkamer's policy of supporting economic exploitation by trading and plantation companies made him a clear advocate of economic colonialism. He opposed both large-scale white settlement in Africa and noneconomic conceptions of colonialism.[15] Although the Cameroon budget was always in deficit, Puttkamer still believed that his policy was correct since it had enabled several companies to make a profit and had set the stage for future solvency. Puttkamer, like Zintgraff, envisioned as the basis of economic development, not a rise in trade with independent African farmers (the standard line in Togo), but the imposition of fully developed capitalism and the creation of an African working class. Puttkamer saw his job as assisting in this kind of development, rather than regulating it. The implications of this conception for native policy were worked out in the 1890s: direct taxation to force Africans to work for wages, labor conscription, and land expropriation, as well as the establishment of training schools and public-health facilities. Puttkamer's thinking was oriented originally toward development through fairly small companies, but the establishment of large concession companies in the late 1890s led to a full-scale policy of support for big business in Cameroon.

It was the nature of Puttkamer's policy, rather than the brutal manner in which he enforced it, that really created criticism of the Cameroon government and Puttkamer's eventual fall. Given the limited resources of colonial government, brutality was often regarded as a regrettable necessity in colonialist circles. To criticisms of arbitrary behavior made by the political left, the colonialists responded with praise for Puttkamer's "firmness."[16] Yet when official policy in Cameroon began after 1900 to alienate many colonialists, Puttkamer was in deep trouble. He came to be opposed by some of the missionary societies and trading companies operating in the colony, by a significant segment of right-wing colonialist opinion, and increasingly by many professional colonial officials.

The missionary attack, led by the Baseler Mission, was based both on humanitarian revulsion against Puttkamer's native policy and on a conception of colonialism that the mission's leadership shared with many merchants and economic colonialists.[17] They believed that tropical colonies should not become exploited industrial societies but rather agricultural economies centering around independent African farmers producing for a market. Such economies would be more capable of supporting European, Christian virtues in Africans and would also be more likely to be profitable. Missionary and merchant critics therefore sought a policy of native protection and government regulation of larger businesses. The trading companies, except for those with big coastal plantations, were also interested in preventing large concession companies from monopolizing interior trade and interfering with the systems of transport on which much of their trade depended.

Radically conservative groups such as the Pan-German League took the Cameroon administration under fire around 1900 as part of a general attack on the influence of big business in government. More attention was paid to the concession companies in Southwest Africa, but Cameroon was not immune. The approach of the Pan-Germans contrasted a business-oriented colonial policy with a more "patriotic" settlement one —which was easier to do for Southwest Africa, with its sizable white population, than for Cameroon. In the absence of a white agricultural population in Cameroon of the sort that the right radicals usually favored, Pan-German spokesmen were sometimes driven to support a black peasantry as an alternative to "industrialization."[18] It is doubtful that such suggestions, considering their source, were made very seriously, but they illustrate the way in which quite dissimilar groups with different motives could adopt very similar prescriptions for colonial policy.

Some colonial officials also eventually opposed Puttkamer's policy. As we shall see, colonial officialdom began around 1900 to acquire a bias against both white settlement and unrestricted capitalist development. To this group the pattern set by Togo came close to the ideal; the function of the colonial administration was to direct economic development and to protect native social structures. This was not a self-consciously humanitarian view but rather a seemingly reasonable approach based on Germany's best economic interests. Official resistance within Cameroon to Puttkamer's policies was not overt, but it probably avoided some of the worst aspects of their enforcement. Opposition to policy in Cameroon was, however, expressed in the *Kolonialrat* and, with the coming of the colonial crisis in 1905, in the Reichstag as well. The Colonial Department was unable to withstand the pressure; Puttkamer, recalled at the end of 1905, returned to Germany in 1906.[19]

Cameroon was brought particularly to public attention by the establishment of two chartered companies in the late 1890s to work concessions in the interior.[20] Of the two, the *Nord West Kamerun Gesellschaft* (NWKG), founded in 1898, was the more typical of concession companies elsewhere. The NWKG's land concession was very large and covered some productive regions in the north central part of the country. However, the company was underfinanced and was required to make heavy contributions toward exploration and the construction of transportation facilities. It also had to compete with other companies already engaged in commerce and had to pay for military support in order to set up plantations and trade routes in hostile territory. The NWKG was therefore an unprofitable venture, and it did not survive.

The other company, the *Gesellschaft Süd-Kamerun* (GSK), made much more money, partly because of its smaller obligations and free government support. The GSK was internationally financed, with heavy participation by Belgian interests, and it had more capital than the NWKG. It was also closely associated with the Congo enterprise of King Leopold. Convenient transportation routes into the Congo Free State from the company's approximately nine million–hectare concession were eventually developed along tributaries of the Congo. The connection between the GSK and the Belgian Congo was one of the factors leading to Germany's attempt to expand Cameroon during the Moroccan Crisis of 1911.[21] The GSK was not required to do much except to pay the government a share of its profits in return for its concession. Therefore, with little superimposed overhead the company could choose when and where to invest capital resources. Also, the government undertook very little supervision of the GSK's activities. (Puttkamer claimed that one reason for the NWKG's failure was excessive government regulation.) This combination of circumstances, together with the kind of business in which the GSK was engaged, led to a great number of excesses, which gave the GSK an unsavory reputation.

At its founding in 1898, the GSK was intended to establish rubber plantations like those in the Congo Free State. This in itself ensured that the GSK's activities would have a destructive impact on the societies and economic systems of the southern Cameroons. A late nineteenth-century rubber "plantation" was usually just a central point within a large and generally unculti-vated area in which large numbers of rubber trees grew. Its location was determined mainly by proximity to transportation facilities. Rubber harvesting was a gathering process requiring large amounts of seasonal unskilled labor, who frequently worked under extremely adverse conditions. In southern Cam-eroon the GSK, assisted by the government, followed the Congo pattern of assembling gangs of workers, often ruthlessly im-pressing people into its service when a labor force was needed. Even when purely economic influences such as monetary wages were used to attract labor, the effect on local social systems was still destructive since large numbers of people were seasonally forced into a proletarian status without possessing any inter-mediate social structure, such as the Duala had, to protect them.[22]

The provision of labor became a prime question in Cameroon, not just because of the concession companies, but also because of the nature of transportation in the colony. Until railways were built, and even afterward in most areas, the prime means of transportation in Cameroon was porterage. In Cameroon, both before and after the German takeover, transport was conducted by peoples whose members partly specialized in carrying, a very important function of the middlemen of whom the larger trading companies so often complained. As soon as large companies started operating in the interior, established carriers became re-luctant to assist in the destruction of their own monopolies. In any event, the existing system was inadequate for transporting large amounts of produce. The concession companies and other big concerns therefore organized their own porterage systems, thereby putting additional pressure on limited labor resources and increasing the tendency toward compulsory labor.[23] Be-sides this, with respect to both plantation and transport labor, the companies naturally wanted to keep costs as low as possible and to break down independent economic units that might bargain to raise wages. The profits of colonial companies tended to be low, and the demand for primary tropical goods, even rubber, fluctuated widely. Combined with the presence of a German colonial administration willing to back up commercial operations, these factors made Cameroon, at least in some areas, a clear example of a colony that thoroughly exploited its indigenous population.

The labor question in Cameroon was very complex, perhaps more so than in other German colonies. The plantation operators and the concession companies both wanted the government to assist them in acquiring native labor through conscription and hut taxation, but since the two interests were in competition with each other for labor, the government was caught in the middle of a political fight. The coastal trading companies, some with plantations in the interior, frequently opposed forced labor because it tended to disrupt their own more traditional trade routes. Yet some of the same companies were willing to have the government expropriate Duala land in order to establish new plantations. Missionary societies and their political supporters continually opposed the forcible transformation of Africans into proletarians but at the same time favored breaking down African social structures through education and a market economy and occasionally suggested the establishment of a white farming economy.[24]

Presiding over these conflicts of interest was the Cameroon administration, which was small but which had a good reputation among the other colonial powers. It was faced with a problem typical of government in Germany itself during the nineteenth century: having to balance a great many divergent interests while maintaining its own initiative under conditions of inadequate financing. The problem was compounded in Cameroon by the existence of well-organized African interests. This may explain the violence of the colonial administration's reaction to the Duala's appeal to the Reichstag in 1907. At that time further complications of the political situation would have threatened the administration's very limited freedom of action, unless, as Puttkamer tended to do, it simply gave in to particular interests.

In the end the Cameroon government pleased nobody over the labor issue. However, this was not solely due to the government's lack of policy, nor were the administration's highly publicized abuses against Africans due completely to the incompetence or ill will of officials. The very nature of the official policy of opening up the interior and providing labor implied the use of violence and gave ample opportunity for excesses.[25] Yet official policy also encompassed the system of indirect rule in the north and heavy reliance on native structures in the four directly administered *Bezirke* in the southwest. Forced labor was used in Cameroon as elsewhere—sometimes openly, sometimes in the guise of alternative tax payments, but usually according to wider legal and economic conceptions than simple short-range exploitation. Many officials viewed forced labor as legitimate only under government supervision and on public projects, as for example the conscription of the people of Buea to build the colonial capital.[26]

The coming of the big plantation and concession companies after 1897 tended to change all this. Not only was the government pressured into using taxation to force more Africans into a monetized economy, which was considered to be more or less legitimate, but also the concession companies began to call upon the government to take a more active role in direct labor recruiting. The government responded by using military force against peoples who resisted the agents of the concession companies.[27] This naturally gave impetus to continued resistance to German rule, and it produced many incidents that eventually opened the whole colonial operation to heavy criticism within Germany.

The well-publicized abuses of the early years, such as Leist's bloody repression of the mutiny of the Dahomean troops in 1893 and some of Puttkamer's actions, were due to a combination of governmental weakness, the unsavory personalities of some early administrators, and the existence of a state of war. These early, spectacular incidents were replaced after 1900 with a constantly repressive system of exploitation in many areas of Cameroon, which produced far more social dislocation than the earlier system. As the bureaucracy grew and became more competent, it avoided really flagrant incidents. Yet even during its most humanitarian period, the administration of Cameroon was usually willing to apply force to foster economic development.

At the same time excessive use of force tended to spur criticism in the Reichstag, upon which the administration was heavily dependent for operating funds. In addition, a political system based on violence went against the legalistic training of most of the professional officials who began to dominate the colonial administrations after 1900. It also offended their practical sense. Naked force, since it engendered resistance, was an inadequate means of keeping order by itself, unless Germany was willing to increase her expenditures on colonial armies. On the other hand, the economic exploitation of Cameroon was unlikely to occur without considerable change in indigenous social and economic structures. A thoroughgoing system of indirect rule employing existing political entities, which might have reduced resistance, was impractical outside northern Cameroon, since the interests of those entities conflicted with German goals for development. A different method had to be found.

That method was largely based on factors that had been present in the colony from an early period: missionary schools and economic colonialist theory. During the administration of Governor Theodor Seitz (1907–10), attempts were made to establish a new system of African political control in Cameroon.[28] Councils were to be set up to represent African interests and to divert discontent. Local government was to be conducted through elected communes, which would contain both white and black members but would usually be dominated by whites. The communes would control and collect their own revenues, thus helping the government escape Reichstag budget scrutiny. Seitz's plan was intended to protect Africans from excessive exactions by European enterprises and to provide a substitute for irregular violence in forwarding the government's policies of development. It was opposed by most of the European interest groups in the colony, represented in chambers of commerce and in the white Governor's Council. The plan was partly an outgrowth of the whole thrust of German official colonial theory since the 1880s: govern as cheaply as possible, consistent with limited economic aims, and if possible, govern indirectly through those organized structures with a stake in development, whether white or black. Thinking like Seitz's tended increasingly to influence policy in Cameroon after Puttkamer.

Other more indirect means of control evolved over time. By the First World War, the European schools in Cameroon had produced a small Germanized African elite partly separated from traditional African societies, which could be used to provide lower-level governmental and commercial personnel. The Germans, of course, lost Cameroon before they could discover that this elite was potentially an effective source of opposition to colonial rule. In 1914 the westernized elite (as opposed to westernized traditional structures like the Duala chief system) was in its political infancy; little conflict had appeared between it and the administration. This may be one reason for the Germans' comparatively good reputation among educated Cameroonians in the twentieth century. The elite of Cameroon owes some of its origins to the Germans, who never had to be fought by them during the struggle for independence.

A German-educated African elite could be controlled more easily by nonforcible means than could the established, traditional elites of coastal society, and it could be more easily assimilated into a bureaucratic political and economic structure, thereby reducing the need to import German personnel. Since the development of such an elite was very much in keeping with the economic theory of colonialism, it is not surprising that settlement-oriented colonialists were against it. In Cameroon and Togo, with their small white settler populations, the entry of blacks into the civil service was harder to oppose than in East Africa, but it was occasionally questioned in the Cameroon Governor's Council, which represented resident European interests.[29]

Colonialism in Cameroon was not peaceful. As we have seen, both the conquest of the interior and the course of economic development were marked by a considerable amount of violence and African resistance. Because of the highly diversified geography and political structure of the Cameroons, however, it was not possible for a unified resistance to appear as it did in Southwest Africa and East Africa. The absence of a large white settler population was also a factor. Nevertheless, the continual need for military action in Cameroon and the financial limitations under which government and business operated there meant that Cameroon was always open to attack within Germany as an example of the deficiencies of colonialism.[30]

7

German East Africa:
Economic Exploitation
and Colonial Politics

Because East Africa was frequently considered to be the most important of Germany's colonies and because it was subjected to an enormous variety of political and economic problems, we shall concentrate more heavily on it than we have on the other territories.

As we have seen, Bismarck did not want East Africa and accepted it only on the understanding that Germany would avoid conflict with Britain and that German businesses there would pay the costs of government. Neither expectation was wholly fulfilled. Although Britain and Germany avoided armed conflict over East Africa, there were frequent diplomatic confrontations, which in turn created political problems in Germany. Furthermore, German enterprise in East Africa failed to make a profit.

Peters, DOAG, and the Early Years of German Rule, 1885–1890

Neither the Germans nor the British were the first imperial exploiters of the East African mainland, although the merchants of both countries had been active at Zanzibar for some time.[1] Until the 1880s the coastal region of what later became German and British East Africa owed allegiance to the sultan of Zanzibar, who was in turn supported by the British government. Despite British political preponderance German merchants played a major commercial role on the island of Zanzibar by the 1880s. However, neither the British nor the Germans were very active on the coast, which was controlled by a highly commercialized, urbanized Swahili-speaking society of great antiquity. The ruling classes of the coastal cities controlled the three major trade routes to the lakes region and participated directly in the ivory and slave trade. Because Zanzibari and coastal merchants had exercised varying degrees of political control over interior peoples since the 1840s, the major trade routes were essential factors in East Africa's history, both before and after the German takeover. The northern route extended from Mombasa, Tanga, and Pangani to Lake Victoria, through territory that later became largely British. The southern route, which led from Kilwa on the coast to Lake Nyasa, had been disrupted earlier in the nineteenth century by the Ngoni incursion; it passed through the area controlled by the emerging Hehe state. The most important route was the central one, which went from Bagamoyo to Tabora in the center of the country and then branched into two spurs going to Ujiji on Lake Tanganyika and to Uganda. The central route had been used by many of the European explorers of East Africa. In the 1880s it was dominated in many places by the Nyamwezi, who provided porters and taxed coastal caravans going into the interior.

The sultan's actual control on the coast was quite limited, but Zanzibar was the ultimate terminus and transshipment point for all three trade routes. In the late nineteenth century Zanzibar's growing clove production made it less dependent on mainland trade, which allowed its political separation from the coast to occur without massive economic disruption. By 1890 much of the slave trade had ended anyway, which further reduced the importance of Zanzibar's coastal relations.

The treaties that Peters and the *Gesellschaft für deutsche Kolonisation* signed in 1884 and 1885 were mainly with chiefs in the interior; the German protectorate in East Africa officially applied only to regions behind the coastal strip.[2] The coast was still nominally under the control of the sultan. The German government, however, reserved an interest in the coastal region to secure transit into the interior and to stop slave traffic. The GfdK's claims to transit rights were backed up with a naval demonstration in 1885 and were thereafter recognized by Zanzibar and Britain. During the next several years Germany and Britain jockeyed to establish their interior East African boundaries and to settle such questions as the fate of Zanzibar itself, the German claim to Witu in Kenya, and the disposition of kingdoms in the hinterland such as Buganda, Rwanda, and Burundi. These issues were resolved in a series of negotiations, which we shall consider later.

The conflict with Britain over East Africa and its eventual resolution affected both German and East African politics.[3] The locations of the interior trade routes were major factors. The line between British and German territories assigned most of the northern route to the Imperial British East Africa Company, and the central and southern routes became German as far as the lakes. After a further round of treaty-signing competition between Peters and his British rivals Jackson and Lugard, Britain took over Uganda and Germany acquired Rwanda and Burundi.

The central problem of Zanzibar was solved by a major Anglo-German treaty in 1890. Zanzibar and Witu became British spheres of influence in return for the cession of Heligoland in the North Sea to Germany. The boundary on the mainland was drawn from a point between Mombasa and Tanga to Lake Victoria, thereby giving to Germany the Pangani River basin, Usambara, and most of the environs of Kilimanjaro. As elsewhere in Africa, the economic portions of the treaty provided for continued trade and for consultation on tariffs. Zanzibar was not

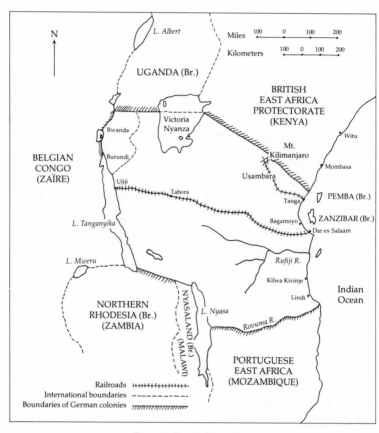

N

L. Albert

Miles   100   0   100   200

Kilometers   100   0   100   200

UGANDA (Br.)

BRITISH
EAST AFRICA
PROTECTORATE
(KENYA)

Rwanda

Victoria
Nyanza

Witu

BELGIAN
CONGO
(ZAÏRE)

Burundi

Mt.
Kilimanjaro

Mombasa

Usambara

Ujiji

Tabora

Tanga

PEMBA (Br.)

L. Tanganyika

Bagamoyo

ZANZIBAR (Br.)

Dar es Salaam

L. Mweru

Rufiji R.

Kilwa Kivinje

Indian
Ocean

NORTHERN
RHODESIA (Br.)
(ZAMBIA)

NYASALAND (Br.)
(MALAWI)

L. Nyasa

Lindi

Rovuma R.

PORTUGUESE
EAST AFRICA
(MOZAMBIQUE)

Railroads   +++++++++++++++++
International boundaries   – – – – – – –
Boundaries of German colonies   ⁊⁊⁊⁊⁊⁊⁊⁊⁊⁊⁊⁊⁊

German East Africa, 1914

cut off from mainland trade, nor was traffic along the northern route halted.[4] In other words, imperial rivalry was not carried to the extreme of self-defeating economic restrictions.

One of the major sources of political difficulty for Germany in East Africa was Carl Peters. He and his company were obviously interested in making a profit in East Africa, but his use of violence in native relations, due apparently to a sadistic streak in his nature, was clearly excessive. In addition, as the darling of the radical right in Germany, he openly advocated massive white settlement and constantly exceeded the limits Bismarck had set for him in claiming land in competition with Britain. Contrary to Bismarck's desires, Peters turned the 1887 German Emin Pasha expedition into an attempt to stake out an enormous African empire for Germany, encompassing Uganda and extending into the Congo basin. Many of Peters's claims, such as that to Uganda, were repudiated by Bismarck, who commented that Peters was a "filibuster," but others were accepted.[5]

The problem of Peters constitutes a useful introduction to the interrelations between German and East African politics in the early period of colonial rule. The replacement of the GfdK in 1887 by the *Deutsch-Ostafrikanische Gesellschaft* (DOAG) was due partly to Bismarck's desire to establish a company that could both govern and develop and partly to the need to control Peters.[6] Even disregarding Peters's unsatisfactory character and his political ties, Bismarck feared that Peters would start an unnecessary war—if not with Britain, then with one or more African states. In the monied interests that controlled the DOAG board of directors, Bismarck found the means of reducing Peters's role.

Peters, however, could not be avoided. His position as the country's most famous colonialist made it difficult for Bismarck or, later, Colonial Director Kayser to attack or ignore him. When DOAG relinquished its political role in 1890, Peters became an imperial commissioner in the area of Mount Kilimanjaro. Peters had selected this area for intensive development of plantations and white settlements producing export crops. He set up an experimental station and exercised almost unchecked political authority in his region, for the official administration tacitly accepted his claim to practical independence. As a result, he was allowed to indulge his rather gross propensities for tyranny against the Chagga, the most important people in his area. This led to unrest and, in 1892, a violent rebellion by the Chagga that was very difficult to put down.[7] Peters was forced to return to Germany, theoretically to respond to press criticisms, and was placed in retirement.

Peters had further sinned against official sensibilities by his key role in creating the precursor of the Pan-German league in 1890 as a protest against the Zanzibar-Heligoland Treaty with Britain, which had directly countered Peters's aspirations for East Africa.[8] As an official in East Africa, Peters had continued to attack the government's foreign policy.

Even in retirement Peters was an embarrassment to the government and the Colonial Department, especially when he criticized Kayser and when in 1895 and 1896 it began to appear that a move was underway to make Peters the next colonial director. Among most colonialists, although not the Colonial Society's leadership, he was as popular as ever. The means of removing Peters appeared in 1896, when the Social Democratic leader August Bebel, in attacking government colonial policy, reported in the Reichstag that Peters, while imperial commissioner, had executed his African mistress and her lover in a fit of jealousy. Kayser gave Peters a pro forma defense that included more than a hint of condemnation. He admitted that Peters had exceeded his authority by ordering executions but said that the executions were the result of suspected plots against the European station on Kilimanjaro. Kayser went on to say that although such extreme action was deplorable, it could be understood in the context of the highly dangerous situation of Peters's station—a situation that was largely of Peters's own making, as Kayser's listeners knew.

Peters was given an administrative trial and was dismissed from government service, going into self-imposed exile in England. He was supported by several conservative political leaders, especially by Wilhelm von Kardorff of the Free Conservatives (*Reichspartei*), but much of his reputation had been destroyed. Peters and his supporters believed, probably correctly, that Kayser had actively sought Peters's fall and had insured that Peters's reputation would be ruined. Whatever his motives, Kayser had gotten rid of an official embarrassment.[9]

By the time of the Peters scandal, the German administration in East Africa was already changing, with government initiative replacing private direction. This process had commenced almost immediately after the establishment of DOAG. Despite its backing by a few big investors, DOAG was actually undercapitalized. Both its major stockholders and the government had miscalculated the immediate profitability of East Africa and had greatly underestimated the costs of exploiting it.[10] It was discovered that trade with East Africa could not be easily expanded. The mechanism for supplying ivory, for example, was not sufficiently elastic to respond to increased demand, and besides, the Germans were committed to putting down slaving, which was traditionally a concomitant of the ivory trade. Also, the German entry into East Africa and their attempt to tax commerce had disrupted coastal trade and had made it even more difficult for DOAG to make money. Between 1888 and 1890 the total value of exports from East Africa was less than three million marks—too small a figure to make a profit.[11]

DOAG also had to pay the costs of government, and this did not turn out to be a cheap proposition. A treaty with Zanzibar in 1887 gave DOAG the privilege of collecting duties and taxes in the coastal region, over which the sultan remained theoretically sovereign.[12] It was hoped that DOAG would thereby be able to profit from long-distance trade, whether its own or other people's. The system did not work as expected. DOAG was unable even to pay for an effective tax-collection system, and the coastal traders naturally evaded payment whenever possible. Finally, the first of the major East African wars, the Abushiri rebellion, irrevocably destroyed German dreams of cheap and solvent empire.

The rebellion began in the late summer of 1888 when coastal chiefs and traders protested DOAG's raising of the German, rather than the Zanzibari, flag over Pangani. It was led by a Swahili merchant and slave trader, Abushiri, who enlisted enough support to create a full-scale war. The war was, of course, caused by more than an affront to Zanzibari national feeling. There was not much real loyalty among mainland subjects to the sultan, whose writ had not run very far even before the Germans. Yet precisely this weakness in the Zanzibari state had made it acceptable to the leaders of coastal society, since it gave them practical autonomy. The coming of the more powerful Germans and British, who clearly intended to govern and control commerce, naturally led to resistance.

Faced with the rebellion, DOAG appealed to the government, which responded with a naval expedition against the coastal towns and a small land army led by a highly able officer named Hermann von Wissmann. Wissmann was given civil as well as military authority as imperial commissioner. His army, in which the officers and noncommissioned officers were mostly Germans, was primarily recruited in the Sudan. The use of Muslim Sudanese soldiers, called *askaris*, set the pattern for the later East African *Schutztruppe*, although the Sudanese were eventually replaced by local Muslim troops. Wissman's policy of refusing to Europeanize his troops or to threaten their religion was, however, retained.[13]

During 1889 Wissmann and the navy managed to reduce most of the coastal cities and clear the trade routes. He defeated Abushiri in a number of fights and persuaded the ruler of Usambara—the region behind Tanga—to stay out of the rebellion. The ruler accordingly turned Abushiri over to the Germans, who hanged the Swahili leader at the end of 1889. The rebellion continued in isolated areas, but with its back broken, resistance petered out in 1890.

It was obvious, however, that the idea of letting DOAG run the East African colony had failed, both politically and economically. The coastal Swahili were clearly not the only people who had to be beaten in order to make East Africa profitable; yet DOAG was unlikely to pay the costs even of the Abushiri rebellion in the near future. The reckoning period in East Africa happened to coincide with the reorganization of the colonial administration in Berlin in 1890. As a consequence of these changes, the German government took over direct political control and tax collection in East Africa, undertaking to make up the colonial deficit through subventions.[14] DOAG was relegated to a purely commercial role, and its monopoly was rescinded in return for a generous financial settlement. The object of official policy remained essentially the same: to make the colony profitable, self-supporting, and as little a strain on the German government as possible. The retraction of political functions was greeted by most directors of DOAG with approval, since it removed an overhead expense and gave a promise (never actually realized) of future profits.

The Establishment of German Political Authority, 1890–1905

Wissmann remained at the head of the infant German administration in East Africa, much to the chagrin of Carl Peters, who had to be satisfied with his commissionership in the northeastern interior. Wissmann was a colorful character, a famous traveler, and an excellent writer with a wide reputation in colonial circles.[15] Perhaps because of this, he was disliked by Chancellor Caprivi and was replaced in 1891 by Freiherr von Soden. Soden was made a full-fledged governor and was empowered to create a regular governmental system like that of Cameroon. The command of the *Schutztruppen* was vested in a separate office, which retained considerable autonomy because of German traditions of civil-military relations and because in the 1890s military authorities frequently conducted local colonial administration. Although the system of employing military personnel in administrative positions continued for a great many years, particularly in interior areas, it was paralleled by a growing system of civil control closer to the coast. When *Bezirke*, or local districts, were established, they were designated either civil or military. Over the long term, however, the balance shifted decisively in favor of the civil authority.[16]

In the 1890s the colonial government also developed staff

functions at the new capital of Dar-es-Salaam. The personnel for the early central departments, like many district officials, were recruited from among the employees of DOAG. The government established financial offices and a regular judicial system, the latter in place of the amateur courts that continued to exist in several other colonies.[17] In the early 1890s the administration began to recruit *Assessoren* (junior career bureacrats), although the colonial service was not integrated into the imperial civil service until 1910.

Even in the early years the administration was heavily committed to agricultural and medical research. An agriculture department was established in 1893, and an experimental botanical garden was built at Dar-es-Salaam. Scientific stations were also set up, mostly with financial help from the KWK. The most important was the research station in Amani, built in 1902.[18] The government-directed scientific effort had successes and failures, but altogether it produced some of the most clearly beneficial contributions that the Germans made to the development of the country. The scientific stations and experimental plantations of Usambara and Kilimanjaro introduced new crops that eventually created an export-oriented agriculture.[19] Usambara became an area of European-run farms and plantations growing coffee, cotton, tobacco, tea, and sisal, from which new crops were expanded into other regions of African peasant agriculture. Sisal, introduced by the Germans early in the 1890s from the United States, eventually became the major export of the country.

The great stumbling blocks to colonial exploitation and profitability, according to colonial theorists, were the inability of East Africa to attract sufficient investment to extend the European-oriented segment of the economy and the government's lack of money to assist in the process. The experience of DOAG made concession companies of the late-Cameroon type seem a poor risk, and smaller private concerns generated only a limited amount of capital. In the early 1890s about half of East Africa's revenue was provided through subvention from Germany. Although the proportion was later somewhat reduced, continual warfare made government in East Africa a financially losing proposition. Tax policy was used as a way of stimulating growth and increasing revenue. In 1897, for example, a hut tax was levied in areas under actual German control. By requiring payments in cash, the hut tax was supposed to expand the monetized economy and increase the labor supply, and it was therefore favored especially by white planters in the northeast.[20]

Many problems facing the Germans in East Africa converged on the question of railways, which were regarded as the key to economic development but which were also capital investments that no private company would bear by itself. In late nineteenth-century colonial thought railways were regarded as absolutely vital agents for economic change and were part of every major East African development scheme.[21] The colonialists' faith in railroads was to some extent irrational, a recrudescence of mid–nineteenth century railway mania, but many of the railroad arguments had merit. A major railroad-building project in an underdeveloped area could encourage a round of economic change and help to monetize a primitive economy, in addition to lowering transport costs.

Initial interest in railway building centered around the northeastern part of East Africa, in the potential plantation area of Usambara. The Usambara Railway was begun in 1893 by a subsidiary of DOAG, but lack of funds and engineering problems forced its abandonment. It was restarted with a Reichstag interest guarantee, but by the time the first section was completed in 1905 the railroad extended only 129 kilometers inland and was not profitable. Nevertheless, the Usambara Railway became important in politics because it served the area where the majority of white settlers established farms. Its extension farther inland became a prime political goal of the settlers and their supporters at home. The *Nordbahn*, as the projected extension was called, was likely to be expensive, and it paralleled an existing railway in British East Africa, but the Colonial Department supported it for political reasons. In 1901 the Reichstag approved funds to continue the *Nordbahn* a short distance and denied funding to a *Zentralbahn* scheme. The *Nordbahn* tended thereafter to be backed by conservative, settlement-oriented colonialists, and the *Zentralbahn* became a main objective of colonial administrators and economic colonialists.[22]

The concept of a *Zentralbahn* was formulated in the late 1890s. It was supposed to follow the old central trade route from the coast to Tabora and later was to be extended to Lake Tanganyika and thence to Rwanda and Burundi.[23] Its purpose was to stimulate African peasant production of export crops, such as peanut growing among the Nyamwezi, by providing convenient access to coastal markets. The KWK became interested in the idea and established the Amani Institute partly to conduct scientific research to back up the *Zentralbahn* scheme. The *Zentralbahn* remained in limbo until 1907, but the whole idea of peasant-oriented economic development became a major component of official policy in East Africa after 1900.

New development schemes began to be taken seriously at about the time the government assumed responsibility for economic development and white planters began settling in the northeast. These two phenomena informed the politics of East Africa after 1900, from disputes over the *Nordbahn* and *Zentralbahn* to more general conflicts. For example, the settlers required large amounts of African labor but had difficulty recruiting it. Even the Nyamwezi, who responded readily to monetary incentives, tended to seek higher wages offered by British concerns across the border.[24] Plantation labor demand, combined with unwillingness to pay attractive wages, led to unsupervised labor recruitment. European agents assembled work crews in areas away from the plantation region, frequently by employing force and fraud and seldom by offering written contracts. Before 1905 the government was usually willing to assist in forcible recruitment. Not only did this create African resistance, but it also made it difficult to establish peasant agriculture in areas where recruiting took place. The settlers resented the *Zentralbahn* because it went through their prime recruiting areas and raised wages through competition for labor. The tendency of the white settlers to organize politically after 1900 was due partly to their vital interest in influencing railway routing and official labor policy.

During the 1890s the outlines of a political administration gradually took shape in East Africa.[25] The system of white district officials was increasingly extended, and particular forms of native administration developed in certain regions. In many coastal areas it became necessary, as the Germans' economic exactions increased, to replace indigenous political structures with more direct control by the bureaucracy and, after 1910, by municipal governments. Elsewhere, the government appointed African chiefs called *akidas*, who reported to white district officers. This was not originally indirect rule, since the *akidas* usually came from outside their districts and operated much like European officials. After 1900, because of resistance to *akidas* in the south, the government tried to recruit them locally, but this change required considerable time to effectuate. One of the reasons for the Maji Maji rebellion in 1905 was southern resentment against alien *akidas* and the economic policies that they were required to carry out.

In areas of central East Africa where large states existed, the Germans tried to rule truly indirectly once the African states had been subjugated. Among certain peoples, especially the Sukuma of the northwest, German district officers ruled through clan heads in segmentary lineage systems. This allowed large areas to be governed economically, but it was often an unsatisfactory system for encouraging economic change. Indirect rule also gave African political structures a means of influencing policy in East Africa, which they exercised increasingly over the years.

In populous Rwanda and Burundi, which were not yet considered ripe for exploitation, it was decided to keep the German presence to the minimum necessary to maintain order and to keep out other powers.[26] A German resident was appointed to advise the rulers of the feudal kingdoms there and to ensure minimal compliance with German policy. Richard Kandt, for many years the resident, was a strong advocate of continued

German acceptance of the existing African political system as the basis of authority. This was regarded, however, as a temporary arrangement that would change when the railroad reached the lakes region.

During the governorship of General Eduard von Liebert (1896–1901), a chancellor's decree created local communal authorities in areas in which there were many Europeans and European interests.[27] The communes were to undertake local government and collect local taxes, thereby reducing the strain on the colony's budget and the requirement for subsidies from the Reichstag. The communes were supposed to contain representatives of significant white and nonwhite political and economic groups within a local area, although Germans were to dominate. Liebert himself—a racist, radical conservative committed to white settlement—did not approve of mixed communes, but he set them up under order. His much more "progressive" successor, Gustav Adolf Graf von Götzen, believed that the communes impeded rational economic development and therefore eliminated their nonwhite elements.[28]

By 1900 the ethnic pattern of coastal colonial society had begun to emerge. The Swahili-speaking Muslims of the coastal towns had become the Germans' major partners, acting as agents for German companies, enlisted *Schutztruppen*, and lower-level officials. Swahili, rather than German, was made the official language of East Africa and was taught in government schools. Islam was protected by the state, despite opposition from missionary societies.[29] Swahili power, however, waned to some extent with the growth of a white settler population in the northeast, the entry of non-Muslim Africans into the lower ranks of European enterprise, and especially the appearance of a sizable Indian population. DOAG had imported Indian laborers into East Africa early in the 1890s. East Africa's close economic connection with India (the official currency in German East Africa was the rupee) led to growing immigration by Indians until by 1914 the Indians were an extremely important economic element in the colony. They operated most of its retail trade and accumulated considerable capital.[30] At the same time they were highly resented by Swahili-speaking Africans and white settlers, who campaigned to have Indian immigration and competition restricted. The white settlers were actually a minority even of Europeans in East Africa. In 1913 there were only 882 planters and settlers in the colony out of a total white population of 5,336. However, their political power was disproportionate to their numbers because of their ability to obtain support from conservative parties in Germany.[31]

The administration of Götzen (1901–1905) was distinguished by a new, elaborate, government-sponsored development policy. Götzen, a general-staff officer and explorer, was one of the most respected German colonial theorists. He believed that the mass growing of cash crops was the key to colonial profitability and that the government itself should direct and invest in their development. In his first years in office, Götzen also supported the KWK's attempt to establish a cotton culture in East Africa.[32]

Götzen's scheme for economic change was multifaceted. He tried to get railway appropriations from the Reichstag in 1901 but failed, except for the short extension of the *Nordbahn*.[33] His removal of nonwhites from the communal governments and his appointment of civil servants to the communes were intended to facilitate economic coordination. He issued orders that made coercive labor recruitment for the northeastern plantations easier. In areas with few whites, he established a program of *Volkskultur* to encourage African farmers, with a mixture of education and fiscal coercion, to grow cash crops for market.[34] *Akidas* in the southeast were ordered to establish exemplary farms, on which African males were required to work for set periods. Götzen recognized no conflict between his aims of encouraging white plantation production in some areas and African peasant farming in others, even though labor and capital scarcities made a contradiction very likely. He did not understand that coerced economic change, however enlightened, was bound to arouse stronger African opposition than had Liebert's brutal collection of hut taxes since it threatened the very foundations of African societies. Götzen did not understand, in other words, why he suddenly in 1905 had to confront an African rebellion more massive than any previously experienced by a modern colonial power.

The Maji Maji Rebellion

African resistance to the Germans in East Africa can be visualized, to an extent, in terms of stages. The first stage, the Abushiri rebellion, was the opposition of a kind of imperial competitor to the Germans and was ended through military defeat and through the series of compromises that the Germans made with coastal society. The next stage consisted of struggle between the Germans, who were expanding their rule largely for economic reasons, and highly organized interior African states such as those of the Nyamwezi and the Hehe. The latter, a military state that had formed in the south during struggles with the Ngoni and Nyamwezi, offered the longest resistance.[35] Under their leader Mkwawa the Hehe fought the Germans constantly between 1893 and 1898. They were finally beaten by the *Schutztruppe* under Tom von Prince and Lothar von Trotha. The Maji Maji insurrection in 1905 was something different from these earlier conflicts. Few of the peoples who had resisted the Germans in the 1890s, including the Hehe, took part in Maji Maji. Maji Maji involved several different peoples of southern East Africa, many without highly organized political systems, who were brought together by German taxes, labor recruitment, and enforced *Volkskultur*.[36] The cement that held Maji Maji together and gave it its peculiar character was magic and popular religion. The rebellion was organized by itinerant religious figures or "medicine men" who developed a magical ideology of resistance to appeal to different peoples. *Maji Maji* itself refers to an incantation that was supposed to turn German bullets into water. Götzen claimed that "native superstition" was the cause of the rebellion, but many other observers recognized that magic was rather a means through which threatened societies mobilized for action.[37]

The socioeconomic causes of the war were evident in its first act, in July 1905, when the men of Kibata refused to work on an exemplary cotton farm and attacked the local *akida*. The rebellion spread quickly, with killings of European farmers and agents throughout the south. The *Schutztruppe* and white volunteers were hard pressed, and the government was forced to recruit soldiers in New Guinea and to ask for army and marine infantry reinforcements. In September a visiting Catholic bishop was killed and a number of mission stations, one quite close to Dar-es-Salaam, were burned. By the late autumn the rebels, joined by the Ngoni, were in control of the southern fifth of the country. With the arrival of German reinforcements, however, the rebels fell victim to superior weapons and their own lack of coordination. By April 1906 the main part of the war was over. Between 75,000 and 100,000 Africans had been killed, and vast areas of the south had been wasted by the Germans. The Ngoni resisted until 1907 before they too were defeated.[38]

The Germans did not escape unharmed. Several hundred had been killed, and considerable damage had been done to European investments. The colonial deficit had increased phenomenally because of the war, and the rebellion, coming on the heels of the Southwest African war, had helped to create a major political crisis in Germany. Götzen's reputation was still largely intact because he had helped to put Maji Maji down. However, it was apparent to his successor, Albrecht Freiherr von Rechenberg, a career diplomat appointed governor in 1906, that major reforms were needed to prevent future rebellions and to meet the enormous costs of the war.[39]

8

The Pacific Colonies and Kiaochow

Except for Kiaochow and Samoa the colonies that Germany acquired outside of Africa were of minor importance, but many of the same processes that occurred in the African colonies took place also in the Pacific. As in Africa theoretical concepts of colonialism altered as a result of colonial realities, the government gradually took over the operation of the colonies from concession companies, and a complex set of relations developed between the Germans and their subject peoples. Since most of the Pacific colonies were economically insignificant and since few major expenditures were required there for military campaigns (although there were some instances of active resistance to the Germans), the politics of the Pacific colonies obtruded on the German public consciousness to a lesser extent than was the case with Africa.[1]

As we have seen, the concession for exploiting and governing Kaiser Wilhelmsland and the adjacent islands of the Bismarck Archipelago was granted to a financial consortium controlled by the Hansemann interest, at whose behest the protectorate was established in the first place. The *Neu Guinea Kompagnie* (NGK), the instrument of this consortium, was charged by its owners with economic development and by the government with almost all the business of administration. The NGK was not the only commercial concern in the area, but it was the largest and it usually prevailed in the making of policy. The NGK also sponsored exploration into the hinterland and established, on paper at least, an elaborate bureaucracy based on current principles of colonial administration. Control was supposed to be exercised from Germany by a board of directors, of which the bureaucracy in New Guinea would be the executive arm, developing new products and collecting taxes. As elsewhere, only perhaps more spectacularly, the enterprise failed.[2] Costs regularly exceeded income, not only on the administrative account, but also on the purely commercial side of the company's operations. German New Guinea and the Bismarck Archipelago were simply not valuable enough to show a profit without extensive, and expensive, development. Costs were multiplied by the NGK's outsized bureaucracy. Because the NGK was unprofitable, the German government had to foot the bill for such essential items as naval patrols. German control was maintained in the Pacific through periodic visits by gunboats, which were sometimes an expensive proposition but which were cheaper than maintaining officials everywhere.[3]

In the end the NGK could not perform the administrative functions assigned to it, and as elsewhere, the German government had to step in and take over. The German New Guinea territories became an official colony in 1899, with the government paying the NGK a high price for the return of the charter. The German presence there was never very extensive, and when war came in 1914, the takeover of the area by Australia and Great Britain was almost unopposed. One of the few advantages that Germany derived from New Guinea was an ability to recruit troops there, particularly in 1905 for use against the Maji Maji rebels in East Africa.[4]

The German experience in the other Pacific island colonies was much the same. The German holdings in the Marshall Islands were expanded by the purchase from Spain in 1899 of

Palau, the Carolines, and the Marianas exclusive of Guam as compensation for the takeover of the Philippines by the United States. The Carolines and the Marianas were administered as official colonies rather than as concessions. The concession companies set up in the earlier island possessions, such as the Jaluit Company, continued to be moderately profitable and extended their operations to the new possessions. However, in the general abandonment of the concession-company system after 1900, the Pacific companies lost their governmental functions everywhere.[5] The Pacific companies made attempts after 1900 to develop new products, but as before the basis of their profits continued to be copra, a commodity whose international market was declining. Since the Pacific island colonies remained marginal throughout the period of the overseas empire, their occupation during the First World War was not seriously opposed.

The one exception to these generalizations about island colonies was Western Samoa, which became a full-fledged German colony in 1900—after German business interests had been profitably entrenched for half a century—and which generally managed at least to pay the costs of its government.[6] As early as the 1870s, German companies, especially the Godeffroy family's *Deutsche Handels- und Plantagen-Gesellschaft* (DHPG), had begun to displace the American, Australian, and New Zealand companies that had long dominated the copra trade there and had also begun to appropriate Samoan land to establish cotton, coffee, and cocoa plantations. The DHPG had sunk a good deal of money into these enterprises, coming close to bankrupting the Godeffroy establishment in the process, but also had developed excellent prospects for long-term profits. As we have seen, Bismarck's first colonial venture was his scheme for a Samoan steamship subsidy in the 1880s. In the process of expanding its interests and holdings, the DHPG increasingly involved itself in Samoan domestic politics, in which it was strongly supported by German consular and naval officials in the area. In 1887 consular and company officials sponsored a coup d'etat, installing as ruler Tamasese, head of one of the constantly warring political factions in the islands. The Germans then attempted to use their position to extend the DHPG's control, and foreign interests, backing the unsuccessful claimants to the throne, called for support from the American and British governments. The German government, not wanting to fight over Samoa, repudiated the actions of its officials and called a conference in Berlin in 1889. From the conference emerged a tripartite system of control, in which Germany, the United States, and Britain were to exercise a loose condominium over the islands and were jointly to rule the capital of Apia and run the European courts there. In fact, most of the officials of the condominium were German.

Throughout the 1890s German interests in Samoa continued to expand, as did American interests in the eastern portion of the islands. Although the condominium worked about as well as could be expected, the system eventually broke down, partly because of conflicts of economic interests and the continuance of civil strife among the indigenous population and partly because of the growth of international tensions at the time of the Spanish-American and Boer wars. After incidents in 1899 that almost resulted in a naval clash between the United States and Germany, the condominium was abrogated, and in 1900 the islands were divided by treaty between Germany and the United States after Britain had pulled out of Samoa. In Western Samoa a regular German colonial government was set up with Dr. Wilhelm Solf, a professional colonial official who had earlier been a judge and municipal president in Apia, as governor.[7]

In the ensuing years German Samoa was a relatively peaceful and profitable colony, although its economic growth was far from spectacular. It is not likely that the establishment of German rule did much to encourage development; the government spent little on improvements. Many of the standard colonial disputes, including one over plantation labor and private land expropriation in which Solf intervened decisively to protect indigenous interests, occurred in Samoa. These disputes seldom penetrated domestic politics, where Samoa was normally regarded as an element of Germany's *Weltpolitik* securing general German interests in the Pacific.[8]

Perhaps the most unusual of all the German colonies in the

Pacific and East Asia areas was Kiaochow, a small colony and naval base established on the Shantung Peninsula in China in 1898. Kiaochow was maintained, not as much for its own worth as a producing unit, but as a base for German economic penetration into China. It was run by the navy, not the Colonial Department, and officially it was designated a "naval base." Yet in its manner of operation, the theory employed to explain it, and its relation to politics within Germany, Kiaochow was clearly part of the overall structure of German colonial enterprise.[9]

The political events leading to the establishment of Kiaochow illustrate the domestic political aspect of German colonialism. The original impetus for the creation of a German colony in Shantung came from the spokesmen for business interests desiring to exploit the area as a location for mines and as a market for German manufactured goods. They argued that a German base would stake Germany's claim to a share of Chinese business vis-a-vis the other powers and the Chinese government. In addition to its direct advantages as a military base, for which it was in fact used in 1900, they contended that Kiaochow would also serve as an earnest of the German government's intentions in East Asia and as a symbol of its commitment to German merchants there. The initial motives behind Kiaochow were therefore commercial, and the interests involved there, unlike those in Germany's African colonies, were very prominent ones, backed by the major banks. This in itself created considerable pressure to establish an official presence in China.

The establishment of Kiaochow resulted immediately, however, from the political needs of the navy. The late 1890s marked the beginnings of the expansion of the German navy and the public campaign led by Admiral von Tirpitz for the building of a heavy battle fleet. Tirpitz attempted to assemble the support of segments of the German political and cultural leadership in order to get the kind of expanded fleet that he desired. To obtain the Colonial Society's support, he portrayed the new fleet as a means of securing, and possibly expanding, the colonial empire. To heavy industry he held out the possibility of new armaments orders. And to overseas investors interested in China, he expressed the navy's desire to establish a naval base on the Shantung Peninsula. The Foreign Office, which had earlier turned down such ideas, despite pressure from the navy and from elements of big business, even in 1897 refused to press for possessions in the Far East that would further aggravate Germany's strained relations with Japan and the other powers in the area. This gave Tirpitz the opportunity to rally procolonial support behind the navy by using the navy command to argue successfully for the grabbing of territory in Shantung.

The navy was portrayed in Tirpitz's propaganda as the most vigorous major branch of the Reich government and the one most conscious of Germany's national requirements. Comparisons were made between the reputed inefficiency of the Colonial Department and the aggressive competence of the naval command. After the takeover of Kiaochow, the navy continually publicized the effectiveness of its administration there and the obvious profitability of the colony, as compared with the territories administered by the Colonial Department. The theme was taken up, in fact, by liberal critics of the Colonial Department, who argued, probably seriously, that the administration of all the colonies should be given to the navy.[10] The popular notion of an efficient Kiaochow government, like the similar notion regarding Togo, was based in part on fact but was greatly inflated as a result of the navy's feud with the Foreign Office.

Tirpitz won a round against the Foreign Office in 1897 and was allowed to acquire a foothold in China as long as he left diplomatic relations with China outside the base to the Foreign Office. Tirpitz found an appropriate excuse in 1898 to land troops on the Shantung Peninsula and to establish a naval base that extended across the mouth of Kiaochow Bay. The Chinese government, beset by a series of similar land grabs by the other major powers as "compensation" for the German move, was forced to agree to a long-term leasehold by Germany on Tsingtao, the principal city of Kiaochow, and its environs and to a German sphere of influence in Shantung Province. In the ensuing years Kiaochow proper was turned into a "model colony" in miniature, and extremely profitable mining and railroad enterprises were created in Shantung. From the point of view of economic advantage, Kiaochow was one of the most successful German colonial endeavors. Its usefulness waned, however, after about 1905, as political developments in China made the German hold on Shantung more tenuous.[11]

As in the case of Togo, Kiaochow was to a large degree exempt from many of the standard disputes over administrative policy. Because the navy was commercially oriented and because the idea of German settlement in China was patently absurd, the question of a settlement versus a trade-oriented policy never seriously came up. Since Kiaochow was seen as the key to more informal interests in Shantung, the colony was not really required to produce profits for German companies within its own boundaries, although profits were actually made there. The prime requirement was that the colony pay the expenses of its own administration from local revenues, and thanks to the thriving commerce of Tsingtao and the efficiency of tax collection, it did so a great part of the time.

An important feature of government in Kiaochow was its heavy use of the Chinese administrative system already in existence there.[12] For several years the amount and the nature of the Chinese taxes previously imposed were continued and were only gradually altered. Chinese officials were kept in their posts and were recruited, at first, according to Chinese civil-service procedures. This permitted the imposition of German rule with minimal expense and dislocation and was to no small degree the secret behind the success of the Kiaochow colony. The affairs of the small number of Germans in the colony were handled by separate offices and courts, but these did not impinge heavily on local Chinese society. Where there were new impositions by the Germans on the local economy—as in the forcible acquisition of railroad rights-of-way or in the seizure of land for building purposes—conflict, but seldom violence, did result.

Kiaochow, then, despite the fact that it was run by the navy rather than the Colonial Department, followed quite closely the administrative theories accepted by most German colonial officials and the general tenets of German economic colonialism.

Kiaochow was a success because its operation met the criteria of success that were accepted for the economic colonial theory. Yet the correctness of the theory itself did not make the colonial system work in Kiaochow as much as did the extremely favorable conditions existing for imperialist activities in Shantung. As in the African colonies, the relative usefulness of Kiaochow to Germany was a function of the total set of circumstances obtaining at that particular place and time, rather than simply the formal practice of the German administration.[13]

PART III

COLONIAL POLITICS IN
GERMANY, 1890–1906

9

Groups and Interests
in Colonial Politics

Economic and Political Background

The politics of German colonialism after 1890 were an integral part of those of Wilhelmian Germany in general and therefore responded to the currents of socioeconomic change that most affected national political affairs. The most important of these was the adjustment of German society to full industrialization. By the 1890s Germany was an economic giant with the world's most advanced technology and with a more efficient business structure and a higher reinvestment rate than Britain, whose volume of international trade Germany was beginning to approach. Germany was more dependent on foreign markets and suppliers than she had been in the 1870s, but with the end of worldwide depression in the mid-90s, such dependence was no longer regarded as being entirely bad. Urbanization had proceeded at a faster rate even than Germany's phenomenal population growth (41 million in 1867 to 67 million in 1914).[1] These and other changes naturally created political disequilibria that were especially difficult to correct, since in Germany social groups fundamentally separated from the forefront of change managed to retain a large share of political power. The major problem of Wilhelmian politics was the difficulty of creating effective consensus within the system, and this difficulty affected colonial politics as much as any other kind.

The groups in German society that benefited the most from industrialization were the owners and managers of major businesses, who had organized into large pressure groups. By and large, the direct economic interest of big business in the colonies continued to be minimal, since investment capital in Germany was limited and financial institutions preferred to put their money into areas of the world with higher potential for profits. The KWK could attract some business interest for schemes like its cotton projects, but normally big business supported an active colonial policy only verbally, as a way of getting the German government to commit itself to generalized support of enterprise abroad and of garnering political support for proindustrial policies from self-consciously nationalist and patriotic segments of the population. Business spokesmen, in other words, used colonialism as a means of creating consensus in favor of policies of which they approved.

Many other groups, not as much in step with industrialization, also used colonialism for similar purposes. These groups ranged from the inordinately powerful Prussian Junkers through the growing organizations of the *Mittelstand* to the Social Democratic party, which represented an amalgam of new working-class and older artisan dislike of industrialization. Since within the political system there was no single, clear center of power, the political process in Germany was literally fragmented. The establishment of consistent policies to confront the problems of rapid economic change was therefore extremely difficult, since no single group or interest could easily assemble a consensus behind what its leaders wanted to do.[2]

To the multitude of groups unhappy with the direction of social and economic change, colonialism was one of a range of ideologies that could be used in politics to mobilize support and to attack other groups. Deficiencies in the existing colonial empire and its operations, measured in terms of any of the commonly accepted varieties of colonialist ideology, were pointed out to discredit the government. The supposed growth of big-business influence in the colonies was decried equally by the radical, middle-class right (represented by the Pan-German League) and by the SPD, although for different theoretical reasons. Colonialism in general reflected both the social and ideological differences present within German society and the way in which politics was conducted. The colonial empire was a rich source of political images: Germany struggling to find her "place in the sun"; preindustrial Germany attempting to reassert itself through farmer-settlers in Southwest Africa; capitalist Germany exploiting helpless Africans. These images could be used in politics, and since the actual economic involvement of most German groups in the overseas empire was very small, the domestic political function of colonialism was the most important feature of colonial politics in Germany.

In the fragmented political system of Wilhelmian Germany, the focus of politics increasingly became the Reichstag, despite the authoritarian tendencies of the governmental structure established by Bismarck. Although the Reichstag had been given little real power and had originally been intended by Bismarck as an empty gesture toward political liberalism, it was the only completely public part of the imperial government and the only one elected through a system of universal manhood suffrage. It was therefore the most obvious place for the symbolic aspects of political compromise and consensus building to occur. As a result, the importance of the Reichstag to policymaking in Germany increased steadily after 1890, even though no real solution to the basic problem of fragmentation was found.

Colonialism and the colonial empire played important roles in the development of the Reichstag as a functioning part of the political system after 1890. The lack of provision for financing the overseas empire in the Imperial Constitution, coupled with the perennial budget deficits of the colonies, made it necessary for the colonial administration annually to seek subventions from the Reichstag. Projects involving the sale of bonds or the construction of expensive transportation facilities normally required interest guarantees from the Reichstag in order to attract capital at reasonable rates.[3] The colonies made the government particularly vulnerable to attack and criticism during the annual budget review by the Reichstag and its Budget Commission. The real control that the Reichstag exercised over general colonial policy after its review powers were confirmed in 1894 made the colonies an ideal subject for the attentions of rival parties of all political persuasions. The Reichstag on several occasions forced the government into policies not favored by the colonial administration, such as the settlement policy in Southwest Africa and the partly successful effort by East African settlers to reverse official native policy after 1908. Of course, the government could have stood up to the Reichstag parties on the colonial issue, as Bismarck had earlier done over the military, but to have done so would have required the expenditure of considerable political capital. The colonies were simply not worth it. A colonial issue in 1906, however, occasioned the first real parliamentary election in Germany in which the government itself openly participated.[4]

In the continuing debate about the importance or lack of importance of economic factors as determinants of late European imperialism, the role of colonialism in domestic German politics is of some significance. Germany's overseas empire was in no sense a major economic asset to Germany, and the interest of big business in the economic potential of the colonies was minimal. There was clearly a very important link between economic and social change in Germany and overseas imperialism, but in the case of the colonies, the link was through domestic German politics, particularly the Reichstag. Participants in the German political system, whose activities were fundamentally determined by their reactions to societal change within Germany, employed colonialism as a tool to get what they wanted and as a means of overcoming some of the major deficiencies in the system, particularly the difficulty of achieving consensus. Much of German colonial politics therefore revolved, not around individual, narrow business interests in particular colonies, but around the varying uses to which colonialism could be put by broader social and economic interests within Germany.

Business Interests

The Hanseatic tropical trading companies were the business interests most directly concerned with colonies for the longest period of time, many of them continuing to operate and expand in their traditional areas between 1885 and 1914. However, success was not evenly distributed. The two major West African companies, C. Woermann and Company and Jantzen & Thormälen, managed to diversify their activities and to establish moderately profitable arrangements with the government, but neither ever became a large company by the standards of German business. Even in Cameroon, where Woermann was most strongly entrenched, a British concern, John Holt and Company, became the largest trading enterprise.[5] Many of the smaller companies did considerably less well since the establishment of colonies did very little to stabilize the fluctuating market in tropical products. In all probability the successful companies would not have been very profitable either if they had actually been forced by Bismarck to pay the costs of colonial administration. In the end the contributions that they made through paying import and export duties seldom covered more than a fraction of the total cost of government.

The tropical trading interest was particularly concerned with native policy, taxation, and economic development. Although the larger companies sometimes undertook extensive projects such as Woermann's plantations in Cameroon, the vast majority of trade in Africa and in the South Pacific was done with small-unit enterprises that gathered tropical products directly from peasant producers.

The nature of the basic economic concern of the tropical trading companies tended to determine their attitudes toward government policy. They naturally favored reductions in tariffs since their prices were most affected by duties on trade. On several occasions in the 1890s, trading representatives in the *Kolonialrat* introduced recommendations to reduce or abolish colonial tariffs from the colonies, but the government, although sympathetic, could not afford such a change.[6] Import and export taxes, which were easy to collect, could be established administratively. The trading companies argued for personal taxes on native populations in place of duties. In theory, personal taxes would not directly affect trade and would encourage the growing of crops for cash. At the same time it was obviously to the disadvantage of companies whose business was done primarily with native commerical structures to encourage the dissolution of African and island societies. Most, although not all, of the trading companies tended to favor a liberal native policy, which implied an effort to protect indigenous social structures to a degree consistent with "progress" and economic development.[7] In terms of domestic politics, the leadership of the more successful trading companies tended toward the National Liberal and *Freisinnige* (left-liberal) parties.

Closely related to the tropical trading companies were the shipping companies of the Hanseatic cities. With the support of banking interests, the Woermann concern diversified its activities in the 1880s and formed the Woermann Steamship Line, which was intended to be a specialized carrier trading to Africa.[8] The Woermann Line maintained a fairly profitable service up to the First World War, mainly because its specialized business was not challenged by the large transatlantic German carriers and because it was awarded the government mail contract. Woermann's activities illustrate several characteristics of German colonial business: the tendency of big business not to involve itself directly in colonial enterprises, the relatively marginal nature even of successful colonial enterprises, and the great importance of the government in the course of commercial development.

The larger shipping interests, the Hamburg-America Line and North German Lloyd, were also involved in colonial affairs, but not directly. H. H. Meier, the founder of North German Lloyd, was also one of the founders of the Colonial Society and one of the major spokesmen of the economic position on colonial development. Albert Ballin, from 1897 the director of the Hamburg-

America Line, was continually involved with the colonial movement and the making of colonial policy. Ballin may have first suggested the appointment of Bernhard Dernburg as colonial director in 1906.[9] However, neither of the major steamship lines did much business with the colonies, and the influence that they exerted through the government, the *Kolonialrat*, and the Colonial Society was seldom narrowly directed toward enhancing their own business, except for their ability to exploit the colonies should the colonies become profitable in the future.

The steamship companies were instead interested in using the colonies for political purposes within Germany. Shipping concerns, for example, wanted a strong navy. Colonialism provided a popular excuse for building a battle fleet, so that individuals and organizations favoring naval expansion tended to involve themselves with the colonial movement. Colonialism, as a set of political ideologies, also offered German business a means of making a patriotic statement in the face of claims by the overtly antiindustrial right that economic development was ruining Germany. To the image of the German warrior or peasant-hero put forward by radical conservatives, the shipping and commercial interests opposed the image of the heroic German merchant battling to win new markets, and thus prosperity for Germany.[10]

Colonialism was also employed by shipping interests to affect foreign policy, especially toward Britain. We shall discuss this aspect of colonialism at greater length in Chapter 11. Shipping officials like Ballin saw both aggressive colonialism and the building of a battle fleet as means, not ultimately of causing conflict with Britain, but of creating an economic understanding with Britain that would allow Germany coequal status as a world power. If sufficiently threatened by Germany in areas of vital British interest, the British would eventually come to an agreement with Germany on common political actions and on allocation of the world's markets. This kind of thinking stemmed directly from the general policies of the major steamship companies and similar interests, which had vigorously challenged British shippers but had recognized their own dependence on trade with Britain and the British Empire. Support of economic colonialism was one means of encouraging the German government to back up the shipping companies by challenging Britain in the colonial area yet constantly showing the advantages to be gained by cooperation with Germany.

The big German banks and investment houses were never very keen investors in colonial enterprises, mainly because the capital shortage in Germany before 1914 made frivolous investment dangerous. Most of the major banks did, however, put enormous sums of money into foreign investment outside the German colonies: in some areas the Germans came first to rival, and then replace, the British as sources of investment capital. Yet even in such areas German investment was intended as a means of increasing overall German business and developing invisible exports, and it was undertaken within much narrower margins of capital availability than the directors of the banks thought to be safe. This explains the financial and verbal backing that many bankers gave to the colonial movement. They reasoned that active colonialism could produce a useful patriotic image and could encourage the government's continued commitment to support both colonial and noncolonial overseas enterprise, since the distinction between the two could easily be obscured. And contributing to the Colonial Society was a great deal cheaper than risking scarce investment capital in an unpromising colony.[11]

This does not mean that there was no investment by large financial institutions in the colonies; we have seen such investment in the cases of DOAG and the New Guinea Company. Heavy participation by wealthier concerns was unusual, however, and was characteristic mainly of the first years of colonial enthusiasm. The investment in DOAG seems, for example, to have occurred for patriotic reasons and in order for investors to present a desirable public image.[12] In the 1890s less investment in the colonies was voluntarily forthcoming from big companies, and this led to the Colonial Department's policy of encouraging private companies and investors to put their money into the colonies. The formation of the *Kolonialrat*, largely dominated by business interests, was intended to assure business concerns that they would have a major voice in the formulation of government policies that might affect investments.[13]

The financial interests that backed concession companies in the 1890s were not usually willing to risk capital by themselves. They desired government guarantees of return or the participation of foreign capital. The individual most clearly associated with the latter approach was Julius Scharlach, a Hamburg businessman and lawyer whom we have already met. Scharlach helped to establish two companies through which foreign capital was applied to German colonial enterprise, the *Gesellschaft Süd-Kamerun* (GSK) and the South West Africa Company, Ltd.[14] We have already seen how the GSK operated in Cameroon and how its profitability was due to the support that it was given by the government in recruiting (and conscripting) labor. The company was founded jointly by German and Belgian investors; the connection between the GSK and concerns operating in the Belgian Congo may have had considerable influence on German policy in central Africa. The South West Africa Company, Ltd. was established with Rhodes money but with a predominately German board of directors (mainly to protect the company against right-wing political attacks within Germany). Like most of the concession companies in Southwest Africa, however, it was more interested in waiting for its land to appreciate in value than in active development.. This made good sense in terms of profitability, but it was contrary to the intention of the concession and aroused considerable controversy.

Although the interests of the larger investors in the German colonies were not the same as those of many procolonial (but noninvesting) big-business leaders, they were nevertheless such that both groups shared the same general ideological positions. They thought that colonial policy should be aimed at efficiently developing the colonies as adjuncts to the German economy. If funds for colonial development were more readily available in foreign countries, then they should be sought abroad. Equally importantly, a policy of sharing colonial development with the British could serve as the first step toward guaranteeing Germany's international economic interests through a cooperative arrangement with Britain.

Around 1900 another sort of business interest in the colonies became evident, although its effect on policymaking was probably not extensive. German financial leaders began to profess concern about Germany's balance of payments as foreign trade began to account for an increasingly high proportion of national economic activity. Some thought that fully developed colonies could help to protect Germany from the adverse effects of a balance-of-payments deficit by keeping some exchanges within a controlled economic area. To an extent this was a continuation of the neomercantilist *Mitteleuropa* concept but within a narrower range. Bernhard Dernburg used the balance-of-payments argument heavily in 1907, during the Hottentot electoral campaign of that year.[15]

A much more significant interest in colonial policy was evinced by certain industries that imported large quantities of raw materials. In the 1870s and 1880s many of these industries had supported colonial acquisition, partly because they supposedly feared being cut off from their sources of raw materials but primarily to reduce competition in overseas markets during the depression. In the period of increasing prices and selling opportunities after the mid-1890s, however, the problem of raw-materials supply came to be regarded as more critical, especially since many raw materials displayed more than average rises in price.[16] The appearance of a rising (although unstable) market for tropical products such as rubber, coffee, and cotton in fact probably did more to bring about the development of colonial economies before 1914 than did any set of deliberate actions by the colonial powers. The rising prices of tropical goods also caused manufacturers using them as raw materials to seek means of holding prices down. The old economic colonialist theory was therefore trotted out once again, in somewhat altered form, to demonstrate that the colonies could be developed as areas in which to produce cheap raw materials,[17] thereby increasing the supply of tropical goods and lowering international commodities prices. These arguments were taken quite seriously by many

German businessmen, but other motives were apparent as well. The advocacy of colonial policy to combat high prices of materials was also intended to encourage the German government to take more far-ranging action to control prices of imported goods. One commodity to which these considerations particularly applied was cotton.

At the end of the nineteenth century, cotton was still the primary raw material for the European textile industry. Demand for cotton had always been high, but new factors affecting cotton supply had come into existence in the late 1890s. Textile manufacturers began to fear that new cotton producers' associations, especially in the United States, were raising the price of raw cotton.[18] In Germany this fear led to the founding in 1896 of the Colonial Economic Committee (KWK), which advocated, as we have seen, the development of the colonies as areas for producing primary economic goods. The KWK shortly afterward associated itself with the Colonial Society, but it retained its independent character throughout its history. Its founder, Karl Supf, was a factory owner, a prominent colonialist, and one of the leaders of the campaign to build a major German battle fleet. From an early period in its career, the KWK undertook development projects in most of the German colonies, but its prime interest was always in cotton, and its most ambitious undertaking was the Togo cotton project of the early 1900s. Between 1904 and 1909 Togo did manage to produce a substantial amount of low-grade cotton, but production was not profitable enough to continue the experiment.[19] The cotton scheme and some of the other work of the KWK did, however, affect colonial politics. The cotton project occasioned a great deal of favorable comment in the Reichstag, not only among those already committed to colonialism, but also among the less orthodox *Freisinnige* whose main previous opposition to the colonies had been their unprofitability. The KWK's activities gave the colonial empire the appearance, at least, of potential solvency.

On the whole, business interests tended to be concerned as much with the political aspects of colonialism within Germany and with the relation of colonial policy to overall German economic policy as they were with the specifics of colonial economic development. Nevertheless, despite the small size of many of the actual colonial businesses, they were very important in determining policy at the local level, as we have seen in the cases of Cameroon and Togo. Their ability to affect policy apparently depended on a coincidence between their interests and those of larger, more influential, but mostly noncolonial concerns and also on the fact that in many cases little else but the interests of small companies could be used as a basis for policy.

Official Interests

Within the German government there were several agencies that affected colonial policy through their normal operations and through competition over their interests. The most important were the Colonial Department, which became the independent Colonial Office in 1907, and the various individual colonial administrations; policy was also affected by the Foreign Office, the navy, and the Imperial Treasury. The navy will be discussed in the context of navalism in Chapter 11, since the navy was frequently an antagonist of the regular colonial administration. The role of the treasury, like that of treasuries the world over, was to economize and to say "no" to unjustifiable expenditures. In Germany this function was amplified by highly circumscribed imperial finances, which increased even further the requirement for economy in nonessential areas of government like the colonial empire.[20] One of the cornerstones of German colonial history, at least until 1906, was the inability or unwillingness of the government to commit extensive funds to colonial development.

The Colonial Department did not enjoy a good public reputation. Its personnel were popularly regarded as being only marginally qualified for their jobs, and within the Foreign Office the Colonial Department was considered to be an unsatisfactory place to make a career. Recent research, however, has indicated that in terms of training and measurable forms of competence, officials of the central Colonial Department were not as deficient as they were thought to have been.[21] The department's low reputation appears to have been the result of its lack of finances, the bad odor that clung to the entire department because of the colonial scandals of the 1890s, and deliberate attacks by parties in the Reichstag and by the navy.

The Colonial Department was headed by a series of directors of varying backgrounds and abilities. Paul Kayser (1890–96), by most reports, was an able official with little experience in foreign affairs and originally with no firsthand knowledge of the colonies.[22] Kayser, a lawyer of Jewish parentage and an expert on labor law, appears to have had some difficulty fitting into the social milieu of the Foreign Office. Committed to a policy of economic colonialism through private enterprise, he created the *Kolonialrat* and packed it with the representatives of business interests to encourage investment. He had been officially involved in several colonial ventures even before taking over the Colonial Department in 1890. Kayser apparently established the economic colonialist outlook that the Colonial Department, with some significant exceptions, retained all through its existence. Whereas Kayser and his immediate successors subscribed to the private-enterprise version of economic colonialism, after 1900 the focus among the department's personnel was on the government as economic initiator. This change in emphasis, which was reflected in individual colonies, was one of the most important events in the development of German colonial policy. It constitutes the essential difference between the policy of Kayser and that of the best known of the colonial directors, Bernhard Dernburg.

Kayser was replaced in 1896 as colonial director and was "kicked upstairs" to the Imperial Supreme Court. He died shortly thereafter. He had come under increasing criticism from people and parties who had discovered the potential of colonial politics for providing issues to be used in the Reichstag and elsewhere.[23] Kayser's policies had especially become the objects of attack by groups such as the Pan-German League that subscribed to the settlement colonial viewpoint. His successor was a senior Foreign Office personality, Oswald Freiherr von Richthofen, who was clearly destined for bigger things. He left few marks on colonial history in his brief period in office (1896–98). Richthofen, incidentally, belies the generalization that the colonial directorship was a career dead-end for professional bureaucrats. Two years after leaving the Colonial Department, Richthofen succeeded Bülow as foreign secretary. One other colonial secretary became foreign secretary: Wilhelm Solf (colonial secretary, 1911–18; foreign secretary, 1918).

Richthofen was followed by Gerhard von Buchka (1898–1900), a mediocre official who followed the standard Kayser line on colonial development. Buchka was bitterly attacked by some segments of the colonial movement for his complete support of the concession companies in Cameroon and Southwest Africa and for a lack of vigor in pressing the colonies' claims to funding before the Reichstag. His successor, Oskar Wilhelm Stübel (1900–1905), was well regarded by many colonialists for his activity and knowledge of the colonies. At his direction the government began to assume responsibility for the economic development of the colonies.[24] Stübel ran into difficulties in the Reichstag because of his insistence on increased colonial appropriations. In order to mobilize support from the entire colonial movement for his proposals, Stübel made gestures to all varieties of colonial opinion. This included support for active settlement policies in Southwest Africa. Stübel left office during the colonial crisis of 1905, at which time nobody of any competence could be found to occupy the job. Prince Ernst von Hohenlohe-Langenburg, the son of the first president of the Colonial Society, accepted the position temporarily for patriotic reasons and made little impact during his brief tenure in office. His successor, named in September 1906, was Bernhard Dernburg, whom we shall discuss in considerable detail later.

The amount of active direction exerted by the Colonial Department depended to some extent on the personality of the colonial director. Yet even the most active directors were hemmed in by inadequate finances, by the colonial bureaucracy, and especially by the obvious difficulties of attempting to rule such a widely spread empire from a single location. The same limitations faced the *Kolonialrat*, which never succeeded in imposing consistent policy on the colonies. As we have seen, the *Kolonialrat* was ostensibly established by Kayser in order to obtain expert business and civil-service guidance in making overall colonial policy. Although the *Kolonialrat* also was intended to encourage investment in the colonies and to allow the colonial director to exert indirect influence on colonial companies, its stated formal purpose appears to have been taken quite seriously by Kayser and his successors. Up until 1908 the colonial budget and other broad policy issues were regularly submitted to its consideration. At the *Kolonialrat*'s semiannual meetings the controversial opinions of junior officials were heard and senior administrators were questioned in detail, since *Kolonialrat* proceedings were published only in summary form.[25]

The *Kolonialrat* served as a focus for interest-group influence on colonial policy, and its debates reflected the variety of such influences. This was considered desirable when the *Kolonialrat* was founded in 1891, but after 1900 it made the council a target for attack both by reformers and by conservatives, since it seemed to symbolize the subservience of the colonial administration to selfish business interests. Furthermore, the *Kolonialrat* appeared to reformers to be an outdated political form that interfered with rational administration precisely because it represented particular interests. By 1908 the *Kolonialrat* was a political liability, and Dernburg abolished it.

In the 1890s individual colonial governments and defense forces also enjoyed rather poor reputations, but over the years their public and foreign images changed. By 1914 many foreign observers believed that German colonial personnel were the best in Africa, at least in terms of formal qualifications, and in all probability they were right.[26] Although, as in other areas, credit for the improvement in official performance was later ascribed to Dernburg, the process of developing a competent bureaucracy had actually commenced long before Dernburg became colonial director in 1906.

In the 1890s full-time colonial officials were few and their backgrounds were diverse.[27] In East Africa the majority were simply taken over from DOAG, which had not been too particular about hiring in the first place. Some of the scandals of the 1890s were due to the presence of unsuitable characters in the administration. After a full-fledged colonial system was established in most colonies, the number of personnel remained limited. Under the governor came a tiny central office presided over by a *Kanzler* and a number of district officials in the areas that the Germans ruled directly. Districts, or *Bezirke*, were headed by white *Bezirksamtsmänner*; in the early years these were frequently military officers or noncommissioned officers. In 1900, there were only forty senior officials in the entire overseas empire. By 1914 the empire was somewhat better stocked with personnel than it had been earlier. In addition, a colonial career pattern had emerged.

The creation of a professional colonial civil service was more easily undertaken in Germany than in many other countries because in the 1890s the German universities produced a surplus of candidates for government jobs. Despite this, certain drawbacks of colonial service tended to limit the quality of the people intending to make a colonial career. Its reputation was not high. Time and again in the memoirs of colonial governors, one finds recollections of warnings against colonial service issued to the authors when young men.[28] Furthermore, overseas colonial officials were contract employees, not regular civil servants, until Dernburg's personnel reforms of 1910. The colonial service therefore did not provide tenure or, for some years, retirement benefits, nor was there provision for transfer to other departments in grade. Therefore, colonial service really was less desirable than service with the major imperial or Prussian ministries; it tended to appeal to budding officials with obscure social backgrounds and those in the governments of the smaller states. The colonial service appears to have attracted a large share of men with unconventional attitudes and people such as Jews who were excluded from successful careers elsewhere in the Foreign Office.

In the 1890s appointments in the colonies began to be made at the level of *Assessor*, the lowest executive rank within the German bureaucracy. By 1914 many of the highest colonial positions were filled by former *Assessoren* from the 1890s. Junior colonial officials received the same, essentially legal, training as all other career civil servants. The colonial service was greatly criticized for this; one of Dernburg's later objectives was to establish a training system more closely attuned to the needs of the colonial service. In fact, the government had by the 1890s made considerable strides in this area. In 1887, for example, the Seminar in Oriental Languages had been established at the University of Berlin to teach languages that officials would need in the colonies. The seminar's emphasis on Swahili was one of the reasons that it was possible to use that language as the official tongue of German East Africa. Still, as in practically every other colonial service, there was little formal, practical training for administrators. Such training had to be acquired through experience overseas.

Perhaps the strongest asset of the German colonial service was the availability of highly competent technical and scientific personnel, who were the envy of foreign colonial services. Not only could the Colonial Department call on the occasional services of scientists such as Robert Koch, who worked in East Africa on sleeping sickness, but it was also able to recruit high-caliber permanent technical officials like Franz Stuhlmann (1863–1928). Stuhlmann was a biologist and cartographer who came to East Africa as an explorer and became in 1903 the director of Amani Institute, where he acquired an international reputation in agricultural science.[29] To technical personnel a colonial career definitely appealed as a means of rapidly acquiring a reputation that could be cashed in for a position of considerable responsibility at home.

Despite variations, certain patterns began to emerge in the backgrounds of colonial officials after a few years. Many governors and high military officers continued to be noblemen, but over time both governors and the senior civil officials tended toward the bourgeoisie.[30] The colonial service showed itself to be an avenue of advancement for those without social connections. Theodor Seitz, governor of Cameroon and Southwest Africa, was recruited from the obscurity of the Baden civil service and Richard Kandt, the German administrator in Rwanda, was a Jewish doctor from Poznan. The colonial service's ability to attract able but slightly disadvantaged people may have helped to offset its general lack of appeal to top civil-service candidates.

The collective influence of the colonial service on colonial policy was very limited; officials had little long-term contact with one another and lacked the means to develop joint positions. By 1914, however, a degree of group feeling had evolved and, more importantly, a collective orthodoxy on colonial policy had developed. In the postwar period, when former colonial officials were the motivating force within the Colonial Society, it was truly possible to describe them as a coherent interest group. However, this was not really the case before 1914.

Nevertheless, the professional colonial officials executed policy on the spot in the colonies. Within the plethora of local factors influencing their decisions, it is possible to identify a vague consensus about the foundations of colonial policy. The main lines of this official consensus grew out of the economic colonial ideology, thoroughly modified by the realities of colonial administration and through adaptation to the Colonial Department's bureaucratic environment.

During the 1890s most colonial officials appear to have shared the views of Colonial Director Kayser.[31] The objective of colonial policy was to keep government expense to the minimum required to provide essential services and to encourage private investment, primarily in trade with native producers and in plantations and mines. It was assumed that the colonial empire would eventually pay the costs of its administration and would constitute a productive component of the German economy, although colonial officials tended to put the date for economic success farther into the future than did nongovernmental enthusiasts. After about 1900 dominant opinion among colonial officialdom shifted within the general context of economic colonialism from an emphasis on the role of private enterprise to a concentration on the economic role of the government.

There were several reasons for this shift. By 1900 private-development policy had pretty clearly failed: it was not an economic success, and it endangered the Colonial Department's relations with the Reichstag. In addition, the fledgling professional colonial service began to adopt an elitist, critical attitude toward other colonial interests simply in the process of developing its self-identity. Officials increasingly believed that they themselves were best qualified to make the colonies profitable, and many nongovernmental colonialists began to agree with them.[32]

Too much should not be made of the collective political opinions of the colonial bureaucracy. As we have seen, they had little opportunity to exert joint influence on the central policymaking process. In addition, alternative views existed within the colonial service itself. One segment of official opinion corresponded fairly closely to settlement colonialism in perceiving the benefit of the colonies to Germany in social, rather than economic terms. Southwest Africa—Germany's only real settlement colony— became the seat of this point of view after Theodor Leutwein was replaced as governor in 1905.[33] Although the existence of official settlement colonialism led to some disputes within Southwest Africa, surprisingly little tension existed within the Colonial Department as a whole as a result of this kind of ideological difference. The leading exponent of settlement colonialism and right-radical politics in the colonial service was Friedrich Lindequist, Leutwein's successor as governor of Southwest Africa. Lindequist's career and reputation were apparently unaffected by basic differences with his colleagues over policy. He became undersecretary under Dernburg and succeeded Dernburg as colonial secretary in 1910. He was undoubtedly assisted by his public identification with settlement colonialism, but this does not seem to have created resentment against him within the colonial administration.[34]

The other major official colonial group was the military, which had been involved in colonial administration from the very beginning. By 1900 every African colony except Togo, which possessed a paramilitary police force, had its *Schutztruppe*. The composition of the *Schutztruppen* varied somewhat, from an all-white volunteer force in Southwest Africa to the more typical arrangement in East Africa and Cameroon, where the officers and noncommissioned officers were mostly Germans and the junior enlisted personnel were Africans.[35]

The *Schutztruppen* were staffed at the start with regular officers detached from the army and were placed under the joint control of the Colonial Department and Imperial Navy Office. In 1896 the *Schutztruppen* were made part of the regular army. Up until 1896 officers had been able to hold only reserve commissions outside of the *Schutztruppen*; from then on they held regular army commissions, which enabled them to transfer to units in Germany without loss of seniority or retirement benefits. The military, in other words, attained a status in 1896 that their civilian counterparts did not achieve until 1910. The higher official status of the military was demonstrated in other ways. Officers were eligible for much higher decorations than were civil officials. No civil official who was not also a regular officer was ever ennobled for service in the colonies, but several military officers were.

The German colonial military service continued to be run in practice by the Colonial Department even after 1896, except during emergencies. In 1907 a regular military command for the overseas empire was set up in the new Colonial Office. Despite their reputation for militarism, the Germans had the smallest military establishment of any major colonial power in Africa, not excepting even Belgium and Portugal. There were about sixty-five hundred troops altogether in the German colonies in 1914; in 1900 there had been only three thousand. The force was very small because the Reichstag was unwilling to finance anything larger, which was a subject of constant complaint from the Colonial Department and Colonial Society. The small numbers of troops available meant that although ordinary forms of coercion could be practiced, emergencies required reinforcements. Units had to be brought from Germany and New Guinea into East Africa for the Maji Maji rebellion in 1905; for the Herero War an entire volunteer army was recruited in Germany and was controlled directly by the general staff.[36] This greatly disturbed colonial budgets, since the entire cost of using regular white troops from Germany was assigned as a debit on colonial balances, leaving any colony in which a major struggle had taken place in permanent debt. The system also ensured that colonial military actions came under the close scrutiny of the Reichstag Budget Commission.

Although the German colonial military had its share of incompetents, especially in the early years, by military standards the overall quality of command appears to have been fairly high. The political capacities of military personnel given civil authority varied greatly, but in terms of combat efficiency most *Schutztruppe* units were fully acceptable. Despite the fact that colonial military service was in normal times a promotion backwater (very few officers who served for long in the *Schutztruppen* ever became generals), it nonetheless held important attractions. To junior officers and noncommissioned officers colonial service offered responsibilities far beyond what could be expected in Germany in peacetime. In several colonies military action was constant for many years, which was attractive to soldiers who enjoyed practicing their trade. Colonial service also attracted somewhat eccentric and adventurous officers who enjoyed the kind of life they could lead overseas and who probably had little chance of advancement in domestic line units anyway. *Schutztruppe* service also appealed to a number of very competent officers from non-Prussian regiments who chafed at being confined to second-class status. Many of these, however, eventually left the colonial military and joined the civil administration. Governor Zech of Togo, possibly the most able of all the German governors, started out as a subaltern in a Bavarian infantry regiment and transferred first to the Togo police and then to the civil administration.[37] Many of the most notable colonial officers, for example Tom von Prince in East Africa and Hans Dominik in Cameroon, represent a type that throve in colonial service but would probably not have done very well in the peacetime army at home.

Especially in the early years military personnel were frequently given civil authority. In East Africa, for example, districts were designated as military or civilian, with officers or noncommissioned officers acting as district officials in the former. Before about 1905 colonial governorships were often assigned to officers such as Liebert and Götzen in East Africa and Leutwein in Southwest Africa. This was sometimes done so that the governor could also command the *Schutztruppe*, since a problem arose when the offices of governor and commander were separate. Despite the legal subordination of the military commanders to the governors, the German tradition of military independence carried over into colonial affairs, and in some areas battle was constant between the civil and military authorities. If the governor were an officer but not military commander, a very severe problem could arise if the military commander outranked the governor.[38]

When a military emergency requiring reinforcement from Germany arose, there was a tendency to make the military completely independent of civilian control and to subordinate the civil government to the military. This happened in Southwest Africa in 1905, when the Colonial Department lost a bureaucratic fight with the army over the conduct of the Herero War.[39] Governor Leutwein, despite his being a professional soldier with vast experience in colonial warfare, was replaced by General von Trotha, who was given both civil and military authority. Trotha, a protégé of Schlieffen, took his orders directly from the chief of the general staff. The unsatisfactory nature of military-civil relations was one reason that Dernburg later moved decisively to strengthen civilian control.

The interests of segments of the German bureaucracy affected the colonial policymaking process, although they were in no sense dominant. The influence of collective bureaucratic ideas seems to have been more effective the more tenuous an area's connections were with Germany. Richard Kandt in Rwanda could strongly impress his ideas on the colonial political system in his region and thereby also implement any collective concepts to which he might subscribe, but the governor at Dar-es-Salaam had to be more circumspect in his actions.

Missionary Interests

The political influence of missionary groups on policymaking in the German colonial empire was, on the whole, less extensive than in Britain or France, and when missionaries did manage to affect policy it was usually because their interests were allied to those of more powerful groups. There were, however, exceptions to this overall assessment.

It might appear that the Catholic missions had an important means of influencing policy through the Catholic Center party. In reality, however, the Catholic missions normally made little use of the Center connection, which was at best tenuous anyway. Colonial governors frequently reported favorably on the Catholic missions because they tended not to play politics against the administration and because they heavily emphasized practical training in their schools.[40] The Catholic missions were apparently too concerned about their status to involve themselves directly with politics.

To the Center party during the 1880s, the issues of German colonial policy and of German Catholic missions in the colonies had both been related to the major question of the status of the Catholic church in Germany.[41] The Center had maintained through the 1880s an anti-Bismarck posture, a carry-over from the *Kulturkampf*. This posture had been evident in the Center's initial vote against the Samoan steamship subsidy and its early opposition to colonial acquisition. However, with Bismarck's declaration of protectorates and the apparent popularity of colonialism among many of the Center's middle-class voters, the Center changed course and tentatively supported the colonial empire. The party then campaigned to get the government to allow German Catholic missionaries in the colonies, primarily as a means of gaining official recognition for the church. In 1889, as a result of an agreement with the curia in Rome, Catholic missions were permitted in the German overseas empire. From that time on, the interest of the Center in colonial policy revolved primarily around the role of colonialism in domestic politics; only occasionally did it concern matters of specific interest to the Catholic missionary societies.

The Protestant missions were generally less hesitant about engaging in politics. What they lacked in direct confessional representation in the Reichstag, they made up for through their ability to play on one of the major ideological justifications of colonialism: the idea that the European colonial presence was supposed to benefit indigenous populations through a process of cultural uplifting. The most important agents of this process were clearly the missions and their schools, whose role was reinforced by the unwillingness of the German government to set up many of its own schools. This gave missionary interests a useful weapon in the Reichstag, in the Colonial Society, and in the *Kolonialrat*.[42]

We have seen in the cases of several of the colonies how the interests of missions led them to engage in politics. In Togo missionary influence was significant in preventing the conversion of the country into a happy hunting ground for concession companies. In Cameroon and East Africa the Protestant societies attacked the government policy of protecting Islam and indirectly ruling through Muslim officials. In Cameroon the Baseler Mission attempted to defend the Duala and other peoples from the government and the concession companies. Friedrich Fabri's Barmen Rhine Mission was one of the leading propagandists for a German takeover in Southwest Africa. In each case, however, ethical and moral considerations behind missionary actions were supplemented by other concerns.

In East Africa, where the missions violently opposed the government's pro-Islamic policy, the basic interest of the missions in monopolizing religion and education was obvious.[43] The interest of missionary groups in protecting existing African social structures in coastal Cameroon and Togo against full-scale capitalist exploitation was only partly due to natural partisanship for societies that were already Christianized. Not only did many missionary societies actually have commercial interests that were threatened by big business operations, but many connections also existed between leading missionary personnel and the owners of trading companies whose operations were even more threatened. J. K. Vietor, for example, was both a director of missionary societies and the owner of the largest trading company in Togo. He was also a leader of the movement to reform German native policy between 1912 and 1914. The arguments of the reform movement centered both around moral considerations of obligations to indigenous populations and around economic arguments that trade with the African peasant in his own social setting was the proper foundation for colonial prosperity.

The missionary interest was hardly ever successful in politics when it acted by itself, as for example when it opposed indirect rule in northern Cameroon. Only when missionary concerns paralleled those of other groups could they be expected to prevail in disputes over colonial policy. This was apparently due in part to a general lack of deep support for missionary work in Germany, as compared for example to Great Britain, and a consequent inability of missionary societies to wield effective political influence in their own rights.

Political Parties and Mass Organization

A great many political organizations and most German parties at one time or another became involved in colonial politics. Here we shall discuss only those most directly concerned with colonial affairs.

We have already examined the Colonial Society and the interests and ideologies represented in it. The Colonial Society was the largest and best-known colonialist organization, although there were several other independent or autonomous groups such as the KWK. The Society itself was by no means unified. Not only were there ideological disputes resulting from the Society's broad-ranging membership, but there were also actual structural splits within the Society.[44] The Society's Berlin section, for example, split into two separate groups in the late 1890s on partly ideological grounds. The breakaway group, the Berlin-Charlottenburg section, devoted itself to scientific colonialism as opposed to the political colonialism practiced by the

main Berlin branch. Some of the sections had political special-
ties. The Meiningen branch was for example a hotbed of right-
radical conservatism, and the Chicago branch naturally
concerned itself with questions of emigration and German nationality for Germans abroad. We shall examine some of the
political activities of the Colonial Society in Chapter 10.

Many other organizations were involved with colonial affairs.
None has aroused as much interest as the Pan-German League
(*Alldeutscher Verband*), the best-known of the radically conservative organizations that formed in Germany between 1890 and
1914 to advance a kind of middle-class, antiindustrial, anti-
socialist program as a reaction to contemporary social and political problems.[45] The League advocated an aggressive foreign
policy, government action to defend the status of the lower
middle and artisan classes, protection of German nationality
abroad and German culture at home, and action against ethnic
minorities—especially the Poles and the Jews. Its program represented a general ideological set, which we shall examine in the
next chapter. Among the components of the Pan-German
League's ideology was settlement colonialism, which the
League's spokesmen applied as a concept both to overseas policy and to Eastern Europe. As we have already seen, German
settlement colonialism has to be understood as part of a more
general popular attitude toward society and government that
gave settlement colonialism much more political influence than
it would otherwise have merited.

The Pan-Germans were associated with colonialism from the
League's beginning. Its parent organization was founded in 1890
to protest the Anglo-German treaty over East Africa, and one of
its early leaders was Carl Peters. The League continually attacked the government for concession-company policy, the lack
of vigorous efforts to expand the empire, and especially for the
government's unwillingness to support settlement anywhere except Southwest Africa.[46] The leader of the League through the
early 1900s, Ernst Hasse, was a Leipzig professor, a National
Liberal Reichstag deputy, and a leading advocate of settling German farmers in the colonies. The Pan-German League, like set-

tlement colonialism in general, tapped an important source of political support by emphasizing ideas that appealed to the self-consciously antiindustrial segment of the middle class. In this sense settlement colonialism was a kind of imperialist counterpart to the anti-Semitic and anticapitalist ideology that became characteristic of much of the German radical right.

Despite the complaints often made by colonial officials and enthusiasts about the Reichstag's negative attitude toward colonial appropriations, no major Reichstag party was invariably anticolonial. This is even true of the Social Democratic party (SPD), which maintained an official anticolonialist line but which softened its stand after developing a colonialist segment around 1907. On the other hand, few parties were completely procolonial. Even the parties that most consistently supported appropriations for the colonial empire—the National Liberals and the Free Conservatives—had large sections that were at best lukewarm about colonialism, and opinion within the parties ranged from limited economic imperialism to radical settlement colonialism. In general, colonial politics were not themselves matters of overriding concern to the parties requiring the enforcement of a consistent line but rather something to be used for varying ends in the domestic political arena.

The SPD had the most consistent record of opposition to colonialism, although in fact it took an active part in anticolonial politics only after the *Freisinnige* and Center had paved the way in 1884 and 1885.[47] Until theorists within the party worked out a full-scale Marxist anticolonial ideology around 1900, the SPD position was essentially a version of the old left-liberal view of colonies as moral evils and obstructions to economic development. In terms of ideological consistency, the early SPD position was somewhat weak, but it attacked the running of the government and pointed out the scandalous behavior of officials. Any kind of opposition to the government was popular among the party's supporters, the majority of whom appear to have been either against colonies or neutral about them. Nevertheless, revisionists such as Edward Bernstein, Gustav Noske, and Ludwig Quessel eventually argued that the colonial empire, by potentially protecting jobs and improving social conditions, could be a worthy object of SPD support.[48] They also thought that colonialism as an ideology could be used to mobilize support for the party among lower-middle-class people who tended to favor colonies. The revisionist position was never fully accepted by the SPD, although total opposition to colonies was dropped in 1907. In practice, the SPD usually attacked specific colonial abuses that could be employed for political advantage. In the annual budget review the Social Democrats almost invariably voted "no" on the colonial section.

The *Freisinnige Partei* (left liberals or Progressives) were the original opponents of German colonialism. Since they spearheaded the efforts to defeat the Samoan steamship subsidy, Bismarck adopted colonialism partly to injure them. In the late 1880s and 1890s, under the leadership of Eugen Richter, the party attacked the overseas empire as economically senseless and as a cause of international rivalries that contradicted all of the principles of free trade.[49] The *Freisinnige Partei* occasionally took a moral stance on colonial issues and was as willing as any other party to make capital out of colonial scandals, but by and large it stuck to the economic issue—where, indeed, it was on very firm ground. By the standard of profit and loss, the colonial empire was a dismal failure. The norm for the *Freisinn*, therefore, was essentially that of the economic colonialists. Even the small-business outlook of many economic colonialists was repeated by the left liberals, who were themselves spokesmen for professional and small-business interests. The major disagreement was over the economic practicality and potential of colonialism. Even under Richter the *Freisinnige Partei* approved colonial estimates for Togo and Kiaochow and professed to be willing to accept colonial rule when it clearly paid for itself, worked to Germany's economic advantage, and performed a cultural function abroad.

In 1893 the *Freisinnige Partei* split into two new parties, the *Freisinnige Volkspartei* under Richter and the *Freisinnige Vereinigung*. The latter party advocated a partial movement away from classical liberal ideology to attract more voters. The *Vereinigung* adopted a more progressive stance on social welfare and concentrated on the issue of governmental reform, which had proven potential for mobilizing electoral support. It gradually adopted a more favorable view of colonies than Richter's, although it still applied the same, essentially economic, standards of colonial success. The gradual shift of left-liberal thinking toward reformist economic colonialism provided part of the impetus behind the emergence of the colonial policy associated with the administration of Bernhard Dernburg after 1906. The *Vereinigung's* support helped make possible the government's victory in the colonial crisis of 1906 and 1907 and obligated the government to a program of reform within the colonial system.[50] The majority of left liberals continued to support government colonial policy in principle after 1907, although they also constituted the core of the movement for colonial reform from 1912 to 1914. As was the case with other parties, the *Freisinn* employed colonial issues to make political points with respect to Germany itself. Colonial reform continued, therefore, to be considered an initial step toward domestic German reform. To some extent, as we shall see, Dernburg subscribed to this view.

The Center, because of its fairly firm base of support and its policy of political opportunism, exercised considerable influence on most issues in the Reichstag. Having helped to secure the entry of Catholic missionaries into the colonies in 1889, the Center continued to involve itself in colonial affairs, mainly when the party wanted to attack the government through colonial policy. For this reason the Center frequently opposed colonial appropriations; it was listed by most colonialist writers as one of the *Kolonialfeinde* (enemies of colonialism).[51] However, segments of the party at one time or another subscribed to almost all of the standard varieties of colonialist ideology.

The Center was the main instigator of the Reichstag colonial crisis of 1906 and 1907, but paradoxically a new and strongly imperialist wing of the party, led by Matthias Erzberger, initiated the attack on colonial policy. The Erzberger wing followed an overall strategy of using political issues and the bargaining power of the Center to make the administrative segments of the government responsible to the Reichstag, as in a normal parliamentary system. For this purpose issues having to do with the power of the Reichstag over colonial policy were employed to create a political crisis. We shall discuss the crisis later, but it should be noted that neither Erzberger nor most of his associates were anticolonialists. Erzberger himself continually supported overseas expansion and was a participating member of the Colonial Society.[52] He claimed that the Center wanted to reform rather than destroy colonial administration and to make it financially responsible. If the victory of parliament over bureaucracy could be won in colonial affairs, he argued, then the precedent would be set for other areas. In other words the Center was primarily concerned with the colonies in relation to major issues of domestic politics. Between 1907 and 1914 the Center generally supported the government on colonial policy, but it also joined in criticizing Dernburg's lack of support for settler interests. In 1914, during the revived reformist onslaught on colonial policy, Erzberger and the Center cooperated with the liberals in pushing colonial-reform resolutions through the Reichstag.[53]

The most consistent colonialists were the National Liberals, the party of bourgeois nationalism and Bismarckian *Realpolitik* and the self-conscious representatives of small and medium-scale business. The National Liberals supported Bismarck's colonialism in the 1880s and regularly voted for the government's colonial estimates.[54] Some National Liberal delegates did criticize the government on colonial matters but usually because the Colonial Department's plans were too modest or were directed away from the "true" goals of German colonialism.

The National Liberals were not, however, a uniform party. The party contained both proparliamentary liberals and radical antidemocratic conservatives. The National Liberals also split on colonialist ideology. Generally the position taken by the party corresponded to the economic view of colonial policy. The National Liberals usually favored expenditures to develop the capital resources of the colonies. Yet a section of the party's Reichstag delegation that employed different colonial theories were sometimes able to bring the rest of the party along with them. Ernst Hasse, the Pan-German president, was also a National Liberal Reichstag deputy and the leader of attacks on the Colonial Department for its concession policy and lack of attention to settlement.[55] Hasse's position was eventually taken up by the entire party, which came out against concession companies. The National Liberals' conception of themselves as spokesmen for small business against big finance and industry also helped the party assimilate settlement colonialism, as did the settlement ideology's apparent electoral popularity.

During and after the Dernburg period the National Liberals continued to support the government's colonial policy, except in cases in which policy seemed to go against the ideological stances of the party. They were critical, for example, of Germany's apparent backing down over colonial expansion during the Moroccan crisis of 1911 and of some of Dernburg's decisions that, it was claimed, favored big business.

The German conservative parties were also fairly consistent supporters of government positions on colonial policy, but again, when their domestic political interests were involved in colonial issues, they were as willing as any other parties to oppose the official line. From the 1880s the Free Conservative party consistently supported calls for increased colonial appropriations. As the representative of big business and a segment of the agrarian upper classes, the Free Conservative party was sometimes forced to adopt positions on colonial policy that were inconsistent with the normal ideological conceptions of the party's leadership. This was done in order to hold together their socially disparate supporters and to appeal for middle-class votes.[56] The probusiness stance of the Free Conservatives normally made them economic imperialists and supporters of private colonial economic development. However, during the bitter conflicts over national economic policy in the 1890s, the Free Conservatives strongly swung to the agrarian, not the industrial, side of the dispute in order to retain the support of the Prussian agrarian classes. This led to a switch in favor of agrarianism's ideological counterpart, settlement colonialism. Therefore the Free Conservatives joined in the attack on the colonial concession companies in the late 1890s and after 1900, despite their original attitudes and the fact that several influential Free Conservatives were investors in concession companies.[57] During the crisis of 1906 and 1907, the Free Conservatives strongly supported the government, but they later opposed Dernburg's antisettler policies.

The Conservative party, the mouthpiece of Prussian Junkerdom, was also normally a supporter of government colonial policy, but its support was not always consistent. The groups whom the Conservatives represented had, for the most part, little direct interest in colonial affairs. However, after 1890 the Conservatives became very conscious of the very narrow basis of their electoral support and the selfish class interests that the policies that they advocated (grain tariffs, the three-class voting system in Prussia, etc.) appeared to the public to represent. They were therefore forced to employ ideologies that allowed them to extend their appeal to at least some segments of the middle classes. Radical, racist conservatism of the sort advocated by the Pan-German League increasingly became part of the Conservatives' repertoire, and the colonial empire provided a number of issues over which radically conservative ideology could be brought into play.[58] The Conservatives were the only party that completely opposed the 1890 treaty with Britain as a sellout of Germany's imperial interests, and because of their stand they received the support of radically nationalist opinion. The Conservatives also opposed the concession companies and consistently favored white agricultural settlement in the colonies. On the other hand, when government colonial policy corresponded to the Conservative view of national interest, as in 1906 and 1907, the Conservatives invariably supported it.

In the next chapter we shall examine the interaction of the parties and interests that have been described above in disputes over particular colonial issues.[59]

10

Issues of Colonial Politics

Colonial politics in imperial Germany cannot be understood apart from the general context of domestic political issues. In the previous chapter we have observed a strong institutional relation between domestic and colonial politics. In the present chapter we shall see that the relation holds for the dynamic aspects of politics as well.

The Tariff Question

By the 1890s the marriage of convenience between Prussian Junker agriculture and big business that underlay Germany's regime of economic protection had begun to collapse. Improving economic conditions and the breakup of the conservative–National Liberal political cartel caused the leaders of business to agitate for a lowering of German tariffs, since German industry had achieved a position from which it could compete successfully in the international market and from which tariffs appeared to be only an impediment to economic expansion, especially in Eastern Europe.[1] Agrarian interests did not take the same view, since German agriculture possessed no comparable advantage over its potential rivals in Russia and the United States. The resulting conflict over tariff policy became the major issue of German politics in the 1890s. It evolved into a general debate on the direction of German society and absorbed other issues, including colonial ones.

In 1891 and 1892 Chancellor Caprivi introduced a policy of reducing tariff levels as existing economic treaties came up for renewal. Over the next few years new tariff arrangements were made with many of Germany's trading partners, and especially with Russia and Rumania, both potential competitors of the East Elbian grain growers. The new economic policy soon proved itself a boon to industry, but agrarian interests attacked it immediately and violently. Caprivi was vilified by his own class, and a powerful agrarian interest group, the *Bund der Landwirte*, was formed to influence the Reichstag. The proagrarian conservative parties desperately played on every weapon of ideology and influence they could muster in order to reestablish tariff protection. Eventually, in 1902, they got their way when Chancellor Bülow passed a revision of the tariff schedules through the Reichstag.

The questions at issue were of course far more significant than the level of tariffs or their effects on German agriculture. The Caprivi tariffs did not actually hurt East Elbian grain sales very much, and German agriculture responded to competitive stimulus in a basically healthy way.[2] The questions really were whether or not a narrow status group such as the Junkers could continue to determine policy for all of Germany and whether Germany should vigorously encourage industrial development or attempt to balance industrialization with the protection of other economic forms. These deeper issues were immensely complicated and not susceptible to immediate resolution. Although the proindustrialists pointed to the material benefits of development, the agrarian conservatives persuasively pointed out the social dangers of unrestrained industrialization, which they claimed that the government's economic policy was intended to promote.

The transformation of the tariff issue into a more general dispute led each side to appeal to widely known sets of ideological conceptions in order to justify its position in terms of the national good. As it happened, this accentuated the split already existing within German colonialism. Even before the tariff disputes economic colonialism had been part of a more general commercial and industrial ideology, and settlement colonialism had been closely related to agrarianism and radical conservatism. Because of this, disputes over colonial policy after 1890 tended to evolve quickly into confrontations between the settlement and economic viewpoints and to become part of the more general conflict over national economic policy. The tendency of national and colonial disputes to interpenetrate each other frequently left organizations like the Colonial Society in awkward political positions.[3]

The dichotomy in German colonialism between the economic and settlement ideologies was a phenomenon of long standing in the 1890s, but it did not inevitably apply to every colonial issue. Many significant colonialists straddled the main divisions within the colonial movement or defied simple classification. The most influential colonial publicist of the post-1900 period, Paul Rohrbach, managed to combine both strains of thinking in his work.[4] Moreover, the relationships between the colonial ideologies and the two sides on the main economic issue were not always clearly drawn. Although economic colonialism was usually considered an aspect of German industrial expansion, it could just as easily be, and occasionally was, represented as a policy of developing the colonies on the basis of small businesses and native peasant farmers, a policy equally opposed to large-scale capitalistic development and European farming settlement.[5] Yet because of the national controversy over economic policy, the split within colonialism was accentuated and the areas of agreement between colonialists were obscured. Colonial issues that might otherwise have been resolved locally in the colonies became intensified because parties to the disputes could appeal to one political faction or another within Germany on the basis of ideological affinities.

The basic features of the general agrarian position included an attack on urban industrial society for lowering the quality of life, creating social fragmentation, and threatening the most valuable classes of the German population. Not only was the industrial side vulnerable on these points, but also through emphasizing them, the agrarian interest acquired support from large segments of the middle classes that had little direct concern with the issues at stake in the tariff question. The agrarian conservatives deliberately adopted ideological positions that had traditionally been aimed at large middle-class groups, and these included settlement colonialism. Despite the ending of emigration from Germany in the late 1890s, conservative politicians dusted off the old emigrationist arguments that showed that Germany was overpopulated and that the survival of the German people required the resettlement of a large number of Germans in colonies abroad.[6] The virtue of settlement colonies remained as always: they permitted peasants and the *Mittelstand* to maintain their traditional modes of living in the face of industrial capitalism, thereby maintaining the social qualities on which the strength of Germany depended. By actively favoring settlement colonialism, the conservative agrarian interest made use of an explicitly antiindustrialist ideology with a positive program of action as a way of mobilizing middle-class support.

Settlement colonialism did not necessarily have to be a politically conservative ideology; it attracted several professed liberals, such as the publicist Paul Rohrbach. Liberals who championed the "little man" against big business often favored the kind of thinking implicit in settlement colonialism. However, during the major political disputes of the 1890s, the identification between settlement colonialism and radical conservatism, which already existed in general, became much more complete. In the 1890s almost exact counterparts to settlement colonialist ideas developed in other areas of radical conservative ideology. The concept of *inner colonization*, the idea that independent German farmers should be settled in underused or predominantly Polish areas of eastern Prussia, was one of the main elements of the Pan-German program and was favored by many of the strongest conservative academic supporters of settlement colonialism.[7] The economists Adolf Wagner and Max Sering and the historian Dietrich Schäfer, who provided the theoretical basis for the overall agrarian, antiindustrial side in the tariff dispute, also actively supported settlement colonialism.

The inner-colonization idea was extended in the 1890s by some of the more radical Pan-Germans into plans for annexation and settlement in areas such as Poland, the Ukraine, and the Balkans.[8] The eastern extension was a logical one in that *inner* colonization, if actually applied to Germany itself, would work to the disadvantage of the Junkers, the core of Prussian conservatism who were the primary employers of Polish labor and who owned most of the land that would presumably have to be used for settlement. In normal times this problem hardly mattered since inner colonization was a largely fictitious concept. However, during the First World War, when Germany was actually in possession of large non-German agricultural areas, the conservative commitment to peasant colonization led to advocacy of German settlement colonization in eastern Europe.[9] Both in the prewar period and, as we shall see, during the 1914-to-1918 war itself, the importance of settlement colonialism has to be considered as a function of the strength of radical conservative ideology in Germany. The strength of that ideology was such that settlement colonialism, a set of ideas that possessed only minimal applicability in the actual German colonial empire, nevertheless was an important factor in German colonial politics and policymaking.

The Colonial Scandals

Among the most notable features of German colonial politics, particularly in the 1890s, was the heavy publicity given to cases of official misbehavior in the colonies. In actual fact, it does not appear that German colonial officials behaved better or worse than those of any other country. In the early years, of course, the lack of trained personnel and the fact of military conquest led to incidents of a fairly revolting nature, but apparently the number of cases of government officials exceeding their authority declined as the quality of colonial personnel improved. Of course, the latitude given to officials was at times extensive, as is indicated by the deaths caused by the suppression of the Herero and the Maji Maji rebellions. The main reason, however, that German colonialism was associated with a series of well-publicized scandals was the political use to which colonialism in general was put by political groups in Germany.

As we have already seen, almost all parties in the Reichstag employed parliamentary review of the colonial budget as a means of taking a position on overall government policy. The Colonial Department served as an unusually vulnerable symbol for the administration, to be attacked as necessary. A case of scandalous behavior was one of the best possible vehicles for criticism since it immediately aroused the interest, and occasionally the indignation, of a great many people who would not normally become exercised about, say, incorrect figures in financial reports by colonial governors to the Budget Commission. For this reason some of the best-known colonial scandals were directly related to major questions of domestic German politics.

The relation between colonial scandals and political issues can be seen in the Peters affair, which has already been discussed in Chapter 7. Many of the positions taken by the Reichstag parties in the 1896 Peters debate were closely related to stances on the larger issues of national policy.[10] Not only was Peters abandoned by the government because he was an impossible subordinate, advocating settlement policies contrary to Kayser's and plotting to replace him as colonial director with the help of the conservative parties, but the attack was laced with clear ideological overtones as well. Procolonial people, especially those within the Colonial Department, thought that Peters's basic outlook on the enterprise of German imperialism contradicted the standard economic colonialist orthodoxy. Peters's settlement ideas and his somewhat lately discovered opposition to concession companies were a conscious part of the radical conservatives' general attack on proindustrial elements of government policy.[11] The economic policy of Caprivi and his successors was intended to help industry by creating new markets and sources of cheap raw materials abroad. Among the reasons for Caprivi's tariff policy was a desire to turn eastern Europe into a kind of German economic empire of the sort that Friedrich List had prescribed as an encouragement to German industrialization.[12] The official policy of *Weltpolitik*, which will be examined in Chapter 11, was designed to create expanded economic opportunities for industrial exports. Economic colonialism, which centered around the concept of colonies for trade and mining, was closely related to the overall official policy and was therefore attacked by opponents of government policy through the alternative, settlement colonial ideology. It is not surprising that Peters's chief supporter in the Reichstag was Wilhelm von Kardorff, the leader of the Free Conservatives and also of the agrarian faction in the chamber—the very person who was responsible for the Free Conservative party's adoption of radical conservative ideologies in order to fight the tariff issue.[13]

The Peters scandal was also used by other groups. For example, a nascent "reformist" position made itself known in the debate over Peters. This position differed somewhat from the socialist and left-liberal attitudes toward the colonial empire, which were mostly negative. Rather, the reformists tended to consider occurrences like the Peters affair, not as reasons for repudiating colonialism, but as opportunities for criticizing the entire German administrative system and suggesting changes.[14] Around the turn of the century, "reform" in Germany was in the process of becoming an ideological entity with some effect on German politics. It suggested political action that could produce beneficial results and put forward a set of attitudes with which people of many different classes could identify. A group seeking access to public support could, therefore, call for reforms in government as a means of obtaining such support. Obviously, many different interests represented themselves as reformist; although most reformist groups shared some ideas with each other, the particular type of reform that a group advocated depended on its political intentions.

Several different reformist tendencies can be identified in the debates over the colonial scandals. One tendency was to call for the extension of regular governmental control over the colonies through increasing the size and improving the training of the colonial bureaucracy and through adopting a rational plan for overall colonial development. The Colonial Department itself generally took this view.[15] A variation on the same theme, less acceptable to officials, held that the degree of Reichstag supervision over the colonial administration should also be increased.[16] This was, of course, an effort to use colonial politics to argue for parallel reforms at home. Some reformers also advocated action to protect African social structures, the employment of moral and religious standards in the making of colonial policy, and changes in colonial economic policy.

Although in the 1890s colonial reformism had been generally a matter of individual groups' reactions to the colonial scandals and to the political opportunities that they presented, a loosely constructed reformist ideological consensus that did not solely depend upon occurrences of misbehavior began to emerge after 1900. It became possible for Dernburg in 1906 and 1907 to use almost all of the existing suggestions for colonial reform (even ones that had already been implemented) as a means of gaining support for the government. The consensus, however, was heavily weighted toward economic colonialism, although there were settlement-oriented colonial reformers such as the liberal Paul Rohrbach and the conservative Ernst Hasse who wanted greater government expenditures on the colonies, an increased white settlement rate, and a reduction of central, bureaucratic control over colonial administration.[17] We shall examine some of these ideas below when we consider the question of *Selbstverwaltung*.

Apart from the Peters scandal almost every year up to 1906 produced cases of official misbehavior—such as Leist's treatment of Dahomean troops in Cameroon, which led to their mutiny in December 1893.[18] Except for the Social Democrats and some of the left liberals, the political groups making use of scandals tended to prefer individual ones of the Peters and Leist variety that pointed up correctable abuses, rather than major, bloody examples of colonialism in operation that the military campaigns in almost all of the colonies produced. In the latter cases officials were not doing anything illegal. Besides, criticism of such actions implied opposition to the whole principle of colonialism and imperialism, which most of the colonial reformists were not willing to accept.

The Colonial Concession Companies

One of the most important and complicated issues of colonial policy in Germany had to do with the nature of capitalist involvement in colonial enterprise. This issue, primarily a matter of domestic politics, was directly related to the dispute over tariffs and national economic policy in the 1890s.

Under Kayser, and in consonance with the generally pro-industrial policy of the imperial German governments of the period between 1890 and 1896, the Colonial Department had attempted to foster private capitalist development in the colonies.[19] The formation of the *Kolonialrat*, a limited effort to discover economic uses of the colonies, and the creation of a semiofficial advertising campaign all were intended to attract reluctant private investors to the colonies. The second major wave of concession grants in the 1890s was a logical consequence of the overall direction of government policy after initial efforts were found inadequate. The conditions under which the new companies were set up—with large territorial concessions, reduced responsibilities to the government, and, at least in Cameroon, the prospect of active governmental support—were intended as means of making colonial investment more attractive. The Rhodes-dominated South West Africa Company, the South African Territories Ltd., the *Otavi Minen- und Eisenbahngesellschaft*, the two Cameroon concession companies (the GSK and the NWKG), and a number of other less prominent concerns in Cameroon and Southwest Africa were all given land concessions of considerable magnitude.[20] Some of them managed to attract foreign capital, but only a few ever made significant profits.

The case for concession companies was stated in its extreme form by the colonial publicist and investor Julius Scharlach,[21] who argued that the companies were the most effective means of fostering rapid economic development. Economic development was defined almost solely in terms of industrial expansion. Private enterprise, if left to itself and supported by the government, would see to it that the colonies became profitable adjuncts to the domestic industrial economy. Government attempts to regulate or alter the direction of economic development would inevitably impede the flow of capital into the colonies, which Scharlach regarded as the key to development. Scharlach was equally scornful of attempts to encourage European farming settlement in the colonies and to protect native peoples from exploitation. He thereby earned himself the enmity of both the settlement colonialists and most colonial reformers,[22] although he appears to have been attacked most consistently by the former. Scharlach's close personal involvement in colonial investment seemed to represent the kind of relation between industrialism and concession-company colonialism that the radical right desired to expose.

The concession companies were in fact wide open to attack, since they really did not work very well as agents of economic development. Most of the companies in Southwest Africa merely waited for something to turn up in their concession areas; they did not actively put capital to work. The DKGfSWA, for example, held its land while prices went up and then, when diamond fields were discovered in its concession in 1908, claimed exclusive rights over the profits.[23] Well before 1900 the Southwest African companies came under attack by organizations claiming to represent the interests of the settlers, ostensibly because the concession companies were preventing good lands from being used for ranching and were driving up land prices.[24] This was a valid enough complaint but was hardly sufficient by itself to create an issue in Germany. The support that the settlers' complaint received from political groups interested in attacking the concession companies as part of a generalized antiindustrial campaign made it important.

Right-wing groups put forward major objections to the high degree of foreign participation in the concession companies.[25] This was again a criticism based on fact, although Scharlach and the Colonial Department argued that it was an irrelevant one since foreign investment in German colonies worked economically for Germany's benefit. To the settlement colonialists and their political associates, however, foreign investment not only introduced the specter of foreign control, but it also helped to turn the colonies into extensions of the industrial part of the German economy, which obviated their purpose. In addition, the radical right had adopted a hard line on foreign policy by heavily emphasizing the threat to Germany from England. The attempt to corner the market in patriotism was one means by which the conservative parties sought to build up generalized middle-class support in the post-1890 period, and it was natural for them to emphasize the nationalist aspect of the concession-company issue.

The question of colonial concession companies became a full-blown political issue between 1900 and 1905, when the Pan-German League, the Conservative and National Liberal parties, and eventually the Colonial Society undertook an active campaign to prevent the issuance of any more land concessions.[26] The Colonial Department defended the concession companies at the start but eventually gave up the struggle. In Chancellor Bülow's new alignment of Reichstag parties, conservative elements had the upper hand. Under the attacks of the right and the colonial reformers, the Colonial Department abandoned the policy of issuing new land concessions, although the existing concessions were confirmed in the face of challenges from other interests. In any event, by 1905 opinion within the ranks of the permanent colonial bureaucracy seems to have turned against concessions because they generally performed poorly and because their operations impeded orderly economic development and exacerbated native problems.[27] The kinds of argument that were employed during the concession debate, however, were repeated continually between 1905 and 1914 by settlement-oriented colonialists concerned about the colonial administration's tendency to see the colonies as economic entities rather than as sites for European settlement.

Disputes over Colonial Development

A complex set of issues concerning colonial development surfaced in Germany at about the time (1900–1905) that the concession-company policy was disintegrating and it was becoming clear that the government was going to have to spend considerably more money on the colonies than it had in the past. The debates in the Reichstag over new forms of government investment naturally brought into play most of the currents of thought about colonies, particularly economic and settlement colonialism as extensions of general industrialism and agrarianism. Although the complexities of the issue are presented in the chapters on the individual colonies and in Chapter 13, some general comments can be made here.

The main bones of contention were the positioning of transportation facilities (especially railroads), policies of taxation and native labor, and in the special case of Southwest Africa, the ownership of mineral resources. On each of these questions, specific interests stood to gain or lose from whatever decisions were made, and these interests actively participated in policy debates. However, if these relatively weak interests were to achieve their purposes, they had to acquire support from politically significant groups in Germany and to make reference to ideologies current in German politics. Thus, for example, the East African planters attempted after 1905 to influence the routing of the East African railways and the nature of native-labor policy by appealing to rightist parties in Germany, and they did so by representing themselves as the vanguard of large-scale German settlement according to the traditional settlement conception. It was, of course, also to the advantage of political organizations in Germany to have concrete issues that could be debated in terms of contemporary competing ideological positions. Although the actual issues in the dispute over colonial development were of little concern to the interests represented by the German conservative parties, it was useful to them to be able to represent themselves as advocating a *völkisch* policy through defending the East African planters.

The question of railway routing was entangled with ideology no matter how it was approached. Those who thought about colonies in terms of white farming settlements or large plantations saw railroads as means of cutting transportation costs and thus possibly gaining a margin of profitability.[28] The justification of railroads in the case of white farming settlements was economic only in a secondary sense. Settlement was defended on social grounds; railroads would simply make it more practical. On the other hand, those who advocated an economic colonial policy, either through the efforts of large concession companies or through increasing trade with African producers, tended to subscribe to the nineteenth-century mystique of the railroad.[29]

The railroad was seen as both the symbol of progress and the prime agent of economic change. Thus it was assumed that the building of a railroad into the central portion of German East Africa would automatically stimulate economic change by increasing the degree of contact with overseas markets of the areas through which it passed. In East Africa, as elsewhere in the world, the railroad builders' confident assumptions were founded to a great extent on an illusion of inevitability of economic change. We shall examine this point further in Chapter 13. Despite the apparently greater hold that economic colonialists usually had on economic realities when compared to radical conservative or settlement colonialists, there was a good deal of fiction in their conceptions as well. Certainly the East African *Zentralbahn* did not radically transform the East African economy even though it did increase its foreign trade.[30]

The native-labor question was one of the most bitterly disputed of colonial issues. A large labor supply was obviously important to certain types of economic development, especially plantations and mining; the methods often proposed for obtaining it would have made alternative forms of development impossible. For example, proponents of East African peasant agriculture argued that official labor-procurement policies in support of the Usambara plantations turned African farmers into proletarians, unable to contribute to the East African economy other than as laborers.[31] The peasant-farming enthusiasts held that plantation agriculture would not work in most of East Africa and that the government's policy would effectively destroy the only economic system that actually would function. The latter assumption was also, of course, a matter of faith.

The native-labor question was fought out in terms of the conflict between economic and settlement colonialism, mainly because settlement colonialism was used by plantation interests as a means of gaining conservative support. In East Africa the settlement ideology was employed to defend forcible labor procurement, and a version of economic colonialism was used to oppose it. In Cameroon labor procurement was seen as a sign of encroaching big business and was attacked both by settlement-oriented conservatives and by liberal reformers who conceived of colonialism in terms of small trading activities.[32] Labor policy was also debated on other grounds. It was argued, for example, that the "civilizing" mission of European colonialism could best be served by rapidly pulling Africans out of their traditional societies and placing them completely in a Western economic situation by making them workers in large capitalist enterprises. The counterargument was that civilization was not achieved by proletarianizing people and that an accommodation between modern and traditional societies was the most productive basis for cultural uplift.[33] On each side existed a large element of noncultural selfish interest, but it was more obvious in the case of the proponents of a forcible plantation-labor policy. In any event, however, the disputes about native labor must be understood in the context of a complex relation among specific interests, domestic German politics, and ideological concepts.

Local Administration

The administration of local government was also debated in terms of major disputes within domestic German politics. Once again, examples of politics affecting local-government policy are considered in chapters on individual colonies. Some of the same disputes arose in the German as in the British and French colonial empires: should government be direct or indirect with respect to indigenous political systems, and should administration be centralized or decentralized with respect to white inhabitants? As was the case with the British and French colonies, however, these general questions were influenced both by actual conditions in each colony and by national political issues.

Some politicians and officials supported firmer oversight of the colonial administration from Berlin and more continuous control of local areas by governors in order to increase efficiency, and others argued for a greater delegation of authority to lower levels as a means of eliminating red tape.[34] This was a legitimate issue of theoretical public administration, but it was also related to an issue of German politics: what should be the role of the bureaucracy in the German government? Although respect for the quality of the German bureaucracy was thoroughly ingrained, political capital could still be made by referring to the stultifying effects of bureaucracy on governmental initiative and the snobbishness shown by officials toward citizens. A relatively unsuccessful aspect of government, such as the colonial empire, could be used by politicians seeking to increase political participation at home as an example of the effects of too much bureaucracy. Even Matthias Erzberger sometimes argued that one of the reasons that Southwest Africa had never fulfilled its promise as a white settlement colony was official interference with the natural development of the area, although the main defenders of the Southwest African settlers were radical conservatives who on other matters seldom agreed with people like Erzberger.[35]

Although the question of self-administration (*Selbstverwaltung*) in the colonies became a major issue during the Dernburg era, it had been a matter of extensive discussion for some time. There were essentially two sets of ideas that went under the name *Selbstverwaltung*, one developed by colonial officials and the other ostensibly voiced by white settlers, especially in Southwest Africa. A certain amount of confusion—which could, as we shall see, be used by politicians and by the Colonial Department—existed between the two. Dernburg used the ideas to his advantage in 1906 and 1907, for example.

The official view centered around the concept of a communal form of government, whereby the leading inhabitants of local areas conducted local administration, subject to fairly strict controls by the central authority. This general concept applied to Germany as well as to the colonies and constituted the cornerstone of the system of local government in Prussia.[36] The main function of the communal authorities that were established in all of the colonies from the late 1890s on was financial. Communes undertook local projects and collected local taxes without the oversight of the Reichstag and the Imperial Treasury. This theoretically permitted the Colonial Department to spend money for other purposes and solved the political problems inherent in budgetary review. Communal governments were also used to implement official policies, but in the bureaucratic view they were clearly not intended to challenge or replace the authority of the central colonial government. On a larger scale self-administration also referred to the status that the Colonial Department sought for all the colonies: fiscal self-sufficiency, so that the expenses of running the colony would be completely covered by funds collected from taxes within the colony.

The other major view of *Selbstverwaltung* was different in many ways. Although the official conception envisioned multiracial (but white-dominated) communal governments, settlers believed that the communal system should represent them alone.[37] The communes were not to be merely fiscal conveniences and, where necessary, were themselves to be subsidized by the central government. The supporters of the white communal system fell into two groups: those who advocated communal self-government because it fostered democracy or encouraged initiative on the part of white communities, and those who saw the communes as means of influencing economic development to their own advantages. These catergories were not mutually exclusive, but the reason that interested parties were able to use *Selbstverwaltung* for their own benefit was that other people in Germany responded favorably to settlement colonialism without having immediate economic reasons for doing so. Paul Rohrbach, for example, favored local self-government in Southwest Africa because it seemed to him that the reason for having the colony in the first place—that it would develop a democratic "frontier" spirit that would find its way back into German society—would be best served by handing over governmental functions to the settlers.

Selbstverwaltung became an especially important issue after the discovery of diamonds in Southwest Africa in 1908. As we shall see in Chapter 13, the question of whether the profits from the diamond fields should go to the DKGfSWA or to the settlers became entangled with the whole question of local government. When Colonial Secretary Dernburg ruled against the settlers, he was attacked harshly by the radical right for having renounced his earlier position in favor of *Selbstverwaltung*. Dernburg—who had actually advocated the official, not the settler, type of self-administration—was caught essentially in a difference of meaning ultimately traceable to the fundamental dichotomies in colonialist thinking that we have previously discussed.[38]

The other major question of local government was native administration. The later distinction between direct and indirect rule was not generally made before 1914, but there were debates over the relative advantages of what would later be called the direct and indirect models of authority. In theory the German system followed the direct (or French) pattern, with lines of authority running from a central colonial administration down through a chain of command to district officers. In fact, however, actual methods varied in different areas. In Togo, for example, where a system of direct rule was established fairly early in the coastal region, the authority of African chiefs was also recognized by law and was integrated into the administrative system. In the northern part of Togo, African authorities were left almost completely to themselves, subject to taxation and a minimal amount of supervision. East Africa displayed the greatest amount of variation, reflecting the radical differences in social structure, geography, and German control among the sections of the country. As we have seen, systems of indigenous administration ranged from direct rule through district officers and *akidas* near the coast to indirect rule using chiefs, as among the Sukuma, to the system of loose supervision employed in Rwanda and Burundi. Variations, usually less extreme, were found in other colonies as well.

The structure of native governance in the colonies was also a matter of political debate within Germany, however, and in such debate the natural variation in practical administrative forms dropped out of sight. Those who argued that promising colonial areas should be developed through large plantations generally favored direct rule, since it was believed that traditional indigenous authorities would resist the movements of people and changes in life-style required by the imposition of a full-scale capitalistic system of production.[39] Colonialists favoring white settlement usually, although not invariably, favored direct rule over native populations in areas near white settlements. The destruction of native political structures was, in fact, one of the main elements of settlement colonialism, which saw local populations either as threats to white immigration or as sources of labor.[40] In either case, indigenous political systems were incompatible with the aims of white settlement. On the other hand, most colonial officials and colonialists who favored economic development based on African producers tended to favor indirect rule through African authorities.[41] Advocates of indirect rule and gradual commercialization of African societies often claimed that African political systems would become Europeanized through the exposure of their personnel to Western ideas over time. There seemed to be little awareness until almost 1914 that the "Europeanized" Africans could constitute the most effective opposition of all to colonial rule. In any event, disputes over the general issue of native governance clearly depended on the requirements of the major German colonial theories with respect to native policy and were, therefore, functions of domestic as well as colonial politics.[42]

11

Colonialism, Navalism, and *Weltpolitik*

Colonialism played several roles in Germany's international relations between 1890 and the First World War. In this chapter we shall discuss two of these roles: colonialism as an influence on naval building and as a factor in the set of official attitudes commonly called *Weltpolitik*.

Colonialism and the Building of the German Battle Fleet

The series of events leading to the German government's decision to expand the navy in the late 1890s has been thoroughly discussed elsewhere.[1] We are concerned here with the relation between naval expansion and the colonial movement.

During the 1890s Admiral Alfred von Tirpitz, state secretary of the Imperial Navy Office from 1897 to 1916, launched a highly successful campaign to transform the German navy into a first-rate naval force. By enlisting the support of the kaiser, big business, and a number of mass political organizations, Tirpitz made naval building an extremely popular issue among the German middle classes and pushed naval laws through the Reichstag in

1898 and 1900 that authorized the construction of large warships. The rapid German naval expansion after 1900 set off a naval-building race with Britain that was one of the factors leading to the First World War. Tirpitz, whose "risk theory" advocated a navy strong enough to deter British aggression without achieving absolute parity, attained his immediate goal of building German naval strength and became an important political figure. However, when it became clear that Britain was reacting in a completely hostile manner to the German program and that Tirpitz might not be satisfied with the limits on building implicit in the risk theory, many of Tirpitz's influential business supporters abandoned him, although he retained his political popularity through the First World War.

Colonialism had been related to naval politics for many years before 1898. One of the early leaders of the Colonial Society was Admiral Livonius, who had proposed colonies for Prussia in the 1860s and 1870s. The navy had a vested interest in colonial acquisitions, since colonies could be used to justify a more powerful fleet in order to protect them. It was possible to reverse the argument once the navy had started to expand by claiming that more colonies were needed as naval bases, but this was less common in the 1890s. The Colonial Society officially favored naval expansion, and connections between a large fleet and a large colonial empire seemed natural to the procolonial public.[2] These connections were used to harness colonialist opinion to the naval-building campaign in the late 1890s and were essentially of two sorts, one meant to apply to business interests and the other to a large middle-class public.

The main instrument in the first category was the risk theory. Tirpitz's thinking had originally been primarily tactical; it had stressed offensive operations and heavy battle fleets. The risk theory was added later to give Tirpitz's ideas a strategic and political dimension. The risk theory was intended to produce, simultaneously, one political reaction from the British and another from German imperialist business interests. With respect to the British, Tirpitz postulated that Germany should acquire naval strength such that the danger to Britain from the

German fleet would prevent Britain's attacking Germany. He argued that Germany should build a high-quality battle fleet, considerably smaller than the British navy, that would do its damage in full-scale naval battles in European waters. It was not necessary to match the British navy in numbers of vessels but rather to make the German threat just large enough that the British would be forced in event of war or high international tension to pull forces in from the rest of the world and thereby to expose their colonies to third-party attack or to internal revolt. According to Tirpitz, this would be a better means of protecting German overseas trade and colonies than would an unrealistic attempt to cover all trade routes with German warships. The British would be forced to accommodate themselves to German aims in the world, either, as Tirpitz suggested, in a state of peaceful hostility or, as others thought likely, in active cooperation with the Germans.

Of course, the British did not react as the theory predicted but rather commenced to increase their own navy. To Tirpitz this may not really have mattered very much, since to him the primary value of the risk theory lay in its allowing him to gain business support for fleet building. The risk theory closely corresponded to a more general view of international relations held in the 1890s by many proimperialist businessmen. Albert Ballin, for example, was a major supporter of Tirpitz in the late 1890s, as was Karl Supf, the head of the KWK and a well-known colonialist.[3] Ballin saw in the new German battle fleet much the same thing that he saw in the German colonial empire: the means through which worldwide cooperation between Britain and Germany could be achieved. He thought that this cooperation would encompass both overseas market allocation and political accommodation so that neither country would have to fear the hostility of the other. Such cooperation could not be reached without convincing the British that it was in their interests. Threatened by imperial competition from the German colonies and military competition from the German battle fleet, British businessmen and politicians would conclude that it was better to be friendly to Germany than to oppose her. Clearly, Tirpitz did not see things this way, but it was to his advantage to allow German businessmen to do so.

Tirpitz used the assumptions of business-oriented economic imperialists in other ways. The navy's occupation of Kiaochow was intended to demonstrate to business interests that even if the Foreign Office and the Colonial Department were not willing to support overseas investment movès with dispatch, the navy was.[4] As we have seen, the administration of Kiaochow was widely publicized to show that the navy could do the job of colonial government better than the Foreign Office and that the navy deserved the active support of colonialists and imperialists. Of course, Tirpitz had available other inducements to business that had little to do with ideology or colonies, such as the prospect of armaments orders.

The other aspect of Tirpitz's political strategy was a public campaign to enlist the support of the broad middle classes, partly through presenting an image of the navy as the manifestation of the German middle class, the bourgeois counterpart to the aristocratic army. The *Flottenverein*, or Navy League, was set up in 1897 to spread propaganda for naval construction, and even before that the aid of many patriotic organizations and ideologies was enlisted for the cause. Colonialism and the Colonial Society were important factors in this process. The *Flottenverein* argued that a strong navy was needed to protect and extend the colonial empire, and the Colonial Society played a significant role in initiating the naval campaign.

The Colonial Society and the proponents of naval expansion in fact needed each other rather badly in the late 1890s. The naval question provided the Colonial Society a popular issue with which it could arouse flagging public interest in colonial affairs.[5] The Society jumped at the chance to participate in a movement likely to appeal to the groups that made up the bulk of the Society's membership and among whom more members had to be sought: middle-class people with strong nationalist sympathies. The most enthusiastic navalists in the Society's leadership were economic colonialists like Karl Supf, who saw the navy and the colonies as an earnest of the government's intention to support worldwide economic expansion.

Tirpitz and the navalists also needed the Colonial Society and the connection of navalism with colonialism. The Colonial Society helped finance the naval propaganda campaign until public contributions could be sought, and it provided space in the *Kolonialzeitung* and speaking time at meetings to naval propagandists. In these respects the Colonial Society's role in the naval-building campaign was significant, but the Society and colonialism in general performed an even more important one. Proponents of major naval construction were politically vulnerable on two fronts. In the first place, many of the agrarian conservative interests in German politics were not basically in favor of expanding the navy. The navy offered competition for funds and public prestige to the army, whose officer corps was the conservative aristocracy's major hold on political influence. Also, it was expected that the heavy demands that a naval building program were likely to make on imperial finances would lead to a national income tax that would fall heavily upon the previously lightly taxed landowning classes.[6] Secondly, naval expansion was easy to represent as a selfish ploy by big business to obtain orders at the expense of the average taxpayer. This was in fact the socialist interpretation, but the danger to the navalists did not lie with the SPD, which could not really affect the outcome of the naval debate. The problem lay with the potential for both left liberals and conservatives to use the same argument to alienate antiindustrial sentiment among the middle classes from the navalists. Colonialism helped solve these problems.

Since the Conservative party and most of the radical right had been committed for some time to supporting the colonial empire, they could not easily come out against something that was represented as being vital to the future of German colonialism. An article of imperialist faith all over Europe held that naval power was the key to empire, and many Germans believed that the British Empire rested on the British navy.[7] The alacrity with which the Colonial Society turned to the support of naval building reinforced the popular image of a necessary link between sea power and colonies and thereby created considerable risks for conservatives desiring to attack naval construction. Only the left liberals, already known as anticolonialists, could be consistent in opposing navalism, but they were split on the issue and their appeal to middle-class sentiment was tenuous at best.

Colonialism and Tirpitz's navalist movement, linked from the mid-1890s, continued to maintain close relations through the First World War. This closeness did not apply to the relations between the Colonial Department and the navy, which were in many senses rivals for colonialist favor and in a very uneven way competitors for appropriations. (The navy consistently got one of the largest shares of the budget after 1898, and the Colonial Department received one of the smallest).[8] However, as the navy's place was made more secure and after the Colonial Office was separated from the Foreign Office in 1907, conflict between the two appears to have declined. By the First World War the navy and the Colonial Office were able to establish joint war-aims positions with only a minimum of friction.

Although Tirpitz assembled a broad base of support for naval expansion in the late 1890s, he could not retain the backing of many of his early big-business adherents, such as Albert Ballin, when it became clear after 1905 that the British were not behaving as expected. To understand this reversal and its relation to German colonialism, it is necessary to turn to a discussion of economic imperialism and *Weltpolitik*.

The Colonies and Weltpolitik

Weltpolitik was a word constantly used in German politics before 1914 by a variety of groups; its exact meaning has never been very clear. Taken simply as "world policy," it signifies no more than Germany's foreign policy on a worldwide scale. As it is frequently used by historians, *Weltpolitik* refers to the aggressive style of German diplomacy between 1890 and 1914 and a kind of adolescent emphasis on expansion and strength as meaningful goals in themselves. However, as it was most often used at the time to refer to the content of policy rather than to the style of diplomacy, the term indicates a definite attitude toward German foreign policy characteristic of a portion of the German political elite. This attitude can be perceived most easily and can be differentiated from other views by approaching it through the economic colonialist ideology, which was closely related to *Weltpolitik*.[9]

As we have seen, the economic and the settlement colonial viewpoints were each related to different conceptions of politics and social change in Germany; they were also related to quite different conceptions of the aims of foreign policy. Economic colonialists and those who thought about colonies in terms of trade, plantations, or mining enterprises generally also subscribed to a form of economic imperialism with respect to the noncolonial part of the world—an imperialism that was basic to the concept of *Weltpolitik*. The expansion of German industry and the securing of markets and sources of raw materials were the key aims of *Weltpolitik* thus defined, in which formal colonization played a subordinate role.[10] There existed, therefore, a close relation between *Weltpolitik* and the industrial side of the 1890s economic-policy debates. Caprivi and his close advisors conceived their policy of economic penetration into eastern Europe as part of an overall move to increase the economic opportunities open to German industry. Even though Caprivi was known to be anticolonial, it was clearly *settlement* colonialism to which he objected. He was in no way opposed to indirect or economic forms of imperialism (including economic colonies), without which his general economic policy would have made no sense. The most vigorous advocates of economic colonialism almost invariably conceived of it as one part of worldwide German industrial expansion.[11] The economic imperialism of *Weltpolitik* was therefore similar to imperialist formulations in many other countries. The imperialist opposition to *Weltpolitik* was uniquely German.

The major alternative to industrial economic imperialism was exemplified in the statements of radical conservative organizations such as the Pan-German League, which almost always contained references to settlement colonialism as a sub-element.[12] Like other colonialist components, *Weltpolitik* and its conservative alternative differed mainly in their attitudes toward German industrialization and social change. The Pan-German League advocated that Germany's goal be to protect "Germanism" and the *Mittelstand* by *restricting* the rate of industrialization and lessening the effect of urban life on society. The radical right's advocacy of "inner colonization," territorial expansion into agricultural areas of eastern Europe, and German settlement in the colonies were all based on this foundation. Radical conservatives also alluded to the necessity of maintaining Germany's "material base" by expanding trade, but this was clearly a secondary factor and was viewed more in terms of an epic struggle with the major industrial power, Britain, than as a coherent economic policy. Radically conservative foreign policy was structured to protect Germany from external threats and internal change by directly opposing every potential challenge.[13] Such a stance was necessarily less consistent and rational than the economic imperialism of *Weltpolitik*, but since it was mainly intended as a means of mobilizing political support among middle-class voters for conservative interests, its appeal to widely shared resentments was more important than its lack of coherence.

The differences between the two major views of foreign policy indicated by their colonial elements can be used to explain some of the politics of Germany's international relations after 1890. The peculiar attitude toward Britain evinced by economic imperialists both inside and outside of the Foreign Office can be partially explained in terms of the aims of *Weltpolitik*. Men like Albert Ballin and Alfred von Kiderlen-Wächter, who favored vigorous German economic expansion overseas, believed that Germany could take one of two attitudes toward Britain: outright hostility toward an economic rival or a more complex stance tending toward cooperation and market allocation that would allow both economies the opportunity to expand. The first position encompassed the possibility of an economic or real war, which Germany might not win. It might also be self-defeating in that it would separate German industry from one of its best trading partners—Britain herself—and would limit the availability of British funds to capital-starved Germany. At the same time, the second alternative required a state of cooperation between Britain and Germany that did not exist in the 1890s. It was therefore necessary to convince British public opinion of the advantages of accommodation with Germany. It was also necessary to convince German public opinion—in the face of conservative, antiindustrial opposition—that such an arrangement would not be a sellout to the British. Like naval construction, colonialism was seen as a means of overcoming both difficulties.

By their sponsors within the Foreign Office, the 1890 Zanzibar-Heligoland treaty with Britain and the abortive 1898 treaty dividing Portugal's African colonies between Germany and Britain were seen as initial steps in working out more general arrangements with the British.[14] By agreeing to mutually advantageous terms on issues of formal colonialism, they hoped that similar agreements that guaranteed informal German interests in China, Latin America, and Central Africa, for example, could be reached. In particular, the idea behind the 1898 negotiations became a commonplace of economic imperialist thought in Germany. Constantly during the period between 1906 and 1914, Dernburg and others sought to revive the question of the Portuguese colonies in order to obtain British agreement to a German sphere of economic influence in the Congo Basin and to avoid conflict between the two countries.[15] The advocates of cooperation with Britain clearly misjudged the degree to which British interests were in line with their own, but a contributing cause of the negative British reaction to *Weltpolitik* was the bellicose way in which German policy was stated and was carried out.

Possible explanations for the pugnacious stance and creation of crises that characterized German foreign policy during the post-1890 period range from the instability of the kaiser to the incompetence of certain German diplomats. It may also have been true, however, that the peculiar style of *Weltpolitik* was the result of the dilemma in which the advocates of economic imperialism in cooperation with Britain found themselves. They had to persuade British opinion that Germany was enough of a threat that accommodation with her was necessary, but clearly their extreme bellicosity over Samoa, South Africa, and Morocco, when the government had no intention of backing up its position with force, was not the best way of achieving this purpose. The official policy of truculence in fact backfired, since it created apprehension of Germany's aims in Britain and added to the difficulty of achieving Anglo-German cooperation.

The better alternative was to tread more softly while accentuating tendencies toward natural accommodation already present in German-British relations occasioned by, among other things, colonial affairs. In the majority of cases, especially when the German press was not involved, colonial disputes between Britain and Germany were settled with little friction and a comparatively large amount of German self-restraint.[16]

The practitioners of *Weltpolitik* faced a problem in dealing with German, as well as British, public opinion and with political interests on the right that did not share the *Weltpolitiker*'s convictions about the aims of German national policy. The radical right, since it favored neither a policy that would extend the ascendancy of industry within German society nor an approach to Germany's leading international rival that would downgrade that rival's threat, could not be expected to follow the lead of the economic imperialists. Although the right also employed the term *Weltpolitik* to refer to German foreign policy, they used it very inexactly to indicate unwavering hostility to Germany's "enemies" and defense of Germany's "rights" in the world.[17] The popular appeal of conservative foreign-policy ideas greatly restricted the options open to the economic imperialists.

To protect diplomatic attempts at accommodation from conservative attack in Germany and to assemble support for economic imperialist aims, German governments were forced to take a hard-line public stand against the English. Thus the secret 1898 agreements had to be accompanied by strongly anti-British public statements to keep the political right from branding the agreement as a sellout of German interest.[18] In 1911 the last of the Moroccan crises was engineered by Foreign Secretary

Kiderlen-Wächter for the limited end of extending Germany's territory in Cameroon to the Congo—an aim perfectly in keeping with widely accepted concepts of economic imperialism. The Foreign Office created a crisis by restating German claims to Morocco, not because Morocco made much sense as an economic dependency of Germany, but because Morocco had become a significant cause to conservative political groups whose support could be used by the government. The crisis was also supposed to convince the British and French that Germany was serious by mobilizing violent public opinion behind the government's position. In the end Kiderlen got what he wanted but at the expense of worsening relations with the Entente and making it appear to the German right that Germany had once again backed down. Much of the confusion of German foreign policy between 1890 and 1914 was therefore due to the domestic political position in which policymakers operated. However, this confusion does not mean that official foreign policy was without content beneath the posturing of the Foreign Office or that the basic aims of *Weltpolitik* were themselves confused.

Both the naval risk theory and the economic imperialists' view of colonial relations with Britain therefore depended on a desire to expand and secure Germany's area of economic activity abroad, particularly by eliciting British cooperation. Ballin and other economic imperialists ceased to support Tirpitz around 1908 because Tirpitz's policy appeared to have increased, rather than diminished, British hostility. Up until the First World War, however, many German imperialists continued to hope that the colonies would occasion a general imperial agreement with Great Britain.[19]

PART IV

THE DERNBURG ERA
AND ITS AFTERMATH

12

The Colonial Crisis of 1906–1907
and the Rise of Dernburg

Only once did an issue of colonial politics become the most important issue on Germany's domestic political scene. This occurred during the autumn and winter of 1906 and 1907, when the Reichstag refused to pass the government's request for an emergency supplement to the colonial budget. The first real parliamentary crisis in the Second Reich's history followed, with a dissolution and an election on the colonial issue, in which the government itself actively participated. The colonial crisis was therefore an important event in German political history, as it was in the narrower history of the German overseas empire. It was also the occasion of Bernhard Dernburg's appointment as director of the Colonial Department.

The Origins of the Crisis

A concerted attack on colonial policy by several Reichstag parties had been building for some time by 1906, but the Herero and Maji Maji rebellions created the immediate issue by bringing into question previous policy and the value of having colonies at all and by presenting opportunities for reform-minded politicians.[1] To the Erzberger wing of the Center, the colonial crisis offered an occasion to press for parliamentary control over the government and an official commitment to political reform. To the SPD it gave an opportunity to put the entire government in a bad light and to increase socialist strength among the electorate. The colonial wars were augmented by other questions that would not have been sufficient bases by themselves for a major attack. For several years before 1905, for example, the accounts of expenditures that the Reichstag required of colonial governors had fallen badly in arrears; they were known to be highly inaccurate. To Erzberger and others this diluted the control that the Reichstag was supposed to exercise over the colonial administration and was therefore intolerable.[2] Such complaints, together with the military crisis, placed opposition forces in a seemingly strong position to criticize, and possibly change, the government.

As it turned out, the strength of the colonial opposition in the SPD and Center was more apparent than real, and Erzberger and August Bebel, the leader of the SPD, probably both knew it. There is little indication that they expected their vigorous criticisms of colonial policy to become the beginnings of a French-style political crisis that would display their own weakness. There was not in 1906 an agreed ideological basis for colonial opposition. Erzberger and the Center openly favored maintaining the overseas empire and making it more efficient through reform, but the SPD advocated abandoning the colonies.[3] The procolonial faction led by Gustav Noske was still weak in the SPD, and in any event its criticisms of the Colonial Department did not correspond to those of Erzberger. A common ground for colonial opposition could perhaps have been provided by the left liberals, but in the period from 1905 to 1907, they were deeply split, both organizationally into two parties and ideologically in their attitudes toward social policy. The *Freisinnige Volkspartei* opposed colonialism but maintained a classical laissez-faire approach to social policy that made effective cooperation with the Center and the SPD impossible. The *Freisinnige*

Vereinigung had long since departed from orthodox liberalism and had come closer to the SPD and the Center on social policy. However, it had also adopted a moderately favorable attitude toward colonies, viewing them as necessary means of securing high standards of living and guaranteeing industrial development.

The *Freisinnige Vereinigung*, like other parties, normally used colonial issues as a way of arguing for reforms in the German political system. It had reacted to the colonial wars in 1904 and 1905 by calling for reform in colonial administration to prevent disorder and make the colonies more profitable according to the standard economic theories of colonialism. To the progressive *Freisinn*, reform, whether applied to the colonies or to the homeland itself, was intended to attract popular support by advocating changes that would accommodate the political system to modern industrial society without unduly threatening the middle and working classes. Reform could also, however, be used by other groups with different ideological concerns to mean different things. Reform as a general aim could be very popular, but it was possible to change public support for one sort of reform into support for another simply by emphasizing a reformist attitude rather than the content of reformist proposals. This was one of the main weaknesses of the colonial reformers.

Not only was the colonial opposition weaker than it seemed, but also the government headed by Prince Bernhard von Bülow was less vulnerable than it appeared to be. Bülow, the only real politician among Bismarck's successors, since becoming chancellor in 1900 had faced severe difficulties in maintaining a firm basis of support in the Reichstag. It was apparent that the chancellor had to be able to manage the Reichstag, and legally or not, he was increasingly coming to play the role of a prime minister in a parliamentary system. Bülow's main source of strength was the support of the kaiser—a second essential ingredient of a chancellor's success, but not sufficient in itself. He had attempted to court the conservative parties through the reimposition of agricultural tariffs in 1902, but the support he had received had been tentative and had been counterbalanced by his alienating much liberal sentiment. Bülow's aim was a successful *Sammlungspolitik*, the gathering together of a bloc of the parties of order that would provide a continuous majority for the government in the Reichstag.[4] Bülow's pronouncements on the socialist threat and on the danger of Germany's diplomatic position were useful means of creating a generalized popular consensus to back up a middle-to-right coalition, but they were not enough by themselves.

Intense criticism of colonial policy in 1906 therefore caught Bülow in a position of seeming weakness, without a clear Reichstag bloc to support him. Bülow was first conciliatory, hoping that the crisis would blow over. Gradually, however, he realized that the colonial attacks provided him with an unlooked-for opportunity to create a parliamentary bloc through an election on the colonial issue. Bülow discovered that it was possible to turn a political liability into an asset by representing the colonial empire as something of great national importance, an attack on which was an attack on the welfare of Germany, by promising reforms in administration, and by using nationalist organizations such as the Colonial Society. The appearance of a full-scale political crisis on the colonial issue in late 1906 was due to a deliberate decision by Bülow to bring matters to a head quickly. The appointment and early activities in office of Bernhard Dernburg must be understood in this context.

Dernburg and the Election of 1907

Colonial Director Oskar Stübel, a competent official whose relations with the Reichstag were not good, resigned in November 1905, partly as a result of the Herero and Maji Maji rebellions. As we have seen, a satisfactory replacement for him could not be found among the groups of people normally considered sources for recruiting high government officials (the imperial and Prussian civil services, the military, and the court); Prince Ernst von Hohenlohe-Langenburg took the job temporarily until a permanent director could be found. To Hohenlohe fell the job of defending the government and of yielding to demands for reform from, among others, the Colonial Society itself. One of the government's concessions was that the Colonial Department would soon be separated from the Foreign Office and would be turned into an independent Colonial Office. The next colonial director would therefore be rewarded eventually with translation to a state secretaryship. This made the appointment of Dernburg in September 1906 such a surprise. Dernburg was a businessman and banker rather than a professional official. He was known to have connections with the *Freisinn* and to be a progressive in political and economic ideology. Moreover, although Dernburg was a baptized Christian from birth, his father had been a Jew; Dernburg himself was usually considered a prime example of the Jewish businessmen who were becoming so important in Germany at the time. In every respect Bülow's appointment of Dernburg was novel indeed.

Dernburg had been born to a wealthy commercial family in 1869 and had been brought up to become a merchant.[5] He had made a reputation and a lot of money in the United States as a representative in the late 1880s and 1890s of the Siemens concern and the Deutsche Bank. While in the United States Dernburg had become familiar with American business and political methods and had become imbued with a peculiarly American idea of economic progress as the goal of social and political activity. He was in favor of political reform in Germany, and his outlook placed him in the proindustrial camp in the economic disputes of the 1890s. Within the banking community Dernburg had acquired a reputation for unorthodoxy and dynamism. Between 1900 and 1905 he acted as a troubleshooter for the far-flung economic activities of the Deutsche Bank, salvaging weak subsidiary banks and performing such feats as reorganizing the draining of Rome's Pontine Marshes. In 1906 he was the managing director of the Darmstädter Bank, where his unusual approaches to finance found more congenial surroundings than in the Deutsche Bank. Many influential imperialists, eager to see Germany's shaky colonial empire placed on a firm economic footing , thought that someone like Dernburg was exactly what the colonial administration needed, and when Dernburg's name was proposed to Bülow (possibly by Albert Ballin), the chancellor decided that Dernburg would also fill his own political requirements.[6]

Because Dernburg's papers have been lost, his personal view of his role in German politics must be reconstructed from inadequate sources. Dernburg was politically identified with the left liberals and in 1919 was one of the founders of the Weimar successor to the *Freisinn*, the *Deutsche Demokratische Partei*.[7] In 1919 he publicly favored representative parliamentary democracy, and he probably had done so earlier. Yet he was also criticized as colonial secretary by other democrats for his autocratic attitude toward settler self-rule. Dernburg responded to such criticism by indicating that self-rule had to follow economic development and fiscal solvency and that advanced political systems depended on the prior establishment of advanced economic ones.[8] Although there were good political reasons for his taking such a position, Dernburg's argument seems to indicate the nature of his actual social attitudes. Dernburg was indeed a progressive and a reformer, but primarily in the sense that he favored rapid economic development in Germany and rational political change in order to accommodate it. The criterion for judging the success of governmental policy was the extent to which it facilitated material progress. Since the colonies had not yet even begun to pay for themselves, they were obviously unready for advanced political systems and they had to be considered mainly as means of assisting in Germany's economic progress. The colonial implications of his basic attitudes were not obvious in 1906 even to Dernburg, whose previous interest in colonial affairs had been minimal.

It would, nevertheless, be wrong to identify Dernburg purely as an advocate of industrialism and big business. Dernburg's political identification with the left liberals was not accidental, and like his friend Walther Rathenau he leaned toward a political philosophy that would protect traditional middle-class values while increasing national economic efficiency and productivity. Rathenau later despaired of averting the social consequences of industrialization, but in the prewar period both he and Dernburg seem to have believed that the state could moderate social dislocation caused by economic change.[9] In his public pronouncements and in many of the policies that he advocated early in his term of office, Dernburg claimed to defend the interests of the small businessman and producer against the encroachment of large business conglomerates, and he apparently was perfectly sincere about it.[10] However, it is equally clear that Dernburg's priorities placed economic development ahead of social policy if a conflict were to arise.

Dernburg's activities in office must therefore be understood in terms both of the existing political situation and of his basic conceptions of German society. In particular, it is necessary to perceive the important role that the state, by implication, had to play in Dernburg's thinking. Since unrestrained big business created monumental social problems and did not necessarily facilitate economic development, the government actively had to direct economic change. Therefore, even before Dernburg became colonial director, his thinking was closely attuned to many of the concerns of the economic colonialists and especially to their increasing emphasis on a more extensive economic role for the government.

Despite the surprise attendant upon Dernburg's appointment to the Colonial Department, he was initially well received by both government supporters and the colonial opposition because of his highly advertised managerial abilities and the hope of colonial reform that he offered.[11] It was not immediately perceived that each group interested in reform had a different conception of what reform was. Dernburg's appointment had other political advantages for Bülow besides the obvious one of appearing to respond constructively to the criticism of colonial policy. As part of his *Sammlungspolitik* Bülow had for some time intended to appoint a businessman to high public office in order to attract business support. It seemed that the projected Colonial Office might be ideal for such an appointment because it would be less important than other ministries and its takeover by an outsider would not threaten the classes that normally held office. Also, a businessman might well be the best-qualified person for the job. Dernburg's appointment also gave official recognition to the ideology of assimilation, although given the growing anti-Semitic cast of conservative propaganda, Dernburg probably turned out to be a political liability to Bülow in this regard.[12]

Dernburg began by trying to defuse criticism in the Reichstag and by assuring the nonsocialist colonial opposition that reforms were to follow.[13] The reforms themselves—including increased railroad construction, an independent Colonial Office, the rearranging of colonial finances, and supporting settlers in Southwest Africa—had been advocated by colonialist groups for years. Dernburg managed by these means to detach some sentiment in the *Freisinnige Vereinigung* and other parties from the colonial opposition. However, Bülow's and Dernburg's gestures did not head off Erzberger completely, nor were they an acceptable response to the SPD's generalized criticism of colonialism. The Center commenced a new round of attacks on particular abuses by officials in the colonies. Yet at the same time Erzberger indicated his overall willingness to compromise and to accept the new direction of colonial policy.[14] He primarily intended to increase parliamentary power, not to create a full-scale crisis. The opposition was therefore surprised in December 1906 when Dernburg deliberately picked a quarrel with the Center Deputy Roeren over a minor colonial matter and signified a change in the government's policy of placation.[15] The government made colonial compromise with the Center impossible by accusing the opposition of disloyalty to the larger interests of Germany. The Center and the SPD were therefore driven to organize the defeat of a supplement to the colonial part of the budget. In response Bülow dissolved the Reichstag and called new elections—a state of affairs that smacked suspiciously of parliamentary democracy.

In a sense the parliamentary crisis and dissolution constituted a victory for people like Erzberger who favored representative democracy in Germany. Yet Bülow, not they, engineered the crisis. Bülow's intentions must be understood in terms of his search for a consensus in politics and a parliamentary bloc to support him as chancellor. Having accepted colonial reform in general, Bülow could, through Dernburg, claim that any further opposition, especially the defeat of the budget, constituted unpatriotic obstructionism and a threat to a vital part of Germany's national interests.[16] By so doing, Bülow could obtain the electoral support of the large nationalist organizations for parties supporting his colonial policy and could provide those parties with a firm electoral base. The key to Bülow's plan was the actual participation of the government in the election as a supporter of the bloc of procolonial, progovernment parties— another first in German political history. Since the election ostensibly concerned colonial policy, Dernburg was chosen to lead the government's campaign. Necessary to Bülow's strategy was a government commitment to treating the colonial empire as though it actually were a matter of great national importance. Thus, political considerations within Germany lay at the root of Dernburg's later reforms.

To the election campaign of December 1906 and January 1907, Dernburg brought an enthusiasm seldom seen previously in German politics. He traveled the country speaking at meetings organized by the Colonial Society and other groups, demonstrating considerable political magnetism and an acquaintance with American campaign practices. The conservative parties, the National Liberals, and the *Freisinnige Vereinigung* scrambled onto the government's colonialist, patriotic platform. The January election was a smashing success for the government and at least a temporary vindication of Bülow's bold experiment. Although the Center held its own in the Reichstag because of its fairly fixed basis of support, the SPD lost a large proportion of its seats; the "Bülow bloc" parties gained correspondingly.[17] The SPD shortly thereafter adopted a less hostile colonial line. Erzberger's influence in the Center was temporarily reduced as the Center also moderated its stance on colonial policy. Bülow did not in the long run achieve a stable base of support; he eventually discovered that he was at the mercy of the leaders of the parties that made up his bloc. Yet by most standards of short-run political success, Bülow and Dernburg had achieved a great deal. Dernburg now had to fulfill his mandate to enact reform under deceptively favorable circumstances.[18]

The Dernburg Era, 1907–1910

Dernburg entered office with a great deal of enthusiasm and public support but with little knowledge of what he was doing. Early in 1907 he set into motion those aspects of colonial "reform" that had been generally agreed on by the Bülow-bloc parties: the creation of a separate Colonial Office and the attempt to procure Reichstag funding of new development projects, especially railroad extensions in East Africa. Beyond these Dernburg had few specific ideas about what to do; yet he had to appear to be doing something. His mandate and inclinations were to conduct a reform, but as a business manager he wanted to base policy on good information. That, at least, was the ostensible reason for Dernburg's decision to visit East Africa in 1907.

Dernburg's Concept of Reform and the East African Inspection

It is clear that Dernburg had several other reasons for the 1907 tour. He was especially concerned to publicize the colonial empire, to develop a continuous base of electoral support for the government's colonial policy, and to emphasize to the public the importance of the colonies and of their reform. The circumstances under which Dernburg came to office and Bülow's expectations of him led him to pay close attention to public relations; he therefore tended to advertise most of his actions as "reforms" even though he knew very well that many of them had already been suggested or implemented. The tour of inspection was supposed to provide Dernburg with information for his reform program, but he also made sure that he was accompanied by journalists so that he would get full value from the publicity of his trip.[1]

The 1907 inspection tour was an important event in later German colonial history. In the course of his trip, Dernburg picked up a set of impressions and ideas that greatly influenced his later policies, although he was eventually forced to retreat from some of these. Governor Rechenberg of East Africa was an especially important influence. Dernburg used his journey to express his ideas about colonial policy to the press and to colonialist groups. These expressions to a large extent created the standard view of Dernburg as a colonial administrator and reformer. It is important to remember, however, that Dernburg went to East Africa with some ideas about overall imperial and colonial policy and that his attraction to Rechenberg's thinking was to some extent predetermined by the similar basic ideas, especially concerning economic imperialism, that both men had brought from Germany.

Dernburg's attitudes before his trip can be discerned in a pamphlet that he wrote early in 1907 delineating his goals in office.[2] Although some of his statements can be discounted as propaganda and others as sheer fantasy, the pamphlet nevertheless gives an accurate overall impression of the assumptions that lay behind Dernburg's attraction to a certain type of economic colonialism.

In the pamphlet Dernburg's argument was based almost solely on economic considerations. The settlement colonialist assumptions about the need to maintain certain social classes in the colonies were almost entirely absent from Dernburg's approach. Although he did advocate measures (which he later repudiated) to accelerate white agricultural settlement in Southwest Africa, they were clearly included in his 1907 pamphlet solely because they were in common currency at the time as colonial reforms. Dernburg still felt the need to maintain the support of organizations like the Colonial Society, which were committed to the settlers in Southwest Africa, and he was at that time unaware of any fundamental difficulty in reconciling an economic colonialist policy with large-scale German farming settlement. In any event, his justification for settlement was economic: settlers would be good trading partners for German industry.

The most important sections of Dernburg's pamphlet were his explanations of the colonial empire's potential value to Germany and of the action necessary to make it realize its potential. Although Dernburg in 1907 exaggerated the economic value of the colonies for political reasons and out of sheer ignorance, it is nevertheless true that he later retained these same basic views. The East African journey probably acted, not to change Dernburg's mind, but rather to tailor his rather wild hopes for the colonial empire to the apparent situation in at least one colony. With allowances for Dernburg's exaggeration, the position that he took was essentially that of the KWK: the most up-to-date version of economic colonialism.

Dernburg argued strongly for the need to make the colonies pay for themselves and to contribute to German industrial expansion. As Scharlach and others had done, Dernburg claimed that this required the input of considerable amounts of initial investment capital, which had not yet occurred. This was, of course, partly a matter of faith in capital and partly a conclusion drawn from the most successful examples of colonization by other peoples. In accordance with newer conceptions of economic colonialism, Dernburg saw the government as the crucial provider of working capital for colonial development, especially for railroads and other elements of social overhead. Dernburg on the whole did not favor reliance on big, private business organizations, despite his background in large-scale banking. In fact, the debate on the concession companies had made such reliance politically inexpedient. Dernburg believed that if the government undertook the really large overhead expenditures and adopted a consistent policy aimed at rapid economic development, substantial private investment would follow. In some cases (such as white agriculture in Southwest Africa) the government could provide loans, but normally private colonial enterprises should be self-financed.[3]

Dernburg also insisted that the government plan colonial development to take maximum advantage of existing technologies and marketing opportunities. This he called "scientific colonialism."[4] In part, scientific colonialism was another public-relations gesture; scientific and technical expertise had always been important in German colonial administration. However, Dernburg's version of it was innovative in that he intended to back planned development with extensive financing and systematic, businesslike management. Dernburg's new direction can be seen in the *Kolonialblatt*, the semimonthly official colonial journal. Under Dernburg the number of scientific articles vastly increased, demonstrating both heightened technical interest and an increase in reportable scientific activities.[5]

Dernburg also repeated the KWK's argument that colonies could guarantee favorable balances of payments and guarantee access to inexpensive raw materials for German industry— which was, he said, increasingly at the mercy of foreign producers' associations and large international companies.[6] Yet although the KWK claimed that colonial production could at best create a bargaining weapon in dealing with monopolistic suppliers, Dernburg claimed that the existing German colonies, if properly developed, could supply most of Germany's industrial raw materials and could obviate the necessity of even dealing with monopolists. He believed that the anticipated savings to German producers in raw-materials costs would more than cover the investment needed for colonial development. This argument was absurdly optimistic about the potential of the colonies, and he toned it down after seeing a real colony later in 1907.

Two things should be noted about Dernburg's statements. In the first place, the kind of neo-Listean thinking that lay behind them could be applied to Germany's relations with any primary producing area. This was done during the First World War by advocates of a German-dominated economic area in Central Europe—including Dernburg himself—and in that case Dernburg's thinking was not necessarily absurd. In the second place, once Dernburg discovered that the colonies could not actually provide a large proportion of Germany's industrial raw materials, he naturally concluded that the colonies would have to be expanded. One of his prime concerns in office was an unpublicized attempt to extend German interests, officially or unofficially, into new areas of the Congo Basin.[7] Once again, the implications of Dernburg's early conceptions demonstrate the close connection between German colonialism and wider imperialist ideas.

Dernburg's reliance on governmental direction of economic development implied a requirement for a highly competent and trained colonial service. Thus despite earlier efforts to create such a service, Dernburg strongly emphasized his role in changing the personnel structure of the Colonial Office.[8] Not only did the education of colonial officials have to break out of the old legalistic civil-service mold and emphasize practical training in colonial economics, but the job security and career opportunities of colonial officials had to be improved. Dernburg continued earlier programs to ensure that officials had received detailed training in the languages, legal customs, and economic backgrounds of the colonies to which they were assigned. More importantly, Dernburg worked very hard to develop a career pattern that would make the colonial service attractive to able people. After considerable political struggle Dernburg finally succeeded in getting an act regulating the status and promotion schedule of colonial officials and giving them the same status as other German civil servants passed by the Reichstag in April 1910.[9] It was a major personal triumph for Dernburg, and it was also his last while in office.

Dernburg's 1907 colonial reforms also included the reorganization of the Colonial Office itself. The reorganized Colonial Office generally followed the pattern for most imperial ministries.[10] It had three major departments: one for political affairs, one for financial and technical matters, and one for personnel. In addition, there was a new military command headed by an officer with his own staff. The novel aspects of the new system were the unusual emphasis given to technical coordination (an obvious consequence of Dernburg's policies) and the military command. The latter was supposed to settle the question of civil authority in military matters, thereby precluding some of the problems that had arisen during the Herero War. Many liberals, of course, would have liked to have extended the colonial system of military subordination into domestic government as well.

Dernburg also eliminated the *Kolonialrat* because of its public identification with private business interests and because it was incompatible with his conception of the role of the government in colonial development and with his own somewhat autocratic methods of management. Few regrets were expressed at its passing.[11]

These, then, were the major elements of Dernburg's colonial thinking prior to his East African visit. However, his detailed policies and his particular brand of colonialism resulted from an amalgamation of these elements with the impression that he received on his tour of inspection.

In July 1907 Dernburg traveled via Zanzibar to the East African coast accompanied by Walther Rathenau (at his own expense) and by a number of journalists.[12] Rechenberg met him, but the governor's influence on Dernburg did not become obvious immediately; in fact the two men were never personally friendly. Under Rechenberg's guidance the state secretary's party traveled by the British Uganda Railway to Lake Victoria and thence by donkey south to Tabora. The route was chosen by Rechenberg in order to impress Dernburg with the enormous difficulties of economic development in East Africa, the unlikeliness of the area as a site for European settlement (Dernburg suffered great discomfort on his donkey ride), and the importance of relying on indigenous people for whatever the Germans wanted to attempt. Dernburg then returned to Mwanza on Lake Victoria, and only then, after he had essentially formed his views of East African policy, did he meet the settlers of Usambara.

His arrival had been eagerly anticipated by the well-organized white-settler population who had hoped that Dernburg would support their pet projects, such as the extension of the Usambara railway, and would protect them from Rechenberg's policies. They were quickly disappointed. Dernburg rejected the settlers' suggestions for forced plantation labor and instead talked, as Rechenberg did, about regulating labor conditions and recruitment. He also refused to limit African competition in products in which the Usambara plantations specialized and instead lectured his hosts on the importance of developing African peasant production of cash crops.[13] Although he did not inform the settlers, he had also decided to follow Rechenberg's recommendations to direct railway construction along the central route through Tabora rather than along the projected *Nordbahn*. On his return to Germany, Dernburg made a series of speeches in which he elaborated his new view of colonial policy and in which his debt to Rechenberg was very obvious.[14]

In order to understand Dernburg's position after his East African visit, it is essential to examine the political situation in East Africa in 1907. We have seen that when Rechenberg arrived in East Africa as a replacement for Götzen, his attitudes concerning policy were undecided and were governed by a desire to avoid future conflicts like the Maji Maji rebellion. He originally leaned toward Götzen's idea of combining plantation settlement in the north with an attempt to develop peasant production in the south. In the course of 1906, however, Rechenberg changed his mind, both because of his reading of the situation in East Africa and because of the direction of his thinking about imperial affairs in general. He observed that part of the reason for recent African resistance had been the government's excessive use of force in encouraging economic change, and especially in procuring labor for the Usambara plantations. The situation of the colony was such that fiscal self-sufficiency and economic success were impossible without concentrating on the development of already-existing economic structures, and this meant encouraging African agriculture through the noncoercive influences of the market.

Rechenberg had several European models in mind. Like Dernburg he came to East Africa with an unconscious adherence to economic colonialism, and he was unsympathetic to the political ideas with which settlement colonialism was connected. His view of general imperial policy was economic. During the First World War he was a major advocate of a German-controlled economic association in Central Europe as an alternative to massive annexations, and his criterion of the success of colonies was their economic benefit to Germany.[15] However, since an argument could be made that plantation agriculture in East Africa stood some chance of economic success, Rechenberg must have had additional reasons for turning against it. In particular, Rechenberg seems to have been genuinely concerned with the welfare of indigenous peoples—both to avoid a future Maji Maji and to protect traditional, agricultural social structures from destruction by uncontrolled capitalism.[16]

Rechenberg was by no means a progressive liberal of Dernburg's type. He accepted economic colonialism because it made sense to him as a professional bureaucrat and because, at least as presented by advocates of small-business, peasant-oriented colonialism, it corresponded to his general social attitudes. As a Catholic and a member of the Center party, Rechenberg held that economic change required social responsibility and the preservation of community structure in Africa as much as in Europe. As a career official he shared the view that a separate, meritocratic bureaucracy, chosen from responsible classes in society, should govern for the general good without undue pressure from interest groups. Rechenberg apparently believed that both big capitalist enterprises and the settler interest represented entrenched minorities that had to be overridden for the greater benefit of Germany and Africa.[17]

Rechenberg therefore decided in 1906 that the future of East Africa lay with the African peasant farmer and that to the extent that white plantation agriculture worked against peasant economic development, it would have to be restrained. He established a comprehensive economic program, which he then tried to sell to Dernburg during the secretary's visit in 1907. Rechenberg's plans revolved around the building of the *Zentralbahn* through Tabora to the lakes and thence northwest to Rwanda and Burundi. It was claimed that this railway and its feeder roads would attract agricultural populations and would allow African producers, for example Nyamwezi sisal and peanut growers, to move their goods to coastal export markets. Although Rechenberg did not believe that railroads by themselves could effect economic change, he did believe that the railway would be economically effective if combined with a more general development plan. It would permit the market to influence interior agricultural economies without government coercion. Although Rechenberg claimed to have no objection to the Usambara Line as a secondary priority, only one railway could be afforded at a time, since the bonds issued to build the railroads had to be serviced by East African revenues. Therefore, Rechenberg's prime conflict with the Usambara planters was fundamentally over the allocation of funds for development in the colony.

In keeping with his basic decision, Rechenberg initiated a series of additional policies. He undertook to dissolve Götzen's purely white local communes to prevent the growth of European opposition and to replace them with a system in which native interests were also represented.[18] He continued the scientific research sponsored by Götzen and the KWK and rejected Götzen's coercive *Volkskultur* scheme. In order to rationalize labor recruitment and to protect people like the Nyamwezi, who were important to the peasant-agriculture scheme, the governor issued regulations to require labor contracts and to prevent abuses in employment.[19] He empowered district officials to enforce the labor regulations and appointed labor-recruitment commissioners. Rechenberg's moderate labor policy was immediately opposed by plantation operators, who claimed that without coercion they could not compete for labor against British employers north of the border. In fact, Rechenberg's labor policies were largely unsuccessful because they could not be enforced. Eventually, Rechenberg was forced to reduce even their theoretical effectiveness and to give employers official assistance in recruiting laborers. More successful was his prohibition of corporal punishment by employers, which the settlers resisted because it reduced their ability to discipline their workers.

This then was Rechenberg's presentation to Dernburg as the logical basis of German colonial policy. Because Rechenberg presented his plan skillfully and because Rechenberg's economic thinking coincided in many ways with Dernburg's, the colonial secretary picked up the Rechenberg line with alacrity. After his return home in October, he laid out a comprehensive program for colonial development in a series of public reports on his trip.[20] Wherever practicable, the African peasant was to become the basis of economic activity. The African was to become a junior colonial partner and was therefore to be protected from undue exploitation. Projects like the *Zentralbahn*, which constituted the core of Dernburg's much-increased appropriation request for 1908, were to be given top priority. Although the appropriation was passed because of Dernburg's still-considerable influence, the first signs of conservative opposition appeared during the debates.[21]

The importance of the northern railway route to the East African settlers was obvious, and those who supported the settlers and the settlement ideology began to question the colonial secretary's priorities. By the end of 1907, the conflict between Rechenberg and the settlers had come to a head and the struggle had spilled over into Germany. These developments apparently caught Dernburg unawares; he had not realized the domestic political implications of his decisions. Nor had he been aware that the settler interest was more powerful than its mere size and economic significance indicated. The settlers, whether bona fide small farmers or plantation operators, were the real-life exemplars of emigrants who maintained traditional virtues in a frontier environment, which the settlement-colonial ideology claimed to be the prime justification for having any colonies at all.[22] By attacking the settlers, Dernburg was mobilizing a considerable segment of colonialist and conservative sentiment against himself.

Dernburg became more sensitive to his political position in 1908 and began to reduce his support of Rechenberg, reopening the question of the Usambara railway and taking the teeth out of some of Rechenberg's policies.[23] He concentrated more on reforms in the organization and training of the colonial administration, which had general appeal, and on getting Bülow to orient foreign policy around the expansion of the overseas empire. Nevertheless his difficulties with the right intensified because, as it turned out, Dernburg straddled a weak point in the Bülow bloc. The difficulty of reconciling business interests with the agrarian and conservative attitudes of the right made the bloc unmanageable, and once again colonial policy became the focus of dispute between the two sides. Although Dernburg was forced to compromise in East Africa, he based his colonial policies on economically justified reform. Once the political right had begun to question Dernburg's conceptions, he was no longer able to hide his differences with conservative, settlement-oriented colonialists beneath a general enthusiasm for reform. He compounded his difficulties by a series of decisions with respect to Southwest Africa in 1908 that concentrated the wrath of all settlement colonialists against him.

The Southwest African Tour and the Diamond Question

Although the Nama rebellion had finally been put down by 1907, Southwest Africa was still in considerable turmoil because of the economic changes that had accompanied the wars. Despite a new railway system and an increase in the European settler population, Southwest Africa was economically unprofitable, with few known natural resources and exports. The only bright spot was the recent development of copper mines in Ovamboland, but copper production was still small. Moreover, Southwest Africa was saddled with the debt from the Herero and Nama wars, which meant that it would probably never be able to pay the expenses of its own government.[24]

The colony was politically divided over its economic problems. Political organization among the settlers had been accelerated as a result of opposition to Trotha's policy of wiping out the Herero, who were the prime source of labor for settlers and other European employers. Four newspapers and a plethora of local organizations grew up to mobilize the fewer than fifteen thousand white inhabitants against government policies, against concession companies, and often against each other.[25] Southwest Africa became even more politicized than East Africa, and because of Südwest's special place in settlement colonialist thinking, political disputes there had more comprehensive repercussions in German politics. In particular, the settlers' continual conflict with the Colonial Office over questions of native policy and labor was taken up by several political parties in Germany. Dernburg himself in 1907 explicitly accepted settler criticism of official red tape and "aloofness."[26]

On the other hand, neither Dernburg nor most colonial officials could reasonably accept the settlers' growing claim that their interests should be the sole criteria for policy in Southwest Africa. Complaints by settlers and their adherents (such as Paul Rohrbach) about the lack of government support obscured the fact that the government had actually done a great deal to assist settlers by providing building loans, by giving grants to farmers with children in school in Germany, and by selling land cheaply. The Herero had been forbidden to own cattle, which forced them into European employment. Europeans possessed the right to inflict severe corporal punishment on Africans. Such support was due to Southwest Africa's peculiar role in colonialist ideology and not to considerations of economic rationality. Yet given his basic conceptions, Dernburg could not justify devoting all of the resources of the colony to the development of European farmsteads of dubious potential. His undersecretary, Lindequist, the former governor of Southwest Africa, disagreed, but in general Dernburg expressed the view of most officials in wanting to restrain desires of the settlers.[27]

The situation changed dramatically on 14 April 1908, when a diamond field was discovered in the hinterland of Lüderitz

Bay.[28] In anticipation of large, but probably temporary, profits, almost all interested groups mobilized to control the distribution of the windfall. Considering both the political situation and his own program for orderly colonial development for the benefit of Germany, Dernburg secretly established a diamond board of bankers and officials to monopolize the export of diamonds, set their prices, and regulate their sale so that international diamond prices would not collapse. The arrangement made political sense. It would give the government control over profits until the problem of their allocation was solved. The state had a partial claim to the diamond profits because of debts incurred during the Herero and Nama wars. Although Dernburg had stated that the cost of defending any part of the empire should be chargeable to the whole, the imperial government had supported unprofitable colonialism in Southwest Africa for years. It had a good case for obtaining return on its investment. The DKGfSWA, in whose concession the diamonds had been found, also had a claim. The settler organizations, on their part, argued that the bulk of the diamond profits should be distributed by locally elected authorities to citizens of Southwest Africa in development grants. They also argued that Dernburg's diamond board should be abolished to allow individual prospectors to sell diamonds at market prices.[29]

Public debate over the diamond question placed Dernburg in a difficult political position. It also made *Selbstverwaltung* in Southwest Africa a major issue. Dernburg, already in some difficulty with settlement-oriented colonialists, was forced to decide whether his theories of colonial development should be applied strictly even at the risk of a further loss of support, which might jeopardize his reforms. The crux of the problem was local self-government. Whoever managed to control the Southwest African government would exert the largest influence on the distribution of the diamond profits and would also set labor and economic policy. In addition, Dernburg had already committed himself to some form of *Selbstverwaltung*, and a program of developing local institutions had already begun.

The system of local government eventually approved by Dernburg and Governnor Schuckmann was a far cry from what the settlers wanted.[30] Although the Colonial Office hinted that once a certain degree of "political education" had been attained by the settlers, more power might be given to local organs, it was clear that immediate fiscal and labor questions would be settled by the colonial bureaucracy. The new arrangements called for the establishment of local advisory, nonlegislative councils representing the white inhabitants of the colony, from which would be elected an equally advisory *Landrat*. The Governor's Council would continue to exist, and the authority of the civil service would remain largely unchecked.

This arrangement, which denied the settlers direct access to authority, was in keeping with Dernburg's overall views and with his attitude toward colonial self-government. However, it opened him up to criticism not only from the prosettler right but also from moderate liberals to whom the maintenance of direct bureaucratic rule over locally elected authorities was unconscionable. These groups might accept such a scheme of very limited local rule in places like Cameroon but not in Southwest Africa with its large white population and its special claim on conservative attention.

As soon as the Reichstag had passed the 1908 colonial estimates, Dernburg set off for a tour of Britain, South Africa, and Southwest Africa. The tour, although billed as a fact-finding venture, was primarily a means of maintaining Dernburg's popular credibility and of deflecting some of the Southwest African attacks on him.[31] He was accompanied, as before, by Rathenau and an entourage of reporters. After making an inspection of diamond mining and marketing in South Africa, Dernburg visited the major towns of Southwest Africa and confronted the leaders of the various settler factions. Unlike in East Africa, Dernburg tried hard to be conciliatory, expressing sympathy with the settlers' views on African labor policy. A rift in fact appeared between Dernburg and Rathenau after their return because of the latter's strongly antisettler report, which was distributed separately from Dernburg's own and which the colonial secretary believed would only inflame conservative opinion against him. In reality, it hardly mattered. Dernburg had refused to compromise his basic positions on the diamond question and *Selbstverwaltung*. He refused to release funds to local authorities and he made sure that the concession company got its share. To the settlers themselves he argued that the colony's economic dependency required control from Germany. "If one Müller were to establish a business with a partner living in Germany, to which he subscribed 5% of the capital and the partner 95%, and if Müller should want to have the same say as the partner, the partner would say to him 'Müller, you are an ass!' "[32] Since the settler's allies in Germany were primarily interested in principles rather than in concrete gains for the settlers, Dernburg's attempts to accommodate on specific items such as increased loans to farmers were of no avail. By the end of 1908, Dernburg was under constant attack from the right and from liberals like Rohrbach—and covertly from the Colonial Society, although the Society was too conscious of the utility of Dernburg's other ongoing reforms to make a full-scale assault on him.

Dernburg's Last Years in Office

Dernburg hung onto office all through 1909 and into 1910, mainly because he believed that he could accomplish some further meaningful changes in German colonial affairs by holding out. In particular, he wanted to ensure the regularization of colonial civil-service status and the funding of the East African railway project. He was also increasingly interested in expanding Germany's African empire in cooperation with Britain. In order to keep on with these projects, Dernburg withdrew on other fronts in the face of conservative pressure, thereby losing some of the support of genuine colonial reformers. In East Africa he reduced his support of Rechenberg's policies, especially as they impinged on the Usambara plantations' revenues and sources of labor. He had some justification for doing so: up to 1910 high world prices for tropical goods created unprecedented prosperity for the plantations, a prosperity that collapsed disastrously in that year. However, as Rechenberg rightly pointed out, the same conditions applied to African peasant agriculture, which was in addition more productive and better able to weather the post-1910 depression.[33] Dernburg also gave in to pressure from Southwest African settlers; for example, he issued new regulations that deprived whites married to nonwhites of civil rights.[34] He would not change his basic policies, which he strove to effectuate while trying to hold onto his office.

In the realm of foreign policy, Dernburg attempted to interest Bülow and the Foreign Office in the idea of an expanded, integral German African empire.[35] He suggested reviving the 1898 colonial discussions with Britain with a view to ensuring German predominance in Katanga and in the Congo Basin, in return for which Germany would support British acquisitions elsewhere. On the basis of a colonial agreement, he thought that it might be possible to reduce tensions between the two countries, to guarantee German (and British) markets abroad, and to direct Germany's imperialist aims away from Eastern Europe. In Dernburg's ideas and those of several groups in the Foreign Office was born the type of thinking that resulted in the German-engineered Morocco Crisis of 1911 and in the attempts of Richard von Kühlmann and his associates to direct German imperial attention toward Africa in the years immediately before the First World War. In foreign affairs, however, Dernburg was singularly unsuccessful. He was unable to convince Bülow or Bülow's successor Bethmann Hollweg of the sense of his ideas. Dernburg did not get along very well with Bethmann, who felt threatened by his strong personality, and his political value to Bethmann was questionable because of conservative opposition to him.[36] Dernburg did not, therefore, manage to direct foreign policy toward African expansion, though the year after Dernburg left office Foreign Secretary Kiderlen-Wächter briefly succeeded where Dernburg had failed.

Although Dernburg was primarily interested in the two largest African colonies (the only ones he visited), his period in office coincided with significant developments in the smaller colonies. Throughout Dernburg's term Graf Zech was governor of Togo.

Zech was one of the most respected reforming governors, like Rechenberg a Catholic who combined a sense of moral responsibility toward African subjects with a positive attitude toward commercial development and unlike Rechenberg a man who made few enemies. Zech sponsored an anthropological research project to determine the basis of Togolese customary law, so that it could be effectively integrated with German law. In this and in Zech's policy of developing the Togolese economy around the small African producer can be seen his conviction that the colonial administration and economy should preserve as much of African society as possible. This was a direct consequence of German economic colonialist thinking confronted with practical realities in Togo, and in the particular case of Togo, the confrontation was a successful one. Zech, even more than Rechenberg, set the tone for post-1910 German colonial reformism, which took Togo as its example of proper colonialism.[37]

Less attention was paid to Cameroon during Dernburg's regime than had been done earlier. The growth of capitalistic enterprise in the interior continued, as did construction of transportation facilities. The *Gesellschaft Süd-Kamerun* managed to establish itself as a profitable enterprise and benefited from the worldwide rise in rubber prices. The other concession company, the NWKG, went bankrupt. Many colonialists began to see Cameroon as the center of a new German colonial expansion into most of Central Africa and as potentially the richest of the German colonies. However, not until Dernburg left office was Cameroon a central factor in German colonial and foreign policy. The conflict between the Duala and the German administration continued to grow. Dernburg himself, although in other cases an advocate of African political and economic participation, generally took the side of the administration and the concession companies against the Duala. In carrying their case to Germany over the Colonial Office's head, the Duala offended Dernburg, for they had given his critics in the Reichstag ammunition for their attacks. The gradual reduction of the Duala's political and economic independence continued to be official policy, as did the program of educating Africans other than Duala for lower-level governmental and business positions. Grounds for future conflict between the Duala and the Germans therefore developed rapidly.[38]

The Pacific colonies were likewise areas of lessened concern, which reflected their marginal value even by German colonial standards. Even Kiaochow lost much of its popular appeal because of the declining profitability of German enterprises in Shantung and the obvious impracticality of German imperialism in competition with Japan and with Chinese nationalism.[39]

On 10 June 1910 Dernburg resigned. His disagreements with Bethmann, especially over foreign policy, appear to have been major factors in his decision, as was apparently the opposition that he had received from conservative colonialists. However, his departure was not greeted with enthusiasm by most organs of the colonial movement. The *Kolonialzeitung*, although admitting past disagreements, pointed out the great many things that Dernburg had done and adjudged his administration a success.[40] Liberal and financial newspapers also reported favorably on Dernburg. Only from the right were there unfavorable comments. Named as Dernburg's successor was Friedrich von Lindequist, a respected professional colonial official, former governor of Southwest Africa, Dernburg's undersecretary, and the foremost official exponent of settlement colonialism.[41]

14

German Colonialism, 1910–1914

Although German colonial affairs between 1910 and 1914 lack the drama of the preceding period, they are still quite interesting. Some historians refer to the period from 1910 to 1914 as a time in which earlier colonial tendencies culminated and in which a stability emerged that would have become permanent had the war not cut short Germany's colonial career.[1] In several of the colonies, it was claimed that financial self-sufficiency was imminent, although the decline in tropical-commodities prices after 1910 casts doubt on such claims. By 1914 the German colonial service had become a permanent and relatively efficient organization with a fairly clear vision of its function, and the settler populations of East Africa and Southwest Africa had attained permanence and considerable influence in their colonies. This indicates that the post-Dernburg period cannot really be viewed as a time of fulfillment. The tension that existed between an increasingly permanent colonial service and an increasingly powerful settler community created an unstable political situation in the colonies, which was matched by tensions all through German colonialism. These unresolved tensions, rather than the

appearance of stability, characterized German colonialism between 1910 and 1914.

Lindequist and the Moroccan Crisis of 1911

Lindequist's appointment was greeted with approval by most
colonialist groups. As a well-known conservative nationalist and
settlement colonialist, he had a firm base of support in the right
wing of the colonial movement. Lindequist was highly respected, even by officials who disagreed with him ideologically,
for he had done a good job (by official standards) as governor
and as undersecretary to Dernburg, even though the two disagreed violently on many issues. To a limited extent Lindequist
attempted to turn colonial policy toward his conceptions of colonialism. While continuing almost all of Dernburg's reforms in
the central administration, Lindequist moved wherever he could
to support settlers and plantation interests and to deemphasize
native protection and peasant economic development.[2] More
powers were given to settler-dominated institutions in Southwest Africa, and official efforts there to protect Africans from
physical abuse and labor exploitation were restrained from Berlin. Administrative means of exploiting the labor resources of
Ovamboland were developed, and the settlers' share of diamond profits were increased to levels that most settler interests
considered satisfactory. Yet Lindequist, as a pragmatist, refused
to meddle with successful colonialism in Togo, and in Cameroon
he continued Dernburg's support of European economic interests against native ones. Lindequist paid little attention to
reformists and missionaries who opposed forced labor and
favored the Duala. In East Africa it was expected that Lindequist
and Rechenberg, who loathed each other, would immediately
come into conflict.

In fact, although Lindequist and Rechenberg fought, their
struggle never reached crucial proportions. Rechenberg lost interest in his job, and Lindequist lasted in office for only a year
and a half. Their main disagreement was over local self-government. Rechenberg, unable to achieve African and Indian repre-

sentation, determined not to have communal self-government at all. Instead, he governed locally through the district officers. He attempted to establish at least some nonwhite representation on the governing bodies of the major coastal towns, and he resisted efforts to create an elected, nonofficial white majority on the Governor's Council. In most of these attempts, Rechenberg was defeated by Lindequist. Although Rechenberg ignored outright orders from Lindequist to effectuate white communal government, he was beaten in the end by a combination of Lindequist and the Territorial League, the settlers' pressure group. Most important of all, although work on the *Zentralbahn* continued, Lindequist as undersecretary had already gotten an extension of the *Nordbahn* approved. Work on an initial extension began in 1911. A further extension, which Rechenberg thought would bankrupt the colony, was begun in 1914 but was never completed.[3]

However, Rechenberg was not fired by Lindequist, mainly because Rechenberg's rule in East Africa had by most standards been a success. Exports had increased threefold and the imperial subvention had dropped. African resistance was minimal. In addition, Rechenberg as a Catholic had the backing of the Center party, which formed the main support for Bethmann's government until 1912.[4] Nevertheless, Rechenberg had little desire to remain in East Africa. He returned to Germany in October 1911 with the intention of resigning. Lindequist himself resigned shortly thereafter, and it fell to Lindequist's successor, Wilhelm Solf, to name the professional colonial official Heinrich Schnee to replace Rechenberg. Rechenberg shortly thereafter retired. Though elected a Center Reichstag deputy, he returned to an influential position in the Foreign Office early in 1914. After the war he became, for reasons not altogether clear, a leading advocate of Zionism.

Lindequist's fall was caused not by his disputes with Rechenberg or by his open advocacy of settlement colonialism, which won him the support of the right and the criticism of reformers and economic colonialists, but rather by his opposition to the resolution of the Moroccan Crisis in 1911. The 1911 crisis arose from the tradition of economic colonialism and imperialism and from the foreign-policy aims that Dernburg had earlier tried very hard to have adopted. Economic colonialists argued that the existing colonies were not adequate to meet the requirements of successful economic colonialism. Expansion was necessary. They began to focus on the acquisition—either formally or informally—of the Congo Basin in order to create a unified German colonial empire in Central Africa. Cameroon was vital as a center for creating such an empire and also for its economic potential and the ties already existing between enterprises in Cameroon and the Belgian Congo.[5] The *Mittelafrika* idea came to be favored by an influential segment of the Political Department of the Foreign Office headed by Alfred von Kiderlen-Wächter, the new foreign secretary. Kiderlen and his associates, together with imperialist business interests, decided that the the first step in African expansion should be the annexation by Cameroon of part of French Equatorial Africa; this would connect Cameroon directly with the Congo River. The problem lay in persuading France and the other imperial powers to concur.

The solution was to revive the issue of Morocco, which was in the process of becoming a French protectorate. During the 1905 Moroccan crisis the press had heavily emphasized German economic interests there and the possibilities of the area for German colonial settlement. Since the potential of Morocco had become part of most major imperialist ideologies in Germany, it seemed in 1911 as though a reopening of the Moroccan issue would whip up the kind of nationalist furor in Germany that would be necessary to convince the French and British that Germany was serious about Morocco and would require some kind of compensation (i.e. an extended Cameroon) to avoid war. Neither Kiderlen nor his advisors were really serious about Morocco itself since it made little sense in their larger scheme of African imperialism. Unfortunately, not everyone, including a great many colonialists and Lindequist himself, agreed with them.[6]

In May 1911 Kiderlen began the crisis by publicly stating Germany's claim to partial interest in Morocco and by sending a gunboat there. He had received the approval of Chancellor von

Bethmann Hollweg and the other ministers, although Lindequist apparently believed that Morocco really was the prime
objective of Germany. Lindequist agreed with most conservative
imperialists that Morocco was a far superior site for German
settlement than any colony Germany actually possessed. The
French and British rejected the German claims, and all three
governments explicitly appealed to nationalist public opinion,
using all ideological tools available to them. The diplomats then
commenced secret negotiations that eventually gave Kiderlen
more or less what he had wanted: the extension of Cameroon to
the Congo, in return for which France got a free hand in Morocco.[7] Yet without anticipating it, Kiderlen had destroyed his
own credibility with the politically conscious middle-class public.
The propaganda campaign that had accompanied Germany's
Moroccan effort had taken Morocco as the genuine object; when
it appeared that Germany had backed down once again and had
accepted a less valuable substitute, the conservative press turned
against Kiderlen and the government. The settlement colonialists were especially violent in their attacks, since by the standards of white agricultural settlement, Morocco was far more
valuable than an extended Cameroon.[8]

As an advocate of settlement, Lindequist had gone against the
opinion of his own department by opposing the terms of the
treaty. He had been derided by the impolitic Kiderlen. Believing
that his conservative nationalist convictions had been com-
promised, he resigned on 3 November 1911. If he expected his
departure to cause a great stir, he was mistaken. Most of the
conservative press's ammunition had been expended, and the
more restrained nationalist organizations—especially the Colonial Society—had been privately pressured into neutrality. The
Kolonialzeitung, although praising Lindequist, temporized on the
issue over which he had resigned.[9] In the next few months the
Colonial Office heavily publicized the advantages of the expanded Cameroon as the beginning of wider German involvement in Central Africa.[10]

It is indicative of the increasingly bellicose spirit in which
policy was made in the immediate prewar period that the possi-

bility of actual conflict would be employed over a matter of such little real importance as German expansion into *Mittelafrika*. Lindequist's resignation and the nature of the public dispute over the 1911 treaty also illustrate the continuing importance of the dichotomy in imperialist thinking between the economically oriented imperialists and those who saw overseas expansion as a response to social decline in Germany and as a means of developing new lands for settlement. The ideological differences that this dichotomy represented continued to be important in politics through the period between 1914 and 1918 and influenced policymaking far more than did the realities of the overseas empire.

Wilhelm Solf and the Rebirth of Reform

Lindequist's resignation left Bethmann Hollweg without a clear candidate for the colonial secretaryship and with a desire to appoint a new secretary in a hurry. The job therefore went to the first available colonial governor, Wilhelm Solf of Samoa, who happened to be in Germany on leave.[11] Solf's selection was not actually as haphazard as it seemed. He was a respected, if somewhat obscure, professional colonial bureaucrat—the first specifically trained colonial civil servant to attain high office. Bethmann appreciated bureaucratic talent and disliked amateur flamboyance like Dernburg's.[12]

Solf was a liberal who resembled Dernburg in his orientation toward German economic development, economic imperialism, and political reform. He also believed that citizens should be protected from the unhampered operation of big business.[13] Unlike Dernburg, Solf possessed the typical intelligent German civil servant's attitude toward his political function: he considered himself an independent arbiter among many different groups whose interests were difficult to reconcile. Whereas Dernburg tended to rush ahead with appealing ideas and then back down under pressure, Solf tended to anticipate pressures and curb flights of colonialist fancy. Therefore, Solf's administration cannot be regarded as decisive in setting new directions in colonial policy. His goal, more or less achieved, was to make peace throughout the colonial establishment and to secure the role of the Colonial Office as the resolver of conflicts. Yet the peace achieved was a tense one, not unlike the political balance of Germany as a whole.

Within these constraints Solf tended toward Dernburg-Rechenberg economic colonialism rather than Lindequist's settlement colonialism, but Solf took care not to antagonize conservatives by directly attacking settlement.[14] He acceded to a strong settler voice in Southwest Africa and to the construction of the *Nordbahn* in East Africa. On the other hand, he was instrumental in establishing a broad new policy of economic development in Cameroon as a keystone to what he, like Dernburg and Kiderlen, believed to be the real future of German colonialism: the exploitation of Central Africa. Solf undertook tours of inspection in Southwest Africa in 1912 and West Africa in 1913, publicly reemphasizing his convictions about colonial development and his willingness to consider all points of view. He explicitly took British policy in Nigeria and the Gold Coast as his model, and he came away from his tours with an enhanced dislike for settlement colonialism.[15]

Governors of the major colonies also displayed some of Solf's attitudes. In East Africa, Heinrich Schnee, a weak governor following a succession of very strong-minded ones, attempted to advance native protection in labor recruitment and the establishment of an African-based economy, and he had some success in both areas. At the same time, he was unwilling to cross the settlers. He agreed to the building of the *Nordbahn* although he was unconvinced of its utility. He agreed to restrict the immigration and property rights of Indians, and he appointed a large settler majority to the Governor's Council.[16] Schnee argued, as Götzen had, that different parts of East Africa required development in different ways—the north by white settlers and plantations, other areas through their African inhabitants. This idea reflected Schnee's practical political position rather than a personal commitment to settlement colonialism as preferable to economic colonialism. In general, Schnee applied economic standards to settlement in East Africa.

Theodor Seitz, the governor of Southwest Africa, faced many of the same problems of reconciling the colonial administration's policy of economic development for Germany's domestic benefit with the fact of settler power. Seitz actually claimed sympathy with the settlers, but official policy required him to retain ultimate authority within the colonial bureaucracy and to attempt to protect African interests to some extent.[17]

Humanitarian concern for native protection was the most notable feature of Solf's period in office, despite the contrary tendency toward guaranteeing settler interests, which created a condition of balanced tension within the German colonial establishment. Solf himself took a firmly paternalistic position on native policy.[18] Since the economic future of Germany's African colonies depended on their black inhabitants, Solf thought that Africans must therefore be brought peacefully into the European economic system to avoid unnecessary resistance. Therefore, restraints had to be placed on the exploitation of African labor and on the tendency to turn them into a plantation proletariat. The government's job was essentially an educational one. The African was, Solf said, a "big child," capable of becoming a reasonable facsimile of a European, but for the foreseeable future he had to be "guided" by responsible European authorities. Solf's greatest interest, besides the expansion of German control into Central Africa, was in African education and in bringing Africans into the lower ranks of colonial government and business.

Solf shared these concerns with a group of reformers who became a force in colonial politics during his administration. Whereas Solf himself stated his attitudes almost completely in terms of Germany's economic advantage, the new reformers heavily used humanitarian moralizing by appealing to a kind of emotional sympathy, or *Fürsorge*, for the plight of native peoples.[19] The reform movement was founded on missionary and trading-company interests. Its two prime nonparliamentary figures were Diedrich Westermann, a renowned linguist and anthropologist who had been a missionary in Togo, and J. K. Vietor, a merchant, a former member of the *Kolonialrat*, and a mission society director whom we have discussed as an opponent of settler control and concession companies. The kind of reform that this group represented, despite the heavy moral emphasis in its propaganda, was closely related to a certain variety of economic colonialism, which made it similar to Solf's view. The common factor in the backgrounds of many of the reformers of 1913 and 1914, their relation with Togo, was not accidental. Togo served as their prime model.[20] To them the economic future of the colonies depended on drawing independent, indigenous farmers into small-scale enterprise. For this to happen in Africa, African social structures had to be protected from destruction and only gradually modified. For this reason it was necessary to avoid massive forced labor and land expropriation and to prevent the breakdown of African societies through miscegenation. *Fürsorge* did not imply immediate equality between Europeans and Africans; the races in Africa were to be separate, supposedly for the benefit of both. The reformists' rationale was therefore strongly in the tradition of economic colonialism, and although their humanitarian expressions were doubtless genuine, humanitarianism was primarily a means of gaining public support rather than a guide to policy. The reformists had access to public opinion through their own newspaper, the *Koloniale Rundschau*, founded in 1909.

A new flowering of scientific colonialism and rationalized economic exploitation characterized late German colonial reform. This new trend began symbolically with the founding of the Colonial Institute, a research and training organization, in Hamburg in 1908.[21] The Institute, which Dernburg lauded as a key to his program, was funded by Alfred Beit, an Anglo-German financier and associate of Cecil Rhodes. The Institute's technical and economic work and its advocacy of economic imperialism in cooperation with Britain represented the broad conceptions shared by the new colonial reformers, by Dernburg, by Solf, and probably by most colonial officials.

Though sympathetic to most of the reform ideology, Solf was precluded from taking an active part in the public colonial reform movement by his precarious position among contending interest groups. Reformists instead turned to the colonial opposition of 1906 and 1907, especially to Erzberger, and to the left liberals. Because of the SPD's previous tradition of complete opposition to colonies, its cooperation was not overtly sought. The SPD, however, took advantage of the colonial-reform agitation to assert its post-1912 position as the largest Reichstag party and to criticize colonial policy. Officially, the SPD accepted the revisionist position, which regarded colonies as economic necessities but which opposed abuses and deviations from economic rationality.[22]

The main reformist attack came during the Reichstag debates on colonial appropriations in March 1914.[23] This time the government decided not to meet the attacks head-on, although the representatives of big business conducted an acrimonious dispute with the reformers. Although claiming neutrality and defending official native and labor policies, Solf obviously sympathized with the reformers, reflecting his own convictions and the government's decision to temporize. In the end the Reichstag adopted a resolution stating that native rights should be respected in labor recruitment, that unjustifiable coercion of natives should be abolished, and that education and example should be used to effect social change in the colonies. Solf claimed that many of these items were already official policy, but he accepted the resolution anyway. The Reichstag resolution was the most complete statement to date by any colonial power of its self-conceived obligation to subject peoples and of the need for limitations on the exercise of imperial power. The resolution had no binding force, and since the German colonial empire ended before anything could be done about it, its full meaning was unclear. Yet the formal victory of colonial reform during the heyday of conservative settlement colonialism indicates that in 1914 the direction of German colonial development was still very uncertain.

The Colonial Empire in 1914

Despite the efforts of the economic imperialists, the 1911 settlement was the only tangible result of the Dernburg-Kiderlen expansionary policy. Germany and Britain agreed in 1913 to divide up the Portuguese colonies should the opportunity arise, but as in 1898 nothing happened. A group of imperialists closely associated with the Foreign Office who supported cooperation with Britain, headed by the future Foreign Secretary Richard Kühlmann, in 1913 produced a well-known anonymous pamphlet, "Deutsche Weltpolitik und kein Krieg!" ("German World Policy and No War!"), that advocated abandoning German ambitions in eastern Europe and the Near East and adopting *Mittelafrika* as the major policy goal.[24] They clearly intended to defuse the dangerous diplomatic situation in Europe by diverting attention elsewhere, but the alternative goal in Africa also corresponded to an established trend in German economic imperialist and colonialist thought.

By 1914, the German colonial empire was worth more in trade and capital investment than it had been earlier.[25] Total colonial trade had increased from around 60 million marks in 1902 to about 260 million in 1912. The white population of the colonies had increased to over twenty-four thousand. On the other hand, the colonial deficit for 1913 was still nearly 38 million marks, and Togo and Samoa were still the only colonies that did not require subsidies in order to operate their governments. The proportion of colonial trade to the total amount of German trade was still minuscule (1.2 percent). Judged objectively, whether by the standards of economic or of settlement colonialism, the German colonial enterprise had been a failure. However, this did not prevent the colonies from continuing to play a role in German politics.[26]

15

The First World War
and the Loss of the Colonies

Although the German colonies had for years been publicly justified as sources of raw materials in the event of war, they were
quickly cut off from Germany when war commenced in 1914.
Actually German strategists had largely written the colonies off
as factors in their planning long before 1914, except as possible
naval raiding bases. The raw-materials argument might have
made more sense in the context of a war in which Britain was an
unfriendly neutral, but the actual colonies produced only a few
materials (rubber in Cameroon and copper in Southwest Africa)
that could be regarded as vital to the German economy.

German colonial strategy in 1914 was based on the assumptions that the war would be very short and that Germany would
win. After winning, Germany was to compensate herself for
temporary colonial losses through territorial expansion in Africa.
It was therefore intended to leave each colony alone to resist
attack as long as feasible in the hope that the colonists would tie
down at least a small part of the enemy's force.

Both the German and enemy commands were surprised that
German resistance lasted as long as it did, requiring the Entente

to commit considerable military resources.[1] The lengthy resistance provided the colonial movement and the government with a useful source of propaganda. Although Togo was occupied almost immediately in 1914 without a significant fight and Kiaochow was lost to the Japanese after a month of siege, Southwest Africa had to be conquered by a large South African force in a hard-fought campaign in the spring of 1915. Cameroon was not occupied until 1916, when it was overrun by a joint British-French expedition. Although the defense of Cameroon was effective and mildly embarrassing to the British, the defense of East Africa became a military legend. Efforts to defeat the *Schutztruppe* in East Africa eventually involved British, South African, Indian, Belgian, and Portuguese forces; the campaign did not end until after the European armistice in 1918. The Pacific colonies were occupied by the British and Australians fairly rapidly in 1914 with little opposition although a small group, which did not conduct military operations, held out in New Guinea to the end of the war. The East African campaign was by far the most interesting of these operations, although it could be argued that the occupation of Southwest Africa was ultimately the most important since it gave South Africa claim to the territory and to a special place in British war councils and since it made Jan-Christian Smuts's reputation as a commander.

That Smuts and the South Africans were not as successful in East Africa as in Southwest Africa was due largely to *Schutztruppe* commander Lt. Col. Paul von Lettow-Vorbeck.[2] In November 1914 an allied amphibious assault on Tanga was surprisingly defeated by Lettow-Vorbeck with an augmented force of *askaris*. Lettow-Vorbeck then attempted to invade Kenya and cut the East African Railway, although he was eventually beaten back. In 1916 a multinational force under Smuts invaded German East Africa from several directions, and from then on Lettow-Vorbeck held out against very heavy odds. He gradually retreated into the southwestern corner of the colony and then in 1917 into Mozambique as his forces dwindled. Through a well-executed guerilla campaign 5,000 *askaris* managed to tie down an allied force of up to 130,000 men, greatly embarrassing British and South African arms. Although by 1918 German resistance was limited to quite a small area, Lettow-Vorbeck's force, which was accompanied by Governor Schnee, managed to support itself without significant assistance from Germany and to maintain local political control. When Lettow-Vorbeck surrendered in 1918, he commanded a coherent force capable of active operations.

Lettow-Vorbeck's success was due not only to his obvious military ability, which made him a national hero, but also to other factors deriving from the nature of the German colonial presence. After the war the Germans constantly pointed to the loyalty of the *askaris* and the continued viability of the German administration in wartime as a vindication of their rule and as a counter to the Allied claim that the Germans were brutal tyrants.[3] There seems to have been considerable evidence for the German position and for the reputation that the Germans later had in some areas of being "firm but fair," although past governments frequently appear in a good light when compared with present ones. There is little question that the German government in 1914 was more efficient than its British successor in the early 1920s; initially the British simply took over the German system. At the same time the German regime was clearly oppressive to many of its subjects. Loyalty to Germany appears in part to have resulted from the differential distribution of oppression; the Africans most loyal to Germany were those most benefited and least antagonized by the colonial authorities. In particular, the policy of favoring and protecting the Swahili-speaking coastal population paid off in their continued support of the Germans and in the loyalty of native-born Muslim troops. The system of local government through *akidas* and legitimate chiefs also stood the test. In addition, the British and the Germans tacitly agreed that neither side would attempt to subvert the other's system of native control so that European dominance would not be opened to question.[4] The loyalty of the *Schutztruppe* can also be explained as the attitude of a professional military force, which the *Schutztruppe's* central cadre certainly was by 1914.

Nevertheless, in explaining the East African campaign one is still brought back to Lettow-Vorbeck himself. It may be that part of his success was also due to the lessons he had learned as a protégé of Trotha in China and in the genocidal Herero War[5] and to his acceptance of the utility of exemplary terror, which was an integral part of German (and British, French, and American) colonial military thought. Lettow-Vorbeck may simply have used terrorist tactics more ruthlessly than his opponents, even though they had been trained in the none-too-gentle school of the Boer War.

Whatever the explanation, Lettow-Vorbeck's pinning down of a large enemy army was by far the most significant colonial contribution to the German war effort and quite possibly, from a certain point of view, the most significant contribution that the colonial empire ever made to Germany.

Colonial War Aims

The cutting-off of the colonies from Germany at the beginning of the war did not mean that colonialism ceased to play a role in German politics. The nature of colonialism as an ideology in the German political system guaranteed that mere physical separation was not enough to eliminate colonial affairs from serious political discussion, although they were somewhat downplayed. Even the outright loss of the overseas empire after the war was not enough to remove colonialism from politics. However, wartime colonialism in Germany is more interesting for what it indicates about German imperialism in general than for its actual effect on the colonies, which was nonexistent.

When war came in 1914, the government had no specific scheme for colonial acquisition after victory, but it did possess foreign-policy aims that provided some initial guidance. From 1914 until 1917, a close continuity existed between the prewar assumptions about colonial expansion enunciated by Dernburg and his associates and the official war aims of the chancellor, the Colonial Office, and the Foreign Office.

The first expression of African war aims was contained in

Chancellor Bethmann Hollweg's memorandum of September 1914, which Fritz Fischer has named the "September Program."[6] The September Program was couched in fairly vague terms, but taken in conjunction with an earlier memorandum on war aims from Solf to Bethmann, it permits a comparison with prewar imperialist thinking. The single most important item in the September Program was the demand for a Central European customs union (*Mitteleuropa*) dominated by Germany. This had for some time been the central core of much German economic imperialist thinking, to which economic colonialism was clearly adjunct.[7]

Both Solf and Bethmann advocated a large Central African colony (*Mittelafrika*) that would tie together the existing German colonies (except for Togo) and that would supplement Central Europe as a reserve area and market for industrial Germany. Although the geographic neatness of a continuous African empire had some appeal, the concept was mainly an extension of previous efforts to expand the German overseas empire into more valuable areas. The plan's most important aspect was its required annexation of the Belgian Congo, which was thought to be very valuable. Germany would acquire Katanga's copper mines and other resources, in which German investment had been growing and which Dernburg had wanted to pick up with the consent of Britain. *Mittelafrika*, then, was seen both as a part of the economic imperialism of the September Program and as a means of making the overseas empire immediately profitable. Also in keeping with prewar colonialist thinking, Solf was willing to countenance an exchange of territory with Britain in order to achieve *Mittelafrika*. Included in such a deal would have been the old division of the Portuguese colonies.[8]

Therefore, not only was *Mittelafrika* a concomitant of *Mitteleuropa*, but it was also originally the kind of war aim thought to be compatible with a negotiated peace with Britain. It was believed that Britain would accept both German economic dominance in Europe, if there were little territorial annexation, and an expanded German colonial empire, if the expansion were not at the expense of Britain. *Mittelafrika*, defined largely in the 1914 sense, was among the war aims listed by Bethmann to be presented to President Wilson in late 1916 as the bases for a negotiated peace, and although by that time the Colonial Office, the Foreign Office, and the navy had become greedier, the basic diplomatic idea remained the same.[9] The continuity between the economic imperialists' wartime view of what the British would accept and their prewar idea of what the British would accept was very strong.

A great many other people were interested in colonial aims, both inside and outside the government, despite official prohibition of public war-aims discussion. The Foreign Office by and large concurred with the Colonial Office, although under Jagow and Zimmermann it put less emphasis on negotiations with the British. When Kühlmann became foreign secretary in 1917, the economic imperialism dominant in the Colonial Office became characteristic of the Foreign Office as well, since Kühlmann had been one of its main prewar spokesmen.

The navy's interest in colonial war aims was generally backed up by the Army High Command. Although the potential for conflict between the Colonial Office and the navy was very great, on colonial matters their war aims statements appear to have been fairly well coordinated. The navy usually demanded a series of naval bases from which trade routes could be protected and enemy commerce attacked in wartime and from which *Mittelafrika* could be defended. In preparation for possible negotiations in 1916 and 1917, the navy and the Colonial Office developed a joint program. The areas the Colonial Office desired included *Mittelafrika*, an expanded Togo, and Nigeria. The navy wanted a series of Atlantic bases, including the Azores and either Dakar or the Cape Verde Islands. The navy also wanted Tahiti and at least one of the major islands of Dutch East Indies (which would in any case be economically connected to Germany through the expected Dutch adherence to *Mitteleuropa*). Thus the navy's aims were not fundamentally contrary to those of the Colonial Office. It appears that both departments were deliberately overstating their aims in preparation for bargaining with the British. Nigeria, for example, would probably have been given up in the course of negotiations, had they taken place.

By mid-1917—after the effective takeover of the German government by the army, the adoption of unrestricted submarine warfare, and the entry of the United States into the war—colonial aims changed perceptibly, in line with an overall change in war aims that occurred with Bethmann's fall. To understand the changes in colonial aims, it is necessary to examine the alternative views of war aims that had emerged since 1914.

The conceptions of Bethmann and Solf were closely linked to ideas put forward by upper-class groups associated with, but largely outside, the government. The *Mitteleuropa* idea was publicly outlined by Friedrich Naumann and his associates, especially Paul Rohrbach.[10] It reflected the views of a large number of businessmen, officials, and academics about the easiest way to end the war to Germany's advantage. The *Mitteleuropa* enthusiasts were joined by others less enthralled with Central European economic domination but equally committed to a vigorous policy of economic imperialism, more or less along the lines of prewar *Weltpolitik*.[11] In 1915 these groups joined in an informal coalition to forward their views on war aims and the need for a negotiated peace. This coalition has been variously described as liberal (although many of its members were not) and antiannexationist (although it consistently advocated limited annexations and indirect extraterritorial control). More precisely, however, the members of the coalition were economic imperialists who wanted to ensure Germany's position as an economic superpower through such structures as *Mitteleuropa*, *Mittelafrika*, and an independent kingdom of Poland. This idea was connected, as it had been before the war, to a desire for political reform consistent with a modern economy and to a desire for a mutually beneficial international understanding with Britain.

These conceptions, basically shared by Bethmann and many of his associates, were the foundation of the Delbrück-Dernburg petition on war aims of 1915 and, to an extent, of the *Reichstag* peace resolution of 1917. Continuity with prewar thinking can be seen in that many of the sponsors of these actions—including Dernburg, Rohrbach, Jäckh, and Karl Helferrich—had been among the leading exponents of economic imperialism before the war.[12] The connection with economic colonialism was also present, although it was a little less clear. Most of the colonial reformers of 1914 favored a "peace of understanding" and the acquisition of *Mitteleuropa*, but so did Rohrbach, a settlement colonialist, and Max Sering, an advocate of internal colonization who also favored annexations in the East.

Economic imperialist thinking predominated approximately as long as Bethmann remained in office—that is, until 1917—although it had some effect on policy until 1918. From the middle of 1917, when the army took over ultimate direction of the government, economic imperialism tended to be displaced by a more radically conservative set of ideas.[13] This change had consequences for colonial war aims as well.

The alternative to the economic imperialist view was formulated quite early in the war, sometimes in "private" memoranda circulated among influential people despite Bethmann's prohibition of public war-aims discussion and sometimes in response to requests from high officials for outside opinions. The latter included memoranda submitted by the *Centralverband deutscher Industrieller*, which argued for massive land annexations in east and west. Within a very short while, however, public discussions of war aims in newspapers and journals became commonplace. The most important figure in the discussion was Heinrich Class of the Pan-German League, whom Bethmann caused to be prosecuted because of his statements on war aims early in the war.[14] Class's prosecution was really due, not to his contravention of Bethmann's order, but to the fact that the ideas he expressed were a direct attack on the foundations of government policy; they could have united the political right against Bethmann.

As early as 1914, Class and the Pan-German League called for German gains after victory far in excess of those laid out in the September Program and obviously based on very different conceptions from those of the economic imperialists. Class wanted the annexation of large amounts of European territory, including much of Belgium, northern France, and Poland. In addition, he thought that Germany should acquire an African empire much larger than the *Mittelafrika* of the official policymakers. On this point the Pan-Germans and the Colonial Society agreed, demanding for Germany almost everything in Africa south of 20°N. Germany's new continental and overseas empires were to be filled with German settlers. Class accepted the *Mitteleuropa* concept, but only as a starting point for outright territorial aggrandizement.

The position stated by Class and other radical conservatives became known as the *annexationist* view, as opposed to the moderate economic imperialist position. Clearly, the term is something of a misnomer since most of the moderates also favored a moderate amount of outright territorial annexation. Yet the annexationists clearly, for different reasons, wanted a great deal more territory. Although to people like Naumann and Delbrück, annexations were allowable only for military purposes or to make the proposed economic union more effective, annexationists sought large, conquered regions in which Germans could be settled as military conquerors and as peasant farmers.[15]

Produced during the war were many dozens of pamphlets that argued, on the basis of German overpopulation, that disabled soldiers and German peasants should be settled in, for example, the Ukraine, either becoming a master race or displacing the indigenous population.[16] These arguments were usually repetitions of the old emigrationist, settlement colonialist ideas and were based on the old assumptions about overpopulation and the social threat to valuable classes within Germany. There was, therefore, an ideological connection between wartime annexationist imperialism and prewar settlement colonialism, as there was in the parties advocating the two ideologies.

The connection between settlement colonialism and annexationism after 1914 was more than a matter of intellectual similarity. Many of the annexationist formulations included explicit provisions for expanded overseas settlement colonies, although in general colonies were less important to the annexationists than they were to the economic imperialists. Africa was the prime area of interest, but some writers suggested German settlement colonies in the Near East and in China.[17] Such proposals were usually linked to proposals for German settlement and massive population movements in eastern Europe.

With the political turnover of 1917, the annexationist view became important because it appealed to many elements of the Army High Command (particularly *Oberost*, the army administration in the occupied eastern regions) and because the annexationist idea was one of the ideological elements cementing the conservative political coalition opposed to a negotiated peace and any attempts at democratization that might arise from the war. The conservative coalition, represented in the Reichstag by the new *Vaterlandspartei*, provided a firm basis of support for the army's control of policymaking.[18] Both eastern settlement annexationism and settlement colonialism rapidly became official policy, and the positions of various government departments began to reflect the new trends in their war aims. The Colonial Office's 1918 war-aims proposals were considerably more extensive than they had been, corresponding closely to those of the Colonial Society. Although negotiations went ahead for the creation of a German-Austrian customs union, government policy began to shift more toward plans for actual long-term occupation in eastern Europe, especially after Germany acquired control over the Ukraine in the Treaty of Brest-Litovsk in March 1918. In terms of eastern European and colonial policy, therefore, the German government was shifting in 1917 and 1918 from an economic imperialist line to one emphasizing radically conservative concepts and policies.[19]

A personal connection between moderate war aims and economic colonialism and between annexationism and settlement colonialism can also be seen. When the army decided in 1918 to establish German settlement colonies in the Transcaucasus, Friedrich Lindequist was appointed to run the project.[20] The duke of Mecklenburg, president of the Colonial Society and a prominent settlement colonialist, was also president of the *Vaterlandspartei* and a leader of the conservative reaction in 1917.[21] On the economic imperialist side an interesting example is provided by the wartime career of former governor Rechenberg, a leading economic colonialist.

After a brief period of retirement, Rechenberg rejoined the Foreign Office in 1914 and became involved with policy toward eastern Europe almost from the start of the war. He was one of the architects of the independent kingdom of Poland, which was envisioned as a key link in the chain of German economic control to be embodied in *Mitteleuropa*. In February 1917, during intensive disputes over war-aims policy, Rechenberg volunteered to state the economic imperialist position in a journal article.[22] In his article he laid out a general program for settling the war profitably through negotiation and rejected military control of war-aims policy as something beyond the army's competence. Rechenberg argued that a proper settlement would involve an avoidance of annexations and a concentration on securing Germany's economic interests. He specifically rejected annexations in the Baltic area, which even Rohrbach and Hans Delbrück accepted. Although Rechenberg did not say so in public, he was not completely opposed to annexation for military reasons, having been in charge of planning for a narrow extension of Germany's Polish border, but apparently that was the extent of his support for annexation. He thought that the objective of eastern policy should be an integrated economic area that would provide agricultural products, raw materials, and markets for the industrial regions of Germany and Austria-Hungary. Rechenberg claimed that the economic union would even help Prussian agricultural interests since it would provide a means of controlling agricultural production elsewhere in eastern Europe and would open up the Austro-Hungarian market. An independent kingdom of Poland, and perhaps other independent areas removed from the Russian Empire, would be essential to the economic union.

Rechenberg also rejected schemes to establish German settlement colonies in Africa and elsewhere and instead, in keeping with official policy, came out for a continuous central African empire. He explicitly justified *Mittelafrika* on grounds of the economic utility of new territories in the Congo Basin but cautioned against taking more than was economically viable. Even in 1917 he was willing to give up Togo in return for *Mittelafrika*.

In defending the central African empire, Rechenberg repeated arguments put forward both before and during the war by many economic colonialists. The publicist Emil Zimmermann, for example, called in 1917 for complementary central European and central African empires as constituents of a self-supporting economic area able to secure German power and prosperity for the foreseeable future.[23] Before the war Zimmermann had been a leading advocate of expanding Cameroon into the Congo Basin as the basis of a German *Mittelafrika*. In the cases of both Rechenberg and Zimmermann, therefore, close connections can be shown between prewar economic colonialism and wartime advocacy of economic imperialist aims.

By 1918 the struggle for power in Germany had been won by a broad, right-wing coalition, and war-aims policy began strongly to emphasize colonialism and annexation in the East. The regular personnel of the Colonial Office were increasingly ignored in policymaking, even when their expertise would have been valuable. However, the practical effect of the change in war-aims policy was of course minimal, except in the Ukraine, since after April Germany began losing the war. By November the only overseas German colonial presence was Lettow-Vorbeck's force, and it surrendered immediately after the armistice.

Postwar Colonialism

After the armistice Germany campaigned at Versailles to have her colonies returned to her, but to no avail. Basing their action on a wartime propaganda campaign that had been designed to show that the Germans had mistreated their colonial subjects, the Allies turned the colonies into Mandates of the League of Nations. A large German population remained in Southwest Africa, but most Germans in Cameroon and East Africa were effectively expelled. (Many, however, returned in the 1920s.) Even though the colonies had been lost, colonialism was not quite dead in German politics.

The Colonial Society continued to exist and to propagandize for the return of the colonies, and many earlier colonial figures became important in Weimar politics.[24] The colonial movement came to be controlled by former colonial officials and increasingly reflected their views. Many of the disputes that had divided German colonialism for years were dropped; in the absence of real colonial issues, a new ideological line composed equally of settlement and economic colonialist elements tended to form. Settlement colonialism, which remained part of radical conservative political ideology, was adopted by the Nazis, together with the argument that Germany had a real economic need for colonies. After the Nazi takeover the Colonial Society was integrated into the government. Hitler listed as one of Germany's foreign-policy goals the return of the African colonies. In actual policymaking, however, Hitler largely ignored the Colonial Society and the corps of retired colonial officials. In 1938, when offered the African colonies in return for passing up Czechoslovakia, Hitler had no reluctance in choosing continental expansion over colonial. In its final existence, as in its heyday, the colonial empire was a peripheral aspect of German life. Its role in German politics was more important than its intrinsic material value, a fact which Hitler recognized in his 1938 decision.

The German colonial empire thus exemplifies, perhaps in an extreme form, the nature and results of late nineteenth-century European imperial expansion. Largely founded as a product of the complex interplay of domestic political forces resulting from rapid socioeconomic change, the empire itself was never a practical economic success. One could argue that in most cases of expansion between 1880 and 1900, economic success occurred only by accident and that in other countries, as in Germany, the real meaning of colonialism must be found in its domestic political function. Even German colonialism had a profound effect on non-European societies, but in terms of overall colonial policy and politics, the significant elements of causation were to be found at home.[25]

Notes

ABBREVIATIONS IN NOTES

A.A. Grenzkomission	Auswärtiges Amt, Abt. A., Akten betr. Grenz-komission
A.A. Kolonialrat	Auswärtiges Amt. Akten betreffend den Kolonialrat
DKG Vorstand	Deutsche Kolonialgesellschaft, Vorstand files
DOAG	Deutsch-Ostafrikanische Gesellschaft files
DZA	Deutsches Zentralarchiv
Sten.Ber.	*Stenographische Berichte über die Verhandlungen des Reichstages*

PREFACE

1. The final note to each of the following chapters will contain a brief discussion of current trends in research on the subject of the chapter. Significant recent work relating to German colonialism has been concentrated in three general topic areas: the conflict and interaction between European and indigenous societies under German colonial rule, social and economic roots of German imperialism, and the overall causes of late nineteenth-century European overseas expansion. Of these topics the second is given the greatest attention in the present study, which is quite deliberately oriented toward the domestic aspects of German colonialism. It is hoped that in the bibliographical notes sufficient information will be presented to guide readers to current publications in the other two areas.

CHAPTER 1

1. Franz Wigard, ed., *Stenographischer Bericht über der deutschen constituierenden Nationalversammlung zu Frankfurt am Main*, 2:1055–62; *Protokallischer Bericht über den am 16. Okt 1848 zu Frankfurt a. M. abghaltenen Congress der Vereine für deutsche Auswanderung und Ansiedlung*.

2. Friedrich Hundeshagen, *Die deutsche Auswanderung als Nationalsache*, pp. 1–4, 6–8, 21.

3. Mack Walker, *Germany and the Emigration, 1816–1885*, pp. 38–41, 82–85.

4. *Deutscher Liberalismus im Vormärz*, pp. 242–45, 277–80.

5. Heinrich Sieveking, *Karl Sieveking, 1787–1847*, pp. 518–25.

6. Alfred Zimmermann, *Geschichte der Deutschen Kolonialpolitik*, p. 203; *Norddeutsche Allgemeine Zeitung*, 16, 17, 19, 21, and 22 February 1867.

7. Lothar Bucher, *Kleine Schriften politischen Inhalts*, pp. 180–219.

8. Mary E. Townsend, *The Rise and Fall of Germany's Colonial Empire, 1884–1918*, pp. 55–57.

9. Friedrich List, *Das nationale System der politischen Ökonomie*, pp. 280–90; Bucher, *Kleine Schriften*, pp. 180–219.

10. See, for example, Max Buchner, *Aurora colonialis*, pp. 1–4.

11. The best study of the relation between Hamburg economic interests and colonialism is Helmut Washausen, *Hamburg und die Kolonialpolitik des Deutschen Reiches, 1880 bis 1890*.

12. Hans-Ulrich Wehler, *Bismarck und der Imperialismus*, pp. 258–372. Investors in colonial companies are listed in responses to queries from the Colonial Department, Auswärtiges Amt. Akten betreffend den Kolonialrat,1891, vol. 4, passim; Reichskolonialamt Files. Hoover Institution on War, Revolution, and Peace, Stanford, Calif.

13. Walker, *Germany and the Emigration*, pp. 1–41.

14. Donald G. Rohr, *The Origins of Social Liberalism in Germany*, pp. 121–30.

15. Robert [von] Mohl, "Über Auswanderung," pp. 320–49.

16. Hans Rosenberg, *Grosse Depression und Bismarckzeit*, p. 161.

17. List, *Nationale System*, pp. 406–17.

18. Rosenberg, *Grosse Depression*, pp. 38–51.

19. Wehler, *Bismarck*, pp. 95–126.

20. Ernst von Weber, *Die Erweiterung des deutschen Wirtschaftsgebiets und die Grundlegung zu überseeischen deutschen Staaten*.

21. Helmut Böhme, "Big Business, Pressure Groups, and Bismarck's Turn to Protectionism, 1873–1879," pp. 224–35.

22 C. A. Lüderitz, ed., *Die Erschliessung von Deutsch-Südwest-Afrika*, pp. 58–59.

23. Buchner, *Aurora colonialis*, p. 3.

24. A concise statement of Progressive ideology is Rudolf Virchow, *Sozialismus und Reaktion*.

25. Rosenberg, *Grosse Depression*, pp. 88–117.

26. Wilhelm Hübbe-Schleiden, *Deutsche Colonisation*, pp. 3–5, 18–19.

27. Friedrich Fabri, *Bedarf Deutschland der Colonien?*, pp. 1–13.

28. See Woodruff D. Smith, "The Ideology of German Colonialism, 1840–1906," pp. 641–62. On the *Auswanderung*, and its relation to colonialism, see Mack Walker, *Germany and the Emigration*. The relation between the Great Depression of the 1870s and the development of German colonialism is mentioned in Hans Rosenberg, *Grosse Depression*, and in Helmut Böhme, *Deutschlands Weg zur Grossmacht*, although not in great detail. The best study of the socioeconomic origins of German colonialism is Hans-Ulrich Wehler's masterly work *Bismarck und der Imperialismus*, which sparked widespread interest in German colonialism when it appeared in 1969. Wehler's work will be discussed in more detail in the bibliographical note to Chapter 2. In the context of the present chapter, however, it can be said that in the author's opinion Wehler seriously underestimates the importance of emigrationist colonialism and of lower-middle-class interest in colonialism because of his concentration on the development of colonial-policy

aims by business pressure groups. The operation of these groups is, however, very well discussed by Wehler.

CHAPTER 2

1. Hans-Ulrich Wehler, *Bismarck und der Imperialismus*, pp. 112–26.
2. *Deutsche Kolonialzeitung*, 17 October 1891, pp. 142–45.
3. C. A. Lüderitz, ed., *Die Erschliessung von Deutsch-Südwest-Afrika*, pp. 70–72. From the marginal notations on documents concerning Germany's takeover of colonies, it appears that Bismarck primarily paid attention to arguments based on the economic advantages of possessing colonies.
4. German Colonial Society, *Die Deutsche Kolonialgesellschaft*, pp. 9–10, 12–13; Richard Victor Pierard, "The German Colonial Society, 1882–1914," pp. 13–49.
5. German Colonial Society, *Kolonialgesellschaft*, pp. 36–37; Pierard, "Colonial Society," pp. 50–74.
6. German Colonial Society, *Kolonialgesellschaft*, p. 51; Pierard, "Colonial Society," pp. 93–95.
7. Friedrich Fabri, *Bedarf Deutschland der Colonien?* pp. 1–13, 20–32.
8. German Colonial Society, *Kolonialgesellschaft*, pp. 20–21.
9. *Deutsche Kolonialzeitung*, 25 July 1891, pp. 109–11.
10. Wilhelm Hübbe-Schleiden, *Deutsche Colonisation*, pp. 1–13; Wilhelm Hübbe-Schleiden, *Überseeische Politik, eine Culturwissenschaftliche Studie*, pp. 13–14, 74–75.
11. Carl Peters, *Gesammelte Schriften*, 1:17.
12. Peters, *Gesammelte Schriften*, 1:332–41.
13. Carl Peters, *Zur Weltpolitik*, pp. 141–45.
14. Hans Spellmeyer, *Deutsche Kolonialpolitik im Reichstag*, p. 23.
15. Wehler, *Bismarck*, pp. 112–26.
16. Robert Cornevin, "The Germans in Africa before 1918," pp. 385–86, 390–91.
17. A. J. P. Taylor, *Germany's First Bid for Colonies, 1884–1885*, p. 6.
18. Manfred Nussbaum, *Vom "Kolonialenthusiamus" zur Kolonialpolitik der Monopole*, pp. 66–81.
19. Lüderitz, *Erschliessung*, pp. 58–72; Helmuth Stoecker, ed., *Kamerun unter deutscher Kolonialherrschaft*, 1:17–19. In 1880 Germany's exports to Africa were only 0.2 percent of her total.
· 20. Stoecker, *Kamerun*, 1:53–54; Hartmut Pogge von Strandmann, "Domestic Origins of Germany's Colonial Expansion under Bismarck," p. 148. This fear was largely imaginary.
21. Mary E. Townsend, *The Origins of Modern German Colonialism, 1871–1885*, pp. 54–135.
22. Wehler, *Bismarck*.
23. Johannes Lepsius, Albrecht Mendelssohn-Bartholdy, and Friedrich Thimme, eds., *Die Grosse Politik der europäischen Kabinette, 1871–1914*, 4:96.
24. Pierard, *Colonial Society*, pp. 13–49. In 1886 the *Kolonialverein* had 12,400 members.
25. Spellmeyer, *Kolonialpolitik*, pp. 16–28.
26. Hans Rosenberg, *Grosse Depression und Bismarckzeit*, pp. 62–78.
27. Peters's own description of his early activities in East Africa is contained in Carl Peters, *Die Gründung von Deutsch-Ostafrika*.
28. Pogge von Strandmann, "Domestic Origins," p. 147.
29. Lüderitz, *Erschliessung*, pp. 70–72.
30. Wehler, *Bismarck*, pp. 263–400.

31. Friedrich Fabri, *Fünf Jahre deutscher Kolonialpolitik*.

32. A detailed chronology of the events of the German acquisition of colonies is provided by Ernst Kienitz, *Zeittafel zur deutschen Kolonialgeschichte*, pp. 33–34, 53, 64–65, 77–79, 105–108. For Southwest Africa see J. H. Esterhuyse, *South West Africa 1880–94*.

33. Lüderitz, *Erschliessung*, pp. 107–16. For Lüderitz's biography see Wilhelm Schüssler. *Adolf Lüderitz*.

34. Wehler, *Bismarck*, pp. 298–328; Max Buchner, *Aurora colonialis*, pp. 5–83.

35. *Deutsches Kolonialblatt*, 1 April 1896, pp. 187–88.

36. For the first years of German East Africa, see Bruno Kurtze, *Die Deutsch-Ostafrikanische Gesellschaft*, and Fritz Ferdinand Müller, *Deutschland-Zanzibar-Ostafrika*.

37. *Anlagen* to Board meetings of 2 April 1887 and 27 April 1889, Deutsch-Ostafrikanische Gesellschaft files, Hoover Institution on War, Revolution, and Peace, Stanford, Calif.

38. Wehler, *Bismarck*, pp. 391–400; Paul M. Kennedy, *The Samoan Tangle*, pp. 1–97.

39. A. A. Kolonialrat, vol. 2 (Kolonialratsachen 2/6967), contains an 1896 report to the shareholders of the *Neu-Guinea Kompagnie* explaining the company's problems.

40. Ronald Robinson and John Gallagher, *Africa and the Victorians*, contains the best modern description of the scramble for Africa, primarily from the British point of view.

41. See Sybil Eyre Crowe, *The Berlin West African Conference 1884–1885*.

42. Germany's seizure of colonies has been a subject of scholarly dispute ever since the event occurred, and much of the recent work on German colonialism has been concerned with it. The classic question concerns Bismarck's motives in adopting a colonial policy after years of opposing colonies. As is indicated in the text above, there are certain standard responses to the question. Mary Townsend, *Rise and Fall*, argued that Bismarck changed his mind in the late 1870s but only revealed himself later. A. J. P. Taylor, *Germany's First Bid for Colonies*, produced the classic statement of the view that Bismarck was not really interested in colonies but rather wanted to prevent an entente between Britain and France and to draw Germany closer to France by embroiling the major powers in a colonial scramble. Finally, William O. Aydelotte, in his *Bismarck and British Colonial Policy*, made the case that Bismarck was primarily interested in using the colonial issue to damage the political strength of the left liberals. Bismarck's actual motives will never be known with certainty, but it appears from the evidence that of the classic explanations Aydelotte's will stand the test of time.

Most of the recent work on the subject has been concerned, not with Bismarck's motives by themselves, but rather with the political situation and with the interaction of economic pressure groups that produced Germany's decision to seek colonies. Several East German historians, most notably Fritz Ferdinand Müller in the introduction to his *Deutschland-Zanzibar-Ostafrika*, have argued that the new colonial policy resulted from the German government's response to pressure from big business to acquire new investment areas. Most of the available evidence, however, seems to indicate a decided unwillingness on the part even of procolonial businessmen to invest in colonial enterprises. It is very difficult to show that the colonies were an outlet for excess capital. Hartmut Pogge von Strandmann, "Domestic Origins of Germany's Colonial Expansion under Bismarck," convincingly restates the argument that Bismarck was out to hurt the left liberals in the context of social conflicts within the Reich and of Bismarck's desire to create a firm political base in the Reichstag. Henry Ashby

Turner, Jr., "Bismarck's Imperialist Venture," pp. 47–82, describes Bismarck's policy simply as a diplomatic move to secure certain limited German economic interests without long-term intentions with respect to the European power balance.

The most important recent work on the subject is Hans-Ulrich Wehler's *Bismarck und der Imperialismus*, which has revolutionized the study of German imperialism in the 1880s. Wehler's study is based on an analysis of the social structure of Bismarckian Germany and of the tensions within it. Wehler argues that Bismarck's colonialism was an aspect of his "social imperialism," a kind of sham policy intended to make German business interests and the German middle class believe that the state could advance the interests of German commerce abroad (and also help to repress working-class socialism at home) without changing its basic constitutional structure and social composition. Bismarck was primarily interested in preserving the existing order in which classes threatened with political extinction in an industrial society, especially the Junkers, maintained a large share of power. Wehler argues that Bismarck was not much interested in colonies but that he seized the opportunity presented by the appearance of colonialist agitation among groups representing depression-plagued industries to occupy unimportant colonies and to win the support of business without risking basic concessions of political power to commercial interests. Wehler's work is of very great importance. It has succeeded in placing Bismarck's colonialism in the context of the most important social forces at work in imperial Germany. It has already been indicated that Wehler probably underestimates the importance of the popular emigrationist colonial movement. He fails to see the distinctions among the various types of colonialism and the crucial importance of Bismarck's exploitation of these distinctions. This probably comes from Wehler's concentration on social structure as the determinant of political action rather than on the ideologies through which political action is formulated and understood. Wehler has also been criticized for giving too much weight to the resolutions of chambers of commerce, as though these were politically effective statements. In general, however, Wehler's work is by far the most important study produced in the field in the last twenty years.

The question of Germany's initial colonial expansion, of course, is also relevant to the greater question of why Europe in the late nineteenth century suddenly undertook its last effort at formal overseas colonization. This is a subject beyond the scope of this book. However, it would be a useful contribution to the literature on this subject if a rigorous comparison were made, perhaps on the basis of an analysis like Wehler's, between Germany's expansion and that of Britain and the other colonial powers. Prosser Gifford and Wm. Roger Louis's *Britain and Germany in Africa* made a valuable start in that direction, but their book appeared before the publication of Wehler's study and several other recent works, which focused attention, not on the diplomatic and overseas aspects of imperialism, but on its domestic social characteristics. On this question see Michael R. Gordon, "Domestic Conflict and the Origins of the First World War," pp. 191–226.

The dispute over late nineteenth-century imperialism engendered first by Robinson and Gallagher's *Africa and the Victorians* and more recently by the views put forward by D. H. Fieldhouse and D. C. M. Platt is concerned mainly with the motivations of British imperialism. The German case may have some bearing on the question, in that it appears to be fairly clear that certain sets of imperialist ideas (if not the "official mind" of Robinson and Gallagher) were crucial to Germany's decision to colonize and that political factors (however heavily influenced by long-term economic change) probably took precedence over specific economic interests in colonies, much as Fieldhouse suggests.

CHAPTER 3

1. Richard Victor Pierard, "The German Colonial Society, 1882–1914," pp. 138–41.
2. German Colonial Society, *Die Deutsche Kolonialgesellschaft*, p. 52.
3. *Deutsche Kolonialzeitung*, 26 April 1900, pp. 178, 181–84; ibid., 21 May 1903, pp. 197–200.
4. Geo. A. Schmidt, *Das Kolonial-Wirtschaftliche Komitee*, pp. 5–30, *Deutsche Kolonialzeitung*, 24 May 1900, pp. 226–27.
5. German Colonial Society, *Kolonialgesellschaft*, pp. 22, 52, 61–62, 67, 69, 79–80, 133, 173–79, 191–93; German Colonial Society, *Jahresbericht*, 1894, pp. 26–28; ibid., 1895, pp. 29–33, 50–52; ibid., 1896, pp. 137–39; *Deutsche Kolonialzeitung*, 15 January 1903, pp. 22–23; ibid., 5 January 1907, p. 5; ibid., 19 January 1907, p. 22.
6. Pierard, *Colonial Society*, pp. 92–94, 138–40.
7. Hans-Ulrich Wehler, *Bismarck und der Imperialismus* pp. 412–502.
8. *Amtliches Reichstages-Handbuch*, pp. 9–46; John Iliffe, *Tanganyika under German Rule 1905–1912*, pp. 35–40.
9. Hartmut Pogge von Strandmann, "Domestic Origins of Germany's Colonial Expansion under Bismarck," pp. 149–50.
10. Peters's activities as the agent of DOAG are detailed in DOAG, 2 April 1887, *Anlagen* 5 and 6; ibid., 8 September 188, *Anlage* 1.
11. Friedrich Fabri, *Fünf Jahre deutscher Kolonialpolitik*, Wilhelm Schroeder-Poggelow, *Unsere Afrika-politik in den letzten zwei Jahren*, pp. 1–10.
12. J. C. G. Röhl, "The Disintegration of the *Kartell* and the Politics of Bismarck's Fall from Power, 1887–90," pp. 60–89.
13. Pogge von Strandmann, "Domestic Origins," pp. 152–57.
14. The various reorganizations of the Colonial Department are summarized in Prosser Gifford and Wm. Roger Louis, eds., *Britain and Germany in Africa*, pp. 765–66.
15. J. C. G. Röhl, *Germany without Bismarck*, pp. 30, 36, 60.
16. See, for example, *Deutsche Kolonialzeitung*, 8 February 1900, pp. 51–52.
17. Ibid., 27 June 1891, pp. 85–87; A. A. Kolonialrat, vol. 2, p. 4287.
18. Jake Wilton Spidle, "The German Colonial Service," pp. 100–105.
19. See Kayser's speech to the *Kolonialrat* in *Deutsche Kolonialzeitung*, 27 June 1891, pp. 85–86.
20. The major recent study of the Colonial Society is R. V. Pierard's dissertation, "The German Colonial Society, 1882–1914," which has unfortunately never been published. Analyses of colonial politics between 1885 and 1890 are contained in Pogge von Strandmann's article "Domestic Origins" and in Wehler's *Bismarck und der Imperialismus*. No detailed study, however, exists of post-1885 German colonial politics except for Manfred Nussbaum, *Vom "Kolonialenthusiasmus" zur Kolonialpolitik der Monopole*, an East German study that, although based on the resources of the Colonial Office files at Potsdam, is to be read with caution because of its extreme ideological bias and its clear propagandistic objectives.

CHAPTER 4

1. *Deutches Kolonial-Handbuch 1913*, 3:1.
2. Helmut Bley, *South-West Africa under German Rule, 1894–1914*, pp. xxi–xxvi; Heinrich Vedder, *South West Africa in Early Times*.
3. Robert Cornevin, "The Germans in Africa before 1918," p. 385–86.
4. For the detailed history of the DKGfSWA, see Ludwig Sander, *Geschichte der deutschen Kolonialgesellschaft für Südwest-Africa von ihrer Gründung bis zum Jahre 1910*.

5. German Colonial Department, *Denkschrift über die im südwestafrikanischen Schutzgebiete tätigen Land- und Minen-Gesellschaften*, pp. 1–3.

6. Ernst Kienitz, *Zeittafel zur deutschen Kolonialgeschichte*, p. 36.

7. The early years of German rule are discussed in J. H. Esterhuyse, *South West Africa, 1880–94*.

8. Paul Rohrbach, *Der deutsche Gedanke in der Welt*, p. 145.

9. German Colonial Society, *Jahresbericht*, 1894, pp. 26–28; ibid., 1895, pp. 29–33; ibid., 1896, pp. 137–39; *Deutsche Kolonialzeitung*, 30 April 1892, pp. 61–63.

10. *Deutsches Kolonialblatt*, 1 January 1892, pp. 23–24; ibid., 1 March 1892, pp. 144–46.

11. Hans Oelhafen von Schollenbach, *Die Besiedlung Deutsch-Südwestafrikas bis zum Weltkriege*, p. 19.

12. Bley, *South-West Africa*, pp. 3–70, 124–34.

13. Julius Scharlach, *Koloniale und politische Aufsätze und Reden*, pp. 52–57.

14. German Colonial Department, *Denkschrift*, pp. 1–3.

15. Paul Rohrbach, *Um des Teufels Handschrift*, pp. 61–67.

16. Paul Rohrbach, *Dernburg und die Südwestafrikaner*, pp. 284–323.

17. Theodor Leutwein, *Elf Jahre Gouverneur in Deutsch-Südwestafrika*, pp. 428–64.

18. Ibid., pp. 541–49; Bley, *South-West Africa*, pp. 67–70.

19. Bley, *South-West Africa*, pp. 124–26.

20. Oelhafen, *Besiedlung*, pp. 24–33.

21. Leutwein, *Elf Jahre*, pp. 266–78.

22. Bley, *South-West Africa*, pp. 149–69; Leutwein, *Elf Jahre*, pp. 465–525.

23. Bley, *South-West Africa*, p. 159.

24. Leutwein, *Elf Jahre*, pp. 319–22; Horst Drechsler, "Jacob Morenga," pp. 95–105.

25. Two studies of Southwest Africa have been published fairly recently: Helmut Bley's *South-West Africa* (in both German and English editions) and Horst Drechsler's *Südwestafrika unter deutscher Kolonialherrschaft*. The latter is a fairly standard East German analysis, based primarily on the Potsdam archives. Bley's work is interesting and important. It attempts to explain events in Southwest Africa in terms of the conflict between German and African social structures, and on the whole it succeeds. As in the case of other German historians of imperialism, Bley's emphasis on the imperatives of social position for political action sometimes leads to distortions in his analysis of intentions, especially in his consideration of the relations between Southwest African settlers and their political allies in Germany. However, the most significant failing of Bley's analysis (fortunately in a nonessential area) is his acceptance of Hannah Arendt's notion that colonialism was a precursor of twentieth-century totalitarianism. Bley attempts to show that genocide in Southwest Africa in 1904 and 1905 was directly related to genocide under the Nazis without adducing any substantial evidence. One may indeed find a relation, but it is to be found, not in the actions of European authorities in their colonies, but in the social and ideological makeup of colonialism at home in Europe, where Bley does not look. As far as events in Southwest Africa are concerned, however, Bley's study is of first-rate importance.

CHAPTER 5

1. Robert Cornevin, *Histoire du Togo*, pp. 132–98. See also Arthur Joseph Knoll, "Togo under German Administration, 1884–1910."

2. August Full, *Fünfzig Jahre Togo*, pp. 187–219; Knoll, "Togo," pp. 83–133.

3. Paul Rohrbach, *Der deutsche Gedanke in der Welt*, pp. 133–60.

4. Georg Trierenberg, *Togo*, pp. 46–48. *Deutsches Kolonialblatt*, 15 July 1892, p. 378; ibid., 1 August 1908, pp. 337–42.

5. *Deutsches Kolonialblatt*, 1 June 1902, pp. 242–43; ibid., 15 July 1908, pp. 689–90.

6. O. F. Metzger, *Unsere alte Kolonie Togo*, pp. 26–30; Full, *Fünfzig Jahre*, pp. 62–63; Cornevin, *Histoire du Togo*, pp. 167–81.

7. Trierenberg, *Togo*, pp. 20–33; Full, *Fünfzig Jahre*, pp. 124–26. See also Manfred Nussbaum, *Togo–eine Musterkolonie?*

8. *Stenographisches Bericht über die Verhandlungen der deutschen Reichstags*, 19 March 1906, p. 2148.

9. Cornevin, *Histoire du Togo*, pp. 119–34.

10. Knoll, "Togo," pp. 91–95; Acta betr. Westafrika, 138/2, 1343 (1904), Records of German Embassy in London (T-149), National Archives, Washington, D.C.

11. Trierenberg, *Togo*, pp. 6–30; Full, *Fünfzig Jahre*, pp. 50–53.

12. Arthur Joseph Knoll, "Taxation in the Gold Coast Colony and Togo," pp. 417–53; *Deutsches Kolonialblatt*, 1 January 1892, p. 20.

13. *Deutsches Kolonialblatt*, 15 April 1896, p. 220.

14. Ibid., 15 July 1892, pp. 377–78.

15. J. K. von Vietor, *Wirtschaftliche und kulturelle Entwicklung unserer Schutzgebiete*, pp. 76–82.

16. Trierenberg, *Togo*, pp. 43–75.

17. Cornevin, *Histoire du Togo*, pp. 117–18.

18. Metzger, *Togo*, pp. 214–29.

19. *Deutsches Kolonialblatt*, 1 March 1892, p. 143; ibid., 15 March 1892, pp. 168–76.

20. O. Arendt, *Die parlementarischen Studienreisen nach West- und Ostafrika*; Knoll, "Togo," pp. 102–12.

21. Full, *Fünfzig Jahre*, pp. 198–203; Trierenberg, *Togo*, p. 46.

22. *Deutsches Kolonialblatt*, 15 November 1914, p. 836; Metzger, *Togo*, pp. 3–5; Cornevin, *Histoire du Togo*, pp. 169–71.

23. There has been very little work done on German Togo, either on the German administration or on changes in African society under German rule, despite several interesting aspects to Togo's colonial history. The portion of Robert Cornevin's *Histoire du Togo* devoted to the German period is almost entirely derived from the three or four highly inadequate memoirs of Togo by German officials there. The only thorough study is Arthur Knoll's dissertation—which, although useful, deals mainly with questions of administration and covers the Zech period very lightly. When Knoll's work is published in expanded form, it will perhaps help fill the requirement for a comprehensive study of Togo. Manfred Nussbaum's *Togo–eine Musterkolonie?* is primarily an East German polemic and adds little to our knowledge of German rule in Togo.

CHAPTER 6

1. Helmuth Stoecker, ed., *Kamerun unter deutscher Kolonialherrschaft*, 1:133–45.

2. Max Buchner, *Aurora colonialis*, pp. 63–83; Jesko von Puttkamer, *Gouverneursjahre in Kamerun*, pp. 230–31; Auswärtiges Amt, Abt. A., Akten betr. Grenzkommission, Records relating to Franco-German Relations, Library of Congress, Washington, D.C.

3. Karin Hausen, *Deutsche Kolonialherrschaft in Afrika*, pp. 23–31.

4. Stoecker, *Kamerun*, 1:162.

5. Ibid., pp. 151–242; *Deutsches Kolonialblatt*, 1 April 1892, pp. 198–208.

6. Puttkamer, *Gouverneursjahre*, pp. 102–4; *Deutsches Kolonialblatt*, 15 July 1893, pp. 351–54. For Zintgraff's ideas about colonial development, see *Deutsches Kolonialblatt*, 15 February 1892, pp. 104–8; ibid., 1 March 1892, pp. 131–37.

7. Stoecker, *Kamerun*, 1:84–87; *Deutsches Kolonialblatt*, 15 January 1893, pp. 31–39.

8. *Deutsches Kolonialblatt*, 1 January 1892, pp. 14–18.

9. Puttkamer, *Gouverneursjahre*, pp. 96–120.

10. Buchner, *Aurora colonialis*, pp. 84–322.

11. Puttkamer, *Gouverneursjahre*, p. 52.

12. Mary E. Townsend, *The Rise and Fall of Germany's Colonial Empire, 1884–1918*, p. 283.

13. Stoecker, *Kamerun*, 2:57–98.

14. Ibid.

15. Puttkamer, *Gouverneursjahre*, pp. 324–31.

16. *Deutsche Kolonialzeitung*, 8 March 1900, pp. 98–100.

17. Hausen, *Deutsche Kolonialherrschaft*, pp. 229–48; Puttkamer, *Gouverneursjahre*, pp. 104–5, 136–37.

18. E. Th. Foerster, *Das Konzessionsunwesen in den Deutschen Schutzgebieten*, p. 18.

19. Puttkamer, *Gouverneursjahre*, 298–323; A. A. Kolonialrat, vol. 22, 1901, (Kolonialratsachen 2/6975/3).

20. Hausen, *Deutsche Kolonialherrschaft*, pp. 224–29, 312–15; *Deutsche Kolonialzeitung*, 26 April 1900, pp. 131–84; Puttkamer, *Gouverneursjahre*, pp., 237–38.

21. Lamar Cecil, *Albert Ballin*, pp. 175–80; Emil Zimmermann, *Neu-Kamerun*, pp. 80–94.

22. Hausen, *Deutsche Kolonialherrschaft*, pp. 274–90; Stoecker, *Kamerun*, 1:168–80.

23. Hausen, *Deutsche Kolonialherrschaft*, pp. 214–90.

24. Hans Pehl, *Die deutsche Kolonialpolitik und das Zentrum (1884–1914)*, pp. 64–68.

25. Puttkamer, *Gouverneursjahre*, pp. 211–42.

26. Ibid., pp. 96–120; *Deutsches Kolonialblatt*, 1 May 1893, p. 231.

27. Harry R. Rudin, *Germans in the Cameroons, 1884–1914*, pp. 86–193; Hausen, *Deutsche Kolonialherrschaft*, pp. 71–198.

28. Hausen, *Deutsche Kolonialherrschaft*, pp. 252–55.

29. See Paul Rohrbach, *Die Kolonie*, pp. 10–12.

30. Unlike many of the other German colonies, Cameroon has been rather thoroughly studied by highly competent historians. Harry R. Rudin's *Germans in the Cameroons*, for years the standard work on the subject despite its narrow orientation toward administration, has now been replaced by works with a broader perspective and a strong base in primary sources. These include the very useful two-volume collection edited by Helmuth Stoecker, *Kamerun unter deutscher Kolonialherrschaft*, Karin Hausen's *Deutsche Kolonialherrschaft in Afrika*, and Albert Wirz's interesting *Vom Sklavenhandel zum kolonialen Handel*. Ralph Austen's forthcoming study of the Duala will undoubtedly add much to our knowledge of the interactions between African and European societies in the colony.

CHAPTER 7

1. The best source for the periods just before and after the establishment of German rule in East Africa is Fritz Ferdinand Müller, *Deutschland-Zanzibar-Ostafrika*.

2. W. O. Henderson, "German East Africa 1884–1918," pp. 123–26; DOAG, p. 43, *Anlage* to Directors' meeting of 30 July 1887.

3. Robert O. Collins, "Origins of the Nile Struggle," pp. 119–51.

4. DOAG, p. 102, K4480, 8 October 1890.

5. Carl Peters, *Zur Weltpolitik*, pp. 18–27; Hartmut Pogge von Strandmann, "Domestic Origins of Germany's Colonial Expansion under Bismarck," p. 155.

6. Henderson, "German East Africa," p. 127; DOAG, pp. 25–27, Directors' meeting of 2 April 1887.

7. *Deutsches Kolonialblatt*, 15 March 1892, pp. 166–68; ibid., 1 July 1892, p. 360; Henderson, "German East Africa," pp. 135–36.

8. Pan-German League, *Zwanzig Jahre alldeutscher Arbeit und Kämpfe*, p. vii.

9. *Sten. Ber.*, 13 March 1896, pp. 1419–45; *Deutsche Kolonialzeitung*, 1 May 1897, p. 175; Wilhelm von Kardorff, *Bebel oder Peters*.

10. Rainer Tetzlaff, *Koloniale Entwicklung und Ausbeutung*, pp. 25–35; DOAG, p. 154, *Anlage* 1 to Directors' meeting of 8 September 1888.

11. Henderson, "German East Africa," p. 128; DOAG, *Anlage* to Directors' meeting of 30 December 1887.

12. DOAG, p. 43, *Anlage* to Directors' meeting of 30 July 1887.

13. Marcia Wright, "Local Roots of Policy in German East Africa," pp. 623–24.

14. DOAG, *Anlage* 1 to Directors' meeting of 25 June 1891; Henderson, "German East Africa," pp. 131–32.

15. Wissmann's career in Africa is described in Rochus Schmidt, *Hermann von Wissmann und Deutschlands koloniales Wirken*.

16. Ralph A. Austen, *Northwest Tanzania under German and British Rule*, pp. 62–67.

17. Tetzlaff, *Koloniale Entwicklung*, pp. 36–48.

18. Ibid., pp. 141–47; *Deutsches Kolonialblatt*, 1 May 1892, p. 267; 15 February 1896, p. 98.

19. *Deutsches Kolonialblatt*, 15 April 1892, pp. 20–21; Tetzlaff, *Koloniale Entwicklung*, pp. 58–62.

20. *Deutsches Kolonialblatt*, 15 April 1892, pp. 226–29; Henderson, "German East Africa," p. 133.

21. *Deutsche Kolonialzeitung*, 30 May 1891, pp. 77–78.

22. DOAG, *Anlage* 1 to Directors' meeting of 25 June 1891; ibid., p. 38, railroad contract of 3 August 1891; Henderson, "German East Africa," p. 143; Hans Spellmeyer, *Deutsche Kolonialpolitik in Reichstag*, pp. 89–90.

23. Minutes of meeting of 31 May 1900, Deutsche Kolonialgesellschaft, Vorstand files, Hoover Institution on War, Revolution, and Peace, Stanford, Calif.

24. For the labor problem in East Africa, see Tetzlaff, *Koloniale Entwicklung*, pp. 63–100, 193–208, 233–51.

25. Detlef Bald, *Deutsch-Ostafrika, 1900–1914*, pp. 35–71; Austen, *Northwest Tanzania*, pp. 62–67; E. Th. Gunzert, "Native Communities and Native Participation in the Government of German East Africa," pp. 6–10.

26. Gunzert, "Native Communities," pp. 17–18; see also Wm. Roger Louis, *Ruanda-Urundi, 1884–1919*.

27. Bald, *Deutsch-Ostafrika*, pp. 35–71; Eduard von Liebert, *Aus einem bewegten Leben*, p. 159.

28. Bald, *Deutsch-Ostafrika*, pp. 106–15.

29. Wright, "Local Roots," pp. 621–29.

30. G. A. Graf von Götzen, *Deutsch-Ostafrika in Aufstand 1905–6*, p. 25; Tetzlaff, *Koloniale Entwicklung*, pp. 156–64.

31. Henderson, "German East Africa," pp. 154–55.

32. *Deutsche Kolonialzeitung*, 5 March 1903, pp. 95–97.

33. Spellmeyer, *Kolonialpolitik*, pp. 89–90.
34. Tetzlaff, *Koloniale Entwicklung*, pp. 137–39, 209–12; *Deutsche Kolonialzeitung*, 5 March 1903, pp. 95–97.
35. Liebert, *Leben*, pp. 159–60.
36. Robert I. Rotberg, "Resistance and Rebellion in British Nyasaland and German East Africa, 1888–1915," pp. 667–90; John Iliffe, *Tanganyika under German Rule, 1905–1912*, pp. 9–29.
37. Götzen, *Aufstand*, pp. 42–48; Iliffe, *Tanganyika*, pp. 21–22.
38. Götzen, *Aufstand*, pp. 52–56, 70–103; Iliffe, *Tanganyika*, pp. 20–22.
39. German East Africa has also been the subject of attention by a number of talented scholars, as well as others not so talented. For the early period of German rule, Fritz Ferdinand Müller's *Deutschland-Zanzibar-Ostafrika*, which managed to transcend the limits of narrow East German Marxist orthodoxy in a way that few other East German historians have done, is the best source. Rainer Tetzlaff, *Koloniale Entwicklung und Ausbeutung*, is another more recent Marxist study of the later period of German rule that is extremely useful. John Iliffe's *Tanganyika under German Rule* is an excellent analysis of the Rechenberg period and probably the best-written book on German colonial history. Iliffe is fully aware of the significance of the relations among indigenous, colonial, and German domestic politics, and his discussion of the growth of accommodation between African and German power structures is not likely to be surpassed. Iliffe does not, however, sufficiently discuss the reason that East African settlers were able to court conservative support at home, and according to Tetzlaff, he overemphasizes the extent to which the settler interest managed to overturn Rechenberg's policies. Ralph Austen's *Northwest Tanzania under German and British Rule* is one of the few studies of a local area under the rule of two successive colonial powers and also one of the few to make heavy use of oral sources for the African side.

CHAPTER 8

1. See the description of a rebellion in Ponape (Caroline Islands) in *Deutsche Kolonialzeitung*, 25 February 1911, p. 123; ibid., 2 September 1911, pp. 590–92.
2. A. A. Kolonialrat, Kolonialratsachen 2/6967.
3. *Deutsches Kolonialblatt*, 15 February 1893, pp. 88–94.
4. G. A. Graf von Götzen, *Deutsche-Ostafrika in Aufstand 1905–6*, pp. 220–22.
5. Mary E. Townsend, *The Rise and Fall of Germany's Colonial Empire, 1884–1918*, pp. 145–52.
6. For Samoa see R. P. Gilson, *Samoa, 1830 to 1900*, pp. 332–433, and Paul M. Kennedy, *The Samoan Tangle*.
7. Eberhard von Vietsch, *Wilhelm Solf*, pp. 19–41.
8. *Deutsche Kolonialzeitung*, 25 January 1900, pp. 29–30; ibid., 8 February 1900, pp. 49–50.
9. For Kiaochow see John E. Schrecker, *Imperialism and Chinese Nationalism*.
10. Hans Spellmeyer, *Deutsche Kolonialpolitik im Reichstag*, p. 80; Schrecker, *Imperialism*, pp. 218–19.
11. Schrecker, *Imperialism*, pp. 23–30, 140–209.
12. *Deutsches Kolonial-Handbuch 1913*, 4: 51–74.
13. There has been a recent upsurge of interest in Pacific history, particularly among scholars at the Australian National University, which will probably result in substantial publication on the German Pacific colonies in the next few years. R. P. Gilson's *Samoa, 1830 to 1900* is a product of this interest, as is S. G. Firth, "The New Guinea Company, 1885–1899." Paul M. Kennedy's *The Samoan Tangle* will probably remain the definitive diplomatic and policical history of the Sa-

moan question. On Kiaochow, John E. Schrecker's *Imperial and Chinese Nationalism* is the standard study.

CHAPTER 9

1. Friedrich Lütge, *Deutsche Sozial- und Wirtschaftsgeschichte*, pp. 337–79.
2. Ralf Dahrendorf, *Society and Democracy in Germany*, pp. 31–45.
3. Matthias Erzberger, *Die Kolonial-Bilanz*, pp. 15–40.
4. See George Dunlop Crothers, *The German Elections of 1907*. A random examination of the reports of Reichstag debates through 1914 will demonstrate the inordinate amount of attention paid to the details of colonial administration and budgeting.
5. Robert Cornevin, "The Germans in Africa before 1918," p. 398.
6. *Deutsche Kolonialzeitung*, 14 November 1891, pp. 156–57; ibid., 1 March 1900, pp. 85–86; German Colonial Society, *Verhandlungen des Deutschen Kolonialkongress 1910*, pp. 424–41.
7. The complexities of merchant attitudes are illustrated in discussions of native policy reported in German Colonial Society, *Verhandlungen des Deutschen Kolonialkongress 1902*, pp. 518–35, and in the minutes of the *Kolonialrat*, A. A. Kolonialrat, vol. 22, 1901 (Kolonialratsachen 2/6975/3).
8. *Deutsche Kolonialzeitung*, 27 May 1911, pp. 354–55.
9. Lamar Cecil, *Albert Ballin*, p. 134.
10. F. Wohltmann, *Die nationale und ethische Bedeutung unserer Kolonien*, pp. 13–21.
11. Fritz Fischer, *Germany's Aims in the First World War*, pp. 11–20, 41–49; *Deutsche Kolonialzeitung*, 22 January 1903, pp. 31–32.
12. Richard Victor Pierard, "The German Colonial Society, 1882–1914," p. 46; Fritz Stern, *Gold and Iron*, pp. 394–435.
13. A. A. Kolonialrat, vol. 4, 1891 (8748).
14. *Deutsche Kolonialzeitung*, 26 April 1900, *Beilage*, pp. 181–84; German Colonial Department, *Denkschrift über die im südwestafrikanischen Schutzgebiete tätigen Land- und Minen-Gesellschaften*; Karin Hausen, *Deutsche Kolonialherrschaft in Afrika*, pp. 224–29.
15. Bernhard Dernburg, *Zielpunkte des deutschen Kolonialwesens*, pp. 49–50.
16. Arthur Spiethoff, *Die wirtschaftlichen Wechsellagen*, 2:38.
17. Dernburg, *Zielpunkte*, pp. 32–37.
18. Paul Dehn, *Von deutscher Kolonial- und Weltpolitik*, pp. 71–102. This fear was also felt in Britain. See *Times* (London), 23 August 1904; Acta betr. Westafrika, vol. 9, 138/2, 459, 927, (1904–5).
19. August Full, *Fünfzig Jahre Togo*, pp. 235–36.
20. *Deutsche Kolonialzeitung*, 8 February 1900, pp. 51–52.
21. Jake Wilton Spidle, "The German Colonial Service," pp. 100–105.
22. J. C. G. Röhl, *Germany without Bismarck*, pp. 30, 36, 48, 60, 163–65.
23. E. Th. Foerster, *Das Konzessionsunwesen in den Deutschen Schutzgebieten*, p. 7; Pierard, "Colonial Society," p. 174.
24. Foerster, *Konzessionsunwesen*, p. 7; *Deutsche Kolonialzeitung*, 3 May 1900, pp. 186–87; J. K. von Vietor, *Wirtschafliche und Kulturelle Entwicklung unserer Schutzgebiete*, p. 92; Paul Rohrbach, *Der deutsche Gedanke in der Welt*, pp. 146–47.
25. A. A. Kolonialrat, vol. 2 (4287); ibid., vol. 13 (Kolonialratsachen 1/6951); *Deutsches Kolonialblatt*, 20 April 1892, pp. 256–57.
26. Jesko von Puttkamer, *Gouverneursjahre in Kamerun*, pp. 62–63; Wilhelm H. Solf, *Kolonialpolitik*, pp. 58–64.
27. I owe much of the following section on the German colonial service to

discussions with Mr. Lewis H. Gann of the Hoover Institution. See also Spidle, "Colonial Service."

28. Theodor Seitz, *Vom Aufstieg und Niederbruch deutscher Kolonialmacht*, 1:110–12; Eduard von Liebert, *Aus einem bewegten Leben*, pp. 127–29.

29. Ralph A. Austen, *Northwest Tanzania under German and British Rule*, pp. 73–74.

30. Prosser Gifford and Wm. Roger Louis, eds., *Britain and Germany in Africa*, pp. 765–72.

31. See Kayser's general policy statement to the *Kolonialrat* in *Deutsche Kolonialzeitung*, 27 June 1891, pp. 85–87.

32. Karl Helferrich, *Zur Reform der kolonialen Verwaltungs-Organisation, Beilage* number 2 to *Deutsches Kolonialblatt*, 1905, pp. 17–34.

33. Rohrbach, *Der deutsche Gedanke*, pp. 65–67.

34. See *Deutsche Kolonialzeitung*, 11 November 1911, pp. 747–48, for a sympathetic evaluation of Lindequist's attitudes.

35. Johannes Tesch, *Die Laufbahn der deutschen Kolonialbeamter*, pp. 1–2; Theodor Leutwein, *Elf Jahre Gouverneur in Deutsch-Südwestafrika*, pp. 209–15.

36. G. A. Graf von Götzen, *Deutsch-Ostafrika in Aufstand 1905–6*, pp. 57–69, 102, 152–66; Leutwein, *Elf Jahre*, pp. 465–540.

37. *Deutsches Kolonialblatt*, 15 November 1914, p. 836.

38. W. O. Henderson, "German East Africa 1884–1918," pp. 132–37; Liebert, *Leben*, p. 164.

39. Leutwein, *Elf Jahre*, pp. 465–525; Helmut Bley, *South-West Africa under German Rule*, pp. 155–63.

40. Puttkamer, *Gouverneursjahre*, pp. 104–5.

41. Hans Pehl, *Die deutsche Kolonialpolitik und das Zentrum (1884–1914)*, pp. 14–48.

42. *Sten. Ber.*, 13 March 1896, pp. 1422–23.

43. Marcia Wright, "Local Roots of Policy in German East Africa," pp. 625–29.

44. Pierard, "Colonial Society," pp. 171–73.

45. See Alfred Kruck, *Geschichte des alldeutschen Verbandes*.

46. Pan-German League, *Zwanzig Jahre alldeutscher Arbeit und Kämpfe*, pp. 11–13, 82–88; *Deutsche Kolonialzeitung*, 15 March 1900, p. 114.

47. Hans Spellmeyer, *Deutsche Kolonialpolitik im Reichstag*, pp. 14–28.

48. Ibid., pp. 125–40; Gustav Noske, *Kolonialpolitik und Sozialdemokratie*, pp. 207–17.

49. Spellmeyer, *Kolonialpolitik*, pp. 70–79.

50. Ibid., pp. 95–96.

51. Pehl, *Kolonialpolitik und das Zentrum*, pp. 64–65.

52. German Colonial Society, *Kolonialkongress 1910*, pp. lii, 422–23.

53. *Sten. Ber.*, 7 March 1914, pp. 7907–16.

54. Spellmeyer, *Kolonialpolitik*, pp. 12, 56–57.

55. *Deutsche Kolonialzeitung*, 3 May 1900, pp. 186–87.

56. Spellmeyer, *Kolonialpolitik*, pp. 77–78; Kenneth D. Barkin, *The Controversy over German Industrialization, 1890–1902*, pp. 56–58.

57. *Deutsche Kolonialzeitung*, 3 May 1900, p. 187.

58. Spellmeyer, *Kolonialpolitik*, pp. 86–87.

59. Surprisingly little recent work has been done on either the central German colonial administration or the structure of political groups interested in the colonies. On the administration see Jake Spidle's dissertation, "The German Colonial Service." L. H. Gann's and Peter Duignan's new study, *The Rulers of German Africa, 1884–1914* (Stanford: Stanford University Press, 1977), was published too late to be employed here. As is indicated above, however, the present

work has greatly benefited from the advice of Mr. Gann. Studies abound on pressure groups and political parties in Wilhelmian Germany, but none has been published specifically on colonial politics since Spellmeyer's dissertation, *Deutsche Kolonialpolitik im Reichstag*, which was written over 45 years ago. Interest groups are examined in the leading studies of individual colonies, especially Hausen on Cameroon, Bley on Southwest Africa, and Iliffe on East Africa, but a great deal of additional work remains to be done in the field.

CHAPTER 10

1. Kenneth D. Barkin, *The Controversy over German Industrialization* pp. 32–47.
2. Ibid., pp. 103–28.
3. For the ambivalent attitude of the Colonial Society, which as usual straddled the fence on the tariff issue, see *Deutsche Kolonialzeitung*, 9 January 1892, pp. 3–4.
4. Paul Rohrbach, *Die Kolonie*, pp. 9–14.
5. See J. K. von Vietor, *Wirtschaftliche und Kulturelle Entwicklung unserer Schutzgebiete*, for the best statement of this attitude.
6. Dietrich Schäfer, *Kolonialgeschichte*, 1:5–11.
7. Pan-German League, *Zwanzig Jahre alldeutscher Arbeit und Kämpfe*, pp. 11–12; Max Sering, *Die innere Kolonisation in östlichen Deutschland*; Barkin, *Controversy*, p. 154.
8. "Alldeutsch," *Grossdeutschland und Mitteleuropa um das Jahr 1950*, pp. 47–48.
9. See Max Sering, ed., *Westrussland in seiner Bedeutung für die Entwicklung Mitteleuropas*.
10. *Sten. Ber.*, 13 March 1896, pp. 1419–45.
11. *Deutsche Kolonialzeitung*, 26 April 1900, pp. 181–84.
12. Barkin, *Controversy*, pp. 44–102.
13. Wilhelm von Kardorff, *Bebel oder Peters*; Barkin, *Controversy*, pp. 56–58.
14. *Sten. Ber.*, 13 March 1896, p. 1429.
15. Ibid., pp. 1424–28, 1439–43.
16. Matthias Erzberger, *Die Kolonial-Bilanz*, pp. 15–40.
17. Paul Rohrbach, *Der deutsche Gedanke in der Welt*, pp. 133–60; *Deutsche Kolonialzeitung*, 3 May 1900, pp. 186–87.
18. *Sten. Ber.*, 13 March 1896, p. 1435; Harry R. Rudin, *Germans in the Cameroons, 1884–1914*, pp. 86, 193.
19. A. A. Kolonialrat, vol. 2, p. 4287; *Deutsche Kolonialzeitung*, 27 June 1891, pp. 85–87.
20. *Deutsche Kolonialzeitung*, 26 April 1900, pp. 181–84.
21. Julius Scharlach, *Koloniale und politische Aufsätze und Reden*.
22. *Deutsche Kolonialzeitung*, 26 April 1900, pp. 181–84; Vietor, *Entwicklung*, pp. 72–78.
23. Paul Rohrbach, *Dernburg und die Südwestafrikaner*, pp. 1–83.
24. Pan-German League, *Zwanzig Jahre*, pp. 154–57; *Deutsche Kolonialzeitung*, 15 January 1903, pp. 22–23.
25. *Deutsche Kolonialzeitung*, 19 April 1900, pp. 161-62; ibid., 26 April 1900, p. 178; Scharlach, *Aufsätze*, pp. 54–55.
26. Hans Spellmeyer, *Deutsche Kolonialpolitik im Reichstag*, pp. 86–87.
27. See Leutwein's criticisms forwarded to the *Kolonialrat* in A. A. Kolonialrat, vol. 2, 6993.
28. Rohrbach, *Der deutsche Gedanke*, pp. 146–48.
29. *Deutsche Kolonialzeitung*, 26 March 1903, pp. 121–22.
30. Rainer Tetzlaff, *Koloniale Entwicklung und Ausbeutung*, pp. 281–85.
31. *Sten. Ber.*, 7 March 1914, pp. 7912–16, 7921–26.

32. E. Th. Foerster, *Das Konzessionsunwesen in den Deutschen Schutzgebieten*, pp. 15–20; Vietor, *Entwicklung* pp. 109–20, 133–34.

33. Vietor, *Entwicklung*, pp. 129–44.

34. Ibid., pp. 106–7; Rohrbach, *Der deutsche Gedanke*, pp. 151–55.

35. Erzberger, *Kolonial-Bilanz*, pp. 12–13.

36. Ernst Ludwig Radlauer, *Die lokale Selbstverwaltung der kolonialen Finanzen*, pp. 3–26.

37. Rohrbach, *Der deutsche Gedanke*, pp. 151–55.

38. Helmut Bley, *South-West Africa under German Rule, 1894–1914*, pp. 196–201.

39. Scharlach, *Aufsätze*, pp. 26–35.

40. Rohrbach, *Die Kolonie*, pp. 40–43.

41. Vietor, *Entwicklung*, pp. 106–33.

42. Again, there is no specific modern study of German colonial political issues in the period between 1890 and 1914, although one is badly needed. Bley and Iliffe examine issues that related to their specific colonies, but no one has yet attempted to associate the colonial issues with their counterparts in domestic politics. On the tariff issue in general, see Kenneth Barkin, *The Controversy over German Industrialization*, in which differences over the issue are perhaps somewhat overstated, and Hans-Jürgen Puhle, *Agrarische Interessenpolitik und preussischer Konservatismus*. On post-Bismarckian politics in general, see J. C. G. Röhl, *Germany without Bismarck*. The other issues noted in this chapter will have to be followed in the studies of the individual colonies.

CHAPTER 11

1. See especially Eckart Kehr, *Schlachtflottenbau und Parteipolitik, 1894–1901*, and Jonathan Steinberg, *Yesterday's Deterrent*.

2. *Deutsche Kolonialzeitung*, 25 January 1900, pp. 29–30.

3. Lamar Cecil, *Albert Ballin*, pp. 152–56; German Colonial Society, *Jahresbericht*, 1897, p. 39; ibid., 1898, pp. 22–23, 57–61.

4. John E. Schrecker, *Imperialism and Chinese Nationalism*, pp. 20–22.

5. German Colonial Society, *Jahresbericht*, 1897, p. 39; Richard Victor Pierard, "The German Colonial Society, 1882–1914," pp. 178–80.

6. Steinberg, *Yesterday's Deterrent*, pp. 43–45.

7. Ibid., pp. 56–59; Paul Rohrbach, *Der deutsche Gedanke in der Welt*, pp. 178–97.

8. *Amtliches Reichstags-Handbuch 1903/1908*, pp. 396–97.

9. Fritz Fischer, *Germany's Aims in the First World War*, pp. 20–22; Rohrbach, *Der deutsche Gedanke*, pp. 5–10.

10. Fischer, *Germany's Aims*, pp. 11–38; Rohrbach, *Der deutsche Gedanke*, pp. 9–10; Paul Dehn, *Von deutscher Kolonial- und Weltpolitik*, pp. 1–30, 134–316.

11. Kenneth D. Barkin, *The Controversy over German Industrialization*, pp. 32–47; *Deutsche Kolonialzeitung*, 9 January 1892, pp. 3–4.

12. *Alldeutsche Blätter*, 30 April 1899, pp. 145–47.

13. Friedrich von Bernhardi, *Deutschland und der nächste Krieg*, pp. 1–8.

14. Fritz Schwarze, *Das deutsch-englische Abkommen über die portugiesischen Kolonien vom 30. August 1898*, pp. 11–15, 28–30; Walther Rathenau, *Tagebuch 1907–1922*, pp. 88–89; Cecil, *Ballin*, pp. 144–53.

15. Klaus Wernecke, *Der Wille zur Weltgeltung*, 288–310.

16. See, for example, *Deutsches Kolonialblatt*, 1 January 1892, p. 25; Georg Trierenberg, *Togo*, pp. 3–6.

17. Wernecke, *Wille*, pp. 300–303; Pan-German League, *Zwanzig Jahre alldeutscher Arbeit und Kämpfe*, p. 203.

18. Schwarze, *Abkommen*, pp. 92–124.

19. Unlike the issues discussed in Chapter 10, those examined in this chapter have attracted a great deal of attention, although seldom has the specifically colonial side been heavily emphasized. On the fleet-building question, the classic study remains Eckart Kehr's *Schlachtflottenbau und Parteipolitik, 1894–1901*, which incidentally is the major intellectual influence on the present generation of German social political historians, especially Wehler. Kehr regards fleet building as a product of the peculiarities of Germany's political development, which were in turn the result of a social structure that maintained both the old agrarian elite and the new industrial elite in positions of power, competing and accommodating with each other. In his recognition of the primary importance of domestic political considerations rather than foreign policy or the intellectual climate, Kehr revised the standard assumptions of German historiography. Kehr's analysis is not without faults, some of which are corrected by Jonathan Steinberg's *Yesterday's Deterrent*, but it still remains the standard work on the subject. In terms of the present study, Kehr does not clearly differentiate between varieties of imperialistic thinking perhaps because the differences noted here are most apparent when approached through colonialism, which Kehr does not do.

Weltpolitik has also been examined in copious detail by historians, most of whom have emphasized its aspect of economic imperialism. Besides the treatment of the subject in Fritz Fischer's two major works, *Germany's Aims in the First World War* and *Krieg der Illusionen*, see Jacques Willequet's *Le Congo belge et la Weltpolitik*. None of the standard studies of *Weltpolitik* sufficiently differentiates among the types of thinking and ideological traditions that coexisted under that name, and therefore none adequately analyzes the political tension that existed over the direction of German world policy among elite groups. The practice employed here of using *Weltpolitik* only for a particular trend in economic imperialist thinking is, as far as I know, unique.

CHAPTER 12

1. Hans Spellmeyer, *Deutsche Kolonialpolitik im Reichstag*, pp. 90–122.
2. Matthias Erzberger, *Die Kolonial-Bilanz* , pp. 5–14.
3. German Social Democratic Party, *Die deutsche Kolonialpolitik*, pp. 15–16.
4. Prince Bernhard von Bülow, *Memoirs*, 2:292–93.
5. Walter Moszkowski, *Bernhard Dernburg*, pp. 13–15; Werner Schieffel, *Bernhard Dernburg 1865–1937*, pp. 11–37.
6. Bülow, *Memoirs*, 2:293; Hans Spellmeyer, *Deutsche Kolonialpolitik im Reichstag* pp. 118–21.
7. Moszkowski, *Dernburg*, pp. 305; Schieffel, *Dernburg*, pp. 162–75.
8. *Deutsches Kolonialblatt*, 1 March 1908, pp. 216–31.
9. Walther Rathenau, *Tagebuch 1907–1922*, p. 30; Walther Rathenau, *Die neue Gesellschaft* and *Die neue Wirtschaft*.
10. Bernhard Dernburg, *Koloniale Lehrjahre*, pp. 12–13.
11. Bülow, *Memoirs*, 2:293; Schieffel, *Dernburg*, pp. 37–48.
12. Moszkowski, *Dernburg*, p. 6; Bülow, *Memoirs*, 2:293.
13. *Sten. Ber.*, 28 November 1906, pp. 3957–69.
14. Ibid., 30 November 1906, p. 4029.
15. Ibid., 3 December 1906, pp. 4084–85; ibid., 4 December 1906, p. 4154.
16. *Deutsche Kolonialzeitung*, 19 January 1906, pp. 21–23.
17. Ibid., 2 February 1906, pp. 46–47.
18. The political crisis of 1906 and 1907 is examined in George Dunlop Crothers's standard work, *The German Elections of 1907*, and from the point of

view of Erzberger, in Klaus W. Epstein, *Matthias Erzberger and the Dilemma of German Democracy*. See, in addition, the sections on the crisis in John Iliffe, *Tanzanyika under German Rule, 1905–1912*, and in Werner Schieffel's *Bernhard Dernburg 1865–1937*.

CHAPTER 13

1. Dernburg's tour is described by one of the accompanying journalists in Adolf Zimmermann, *Mit Dernburg nach Ostafrika*.

2. Bernhard Dernburg, *Zielpunkte des deutschen Kolonialwesens*, esp. pp. 9–12, 19–20.

3. Bernhard Dernburg, *Koloniale Lehrjahre*, pp. 12–13.

4. Dernburg, *Zielpunkte*, p. 12.

5. *Deutsches Kolonialblatt*, 1 February 1908, pp. 126–28.

6. Dernburg, *Zielpunkte*, pp. 26–48.

7. Helmuth Stoecker, "The Expansionist Policy of Imperialist Germany in Africa South of the Sahara 1908–1918," pp. 129–41; Hartmut J. Pogge von Strandmann, "The German Colonial Office and its Foreign Politics in the Dernburg Era, 1907–1910."

8. Dernburg, *Koloniale Lehrjahre*, pp. 14–16.

9. Jake Wilton Spidle, "The German Colonial Service," pp. 136–37; Werner Schieffel, *Bernhard Dernburg, 1865–1937*, pp. 81–85.

10. Karl Helferrich, *Zur Reform der kolonialen Verwaltungs-Organisation*, pp. 7–16.

11. *Deutsches Kolonialblatt*, 15 March 1908, p. 277.

12. Walter Rathenau, *Tagebuch 1907–1922*, pp. 55–87, Schieffel, *Dernburg*, pp. 67–73.

13. John Iliffe, *Tanganyika under German Rule, 1905–1912*, pp. 78–81.

14. *Deutsches Kolonialblatt*, 15 December 1907, pp. 1195–1207.

15. Freiherr Albrecht von Rechenberg, "Kriegs- und Friedensziele," pp. 131–43.

16. Detlef Bald, *Deutsch-Ostafrika, 1900–1914*, pp. 75–105.

17. Iliffe, *Tanganyika*, pp. 49–81.

18. Bald, *Deutsch-Ostafrika*, pp. 75–105.

19. Iliffe, *Tanganyika*, pp. 103–7.

20. *Deutsches Kolonialblatt*, 15 December 1907, pp. 1195–1207.

21. Ibid., 1 March 1908, pp. 216–31.

22. Paul Samassa, *Die Besiedlung Deutsch-Ostafrikas*, pp. 16, 105–27.

23. Iliffe, *Tanganyika*, pp. 82–117.

24. *Deutsches Kolonialblatt*, 15 May 1908, pp. 467–68.

25. Helmut Bley, *South-West Africa under German Rule, 1894–1914*, pp. 181–208.

26. Dernburg, *Koloniale Lehrjahre*, pp. 14–15.

27. Rathenau, *Tagebuch*, pp. 88–117.

28. Bley, *South-West Africa*, p. 197; *Deutsches Kolonialblatt*, 15 December 1908, pp. 1199–1200; Paul Rohrbach, *Dernburg und die Südwestafrikaner*, pp. 1–44.

29. Bley, *South-West Africa*, pp. 196–97; Rohrbach, *Dernburg*, pp. 45–90.

30. Bley, *South-West Africa*, pp. 185–196; Rohrbach, *Dernburg*, pp. iii–v.

31. Rathenau, *Tagebuch*, pp. 88–117; Oskar Bongard, *Staatsekretär Dernburg in Britisch- und Deutsch-Süd-Afrika*; Schieffel, *Dernburg*, pp. 73–80.

32. Rohrbach, *Dernburg*, pp. 286–87.

33. Iliffe, *Tanganyika*, pp. 82–117, 140–41.

34. Bley, *South-West Africa*, pp. 212–19.

35. Schieffel, *Dernburg*, pp. 120–27; Stoecker, "Expansionist Policy," pp. 129–

41; Hartmut J. Pogge von Strandmann, "The German Colonial Office and its Foreign Politics in the Dernburg Era."

36. Konrad H. Jarausch, *The Enigmatic Chancellor*, p. 73.

37. August Full, *Fünfzig Jahre Togo*, pp. 100–102; J. K. von Vietor, *Wirtschaftliche und kulturelle Entwicklung unserer Schutzgebiete*, pp. 76–83.

38. Helmuth Stoecker, ed., *Kamerun unter deutscher Kolonialherrschaft*, 2:183–257, Emil Zimmermann, *Neu-Kamerun*, pp. 80–94.

39. John E. Schrecker, *Imperialism and Chinese Nationalism*, pp. 140–209.

40. *Deutsche Kolonialzeitung*, 11 June 1910, p. 401; ibid., 18 June 1910, pp. 419–20.

41. Considering Dernburg's highly unusual position in imperial politics and his long and interesting career, it is extremely surprising that no biography of him has appeared until very recently. This has probably been due to the destruction of Dernburg's papers during the Second World War. In addition, however, there is a certain lack of fulfillment in Dernburg's career that may have discouraged biographers. In any event, Werner Schieffel has now filled the gap with a straightforward account of Dernburg's life, essentially putting into one volume all that is generally known about him. It is a pity that Schieffel was not able to go beyond this, but undoubtedly the lack of personal materials precluded him from doing so. On Rechenberg and his troubles with the East African planters, see Iliffe; on the Southwest African diamond question see Bley.

CHAPTER 14

1. See, for example, Mary E. Townsend, *The Rise and Fall of Germany's Colonial Empire, 1884–1918*, pp. 246–304; John Iliffe, *Tanganyika under German Rule, 1905–1912*, pp. 118–41.

2. Iliffe, *Tanganyika*, pp. 118–32; *Deutsche Kolonialzeitung*, 18 June 1910, pp. 417–19; ibid., 1 April 1911, *Sonderbeilag*.

3. Iliffe, *Tanganyika*, pp. 119–23; 203; *Deutsche Kolonialzeitung*, 4 March 1911, pp. 141–44.

4. Iliffe, *Tanganyika*, pp. 119–23, 141.

5. Emil Zimmermann, *Neu-Kamerun*, pp. 80–94.

6. Pan-German League, *Zwanzig Jahre alldeutscher Arbeit und Kämpfe*, pp. 221–22, 245–46, 251–53; *Deutsche Kolonialzeitung*, 19 November 1903, pp. 475–76; Lamar Cecil, *Albert Ballin*, pp. 175–80.

7. *Deutsche Kolonialzeitung*, 7 October 1911, pp. 667; Konrad H. Jarausch, *The Enigmatic Chancellor*, pp. 123–24.

8. Klaus Wernecke, *Der Wille zur Weltgeltung*, pp. 139–43.

9. Ibid., *Deutsche Kolonialzeitung*, 28 October 1911, pp. 715–17; ibid., 11 November 1911, pp. 747–48.

10. Zimmermann, *Neu-Kamerun*; DKG Vorstand, minutes of 21 November 1911.

11. Eberhard von Vietsch, *Wilhelm Solf*, p. 102.

12. Jarausch, *Chancellor*, pp. 72–73.

13. Vietsch, *Solf*, pp. 83–101. Solf's views on imperialism are expressed in his *Kolonialpolitik*.

14. *Sten. Ber.*, 9 March 1914, pp. 7944–53.

15. Colin Newbury, "Partition, Development, Trusteeship," pp. 455–77.

16. Rainer Tetzlaff, *Koloniale Entwicklung und Ausbeutung*, pp. 229–32.

17. Theodor Seitz, *Vom Aufstieg und Niederbruck deutscher Kolonialmacht*, 3:8–18.

18. *Sten. Ber.*, 9 March 1914, pp. 7947–48.

19. J. K. von Vietor, *Wirtschaftliche und kulturelle Entwicklung unserer Schutzebiete*, pp. 136–37; *Sten. Ber.*, 7 March 1914, pp. 7914–16.

20. Vietor, *Entwicklung*, pp. 76–81, 96–99; *Sten. Ber.*, 9 March 1914, p. 7946.

21. Jake Wilton Spidle, Jr., "Colonial Studies in Imperial Germany," pp. 241–43.

22. Gustav Noske, *Kolonialpolitik und Sozialdemokratie*, pp. 217–29.

23. *Sten. Ber.*, 7 March 1914, pp. 7897–9935; ibid., 9 March 1914, pp. 7940–52.

24. *Deutsche Weltpolitik und kein Krieg!*, pp. 1–2.

25. Townsend, *Rise and Fall*, pp. 264–70.

26. On the colonial politics of the period from 1910 to 1914, very little recent work, except Eberhard Vietsch's biography of Solf and Colin Newbury's article on Solf in Gifford and Louis, has been done. On imperialism and its relation to the coming of the World War a plethora of studies exists. Of these, the most influential are the two books by Fritz Fischer, *Germany's Aims in the First World War* and *Krieg der Illusionen*. In these Fischer puts forward the thesis that Germany's active role in bringing on the war was due to the influence of big business and high finance, who anticipated the advancement and securing of their lightly covered investments abroad through German military victories. Fischer's thesis has been much disputed. For a summary of the controversy, see Fritz Stern, "German Historians and the War: Fritz Fischer and His Critics" in Stern's *The Failure of Illiberalism*.

CHAPTER 15

1. A summary of events in the German colonies during the war is contained in Mary E. Townsend, *The Rise and Fall of Germany's Colonial Empire, 1884–1918*, pp. 356–93.

2. Paul Emil von Lettow-Vorbeck, *Meine Erinnerungen aus Ostafrika*.

3. Wilhelm H. Solf, *Kolonialpolitik*, pp. 49–58.

4. Ralph A. Austen, *Northwest Tanzania under German and British Rule*, pp. 109–18.

5. W. O. Henderson, "German East Africa 1884–1918," pp. 155–62.

6. Fritz Fischer, *Germany's Aims in the First World War*, pp. 359–60.

7. Emil Zimmermann, *Die Bedeutung Afrikas für die deutsche Weltpolitik*, pp. 59–65.

8. Fischer, *Germany's Aims*, pp. 359–70.

9. See ibid., pp. 316–18, on colonial aims.

10. Friedrich Naumann, *Mitteleuropa*; Paul Rohrbach, "Das Kriegsziel in Schützengraben," pp. 241–48.

11. Henry Cord Meyer, *Mitteleuropa in German Thought and Action, 1815–1945*, pp. 95–102.

12. Ibid., p. 234; H. Michaelis, E. Schraepler, and G. Scheel, eds., *Ursachen und Folgen vom deutschen Zusammenbruch 1918 und 1945 bis zur staatlichen Neuordnung Deutschlands in der Gegenwart*, 1:364–65.

13. Konrad H. Jarausch, *The Enigmatic Chancellor*, pp. 349–80.

14. See Heinrich Class, *Zum deutschen Kriegsziel*, and Jarausch, *Chancellor*, p. 355.

15. *Preussische Jahrbücher*, November 1916, pp. 355–57; Friedrich von Schwerin, *Kriegersansiedlung vergangener Zeiten*, pp. 1–3.

16. See, for example, H. L. Dannenberg, *Sieg ohne Landgewinn?*; Georg Bernhard, *Land oder Geld*; Hans Siegfried Weber, *Ansiedlung von Kriegsinvaliden*.

17. These views are attacked in Emil Zimmermann, *Kann uns Mesopotamien eigene Kolonien ersetzen?*

18. Michaelis, Schraepler, and Scheel, *Ursachen*, 2:48–51.

19. Fischer, *Germany's Aims*, pp. 586–91; Jarausch, *Chancellor*, pp. 349–99.

20. Fischer, *Germany's Aims*, p. 548.

21. Michaelis, Schraepler, and Scheel, *Ursachen*, 2:50.

22. Freiherr Albrecht von Rechenberg, "Kriegs- und Friedensziele."

23. Emile Zimmermann, *Die deutsche Kaiserreich Mittelafrikas als Grundlag einer neuen deutschen Weltpolitik*; see also Paul Leutwein, *Mitteleuropa-Mittelafrika*.

24. On post-1918 German colonialism, see Klaus Hildebrand, *Vom Reich zum Weltreich*, and Wolfe W. Schmokel, *Dream of Empire.*

25. On the German colonies in the First World War, a number of military histories, particularly concerning Lettow-Vorbeck and the East African campaign, have been written. None has much to do with the long-term history of the German colonies. The question of war aims from 1914 to 1918 is a major topic of modern historical interest; colonial war aims have been examined as a justifiably minor subset of overall German aims by Fischer and others. Fischer's discussion of colonial aims, and to some extent of war aims in general, suffers from an unwillingness on his part to distinguish between *types* of war aims, and especially to accept the distinction between *annexationist* and more limited *economic imperialist* goals. Fischer thus gives an appearance of uniformity to a highly varied assortment of policy goals. Fischer's discussion of the genesis of war-aims policy remains the authoritative one.

Bibliography

I. MANUSCRIPT SOURCES

The main source of documentary evidence on German colonialism is the set of *Reichskolonialamt* files maintained at the *Deutsches Zentralarchiv* (DZA) at Potsdam in the German Democratic Republic, which the author was unable to use. The Hoover Institution, however, possesses microfilms of three sections of these files (cited below), which were used in this study.

Stanford, California.

Hoover Institution on War, Revolution, and Peace.

Auswärtiges Amt. Akten betreffend den Kolonialrat. 1891–1907. Microfilm.

Deutsch-Ostafrikanische Gesellschaft, Berlin. Protocols of Meetings and Other Papers. 1887–91. Microfilm.

Deutsche Kolonialgesellschaft, Berlin. Vorstand files. 1889–1918. Microfilm.

Washington, D.C.

Library of Congress.

Germany. Foreign Ministry. Records relating to Franco-German Relations. 1867–1910. Microfilm.

Prussia. Foreign Ministry. Records relating to Emigration. Approximately 1840–1900. Photostat.

National Archives.

Records of the German Embassy in London. 1867–1914. Microfilm, T-149.

German Naval Records. 1850–1920. Microfilm, T-1022.

German Foreign Office Records. Akten des Auswärtigen Amt im Grossen Hauptquartier. 1914–18. Microfilm, T-137.

II. GOVERNMENT DOCUMENTS

Amtliches Reichstags-Handbuch. Elfte Legislaturperiode, 1903/1908. Berlin, 1903.

German Colonial Department. *Denkschrift über die im südwestafrikanischen Schutzgebiete tätigen Land- und Minen-Gesellschaften. Beilage 6* to *Deutsches Kolonialblatt,* 1905. Berlin, 1905.

Stenographische Berichte über die Verhandlungen des Reichstages. Berlin, 1871–1918.

Das Werk des Untersuchungsausschusses der verfassungsgebenden Nationalversammlung und des deutschen Reichstages, 1919–1930. Vol. 4. Berlin, 1929.

Wigard, Franz, ed. *Stenographischer Bericht über der deutschen constituierenden Nationalversammlung zu Frankfurt am Main.* 9 vols. Leipzig, 1848.

III. PRIMARY SOURCES

"Alldeutsch." *Grossdeutschland und Mitteleuropa um das Jahr 1950.* 2d. ed. Berlin, 1895.

Arendt, O. *Die parlementarischen Studienreisen nach West- und Ostafrika.* Berlin, 1906.

Bastian, Adolph. *Zwei Worte über Colonial-Weisheit.* Berlin, 1883.

Bekerath, Emil, et al., eds. *Friedrich List: Schriften, Reden, Briefe.* 10 vols. Berlin, 1930.

Bernhard, Georg. *Land oder Geld.* Berlin, 1916.

Bernhardi, Friedrich von. *Deutschland und der nächste Krieg.* Stuttgart and Berlin, 1912.

Bongard, Oskar. *Staatsekretär Dernburg in Britisch- und Deutsch-Süd-Afrika.* Berlin, 1908.

Bonn, Moritz J. *Die Neugestaltung unserer kolonialen Aufgaben.* Tübingen, 1911.

Bucher, Lothar. *Kleine Schriften politischen Inhalts.* Stuttgart, 1893.

Buchner, Max. *Aurora colonialis: Bruchstücke eines Tagebuchs aus dem ersten Beginn unserer Kolonialpolitik 1884/85.* Munich, 1914.

Bülow, Prince Bernhard von. *Memoirs.* Vol. 2, *From the Morocco Crisis to Resignation.* Translated by Geoffrey Dunlop. Boston, 1931.

Class, Heinrich. *Zum deutschen Kriegsziel.* Munich, 1917.

Dannenberg, H. L. *Sieg ohne Landgewinn?* Dresden, 1918.

Dehn, Paul. *Von deutscher Kolonial- und Weltpolitik.* Berlin, 1907.

Dernburg, Bernhard. *Koloniale Lehrjahre.* Stuttgart, 1907.

———. *"Unser Friede".* Frankfurt am Main, 1918.

_____. *Zielpunkte des deutschen Kolonialwesens*. Berlin, 1907.

Deutsche Weltpolitik und kein Krieg! Berlin, 1913.

Deutscher Liberalismus im Vormärz: Heinrich von Gagern, Briefe und Reden, 1815–1848. Göttingen, 1959.

Deutsches Kolonial-Handbuch 1913. 6 vols. Berlin, 1913.

Dove, Karl. *Die deutschen Kolonien*. Vol. 3, *Ostafrika*. Leipzig, 1912.

Die Entwickelung unserer Kolonien. Berlin, 1892.

Erzberger, Matthias. *Die Kolonial-Bilanz*. Berlin, 1906.

Fabarius, G. A. *Neue Wege der deutschen Kolonialpolitik nach dem Kriege*. Berlin, 1916.

Fabri, Friedrich. *Bedarf Deutschland der Colonien?* Gotha, 1879.

_____. *Fünf Jahre deutscher Kolonialpolitik*. Gotha, 1889.

Foerster, E. Th. *Das Konzessionsunwesen in den Deutschen Schutzgebieten*. Berlin, 1903.

Fonck, Heinrich. *Farbige Hilfsvölker: Die militärische Bedeutung von Kolonien für unsere nationale Zukunft*. Berlin, 1917.

Friedrich, J. K. Julius. *Kolonialpolitik als Wissenschaft: Ein neues Forschungsgebiet der Rechtsphilosophie*. Berlin and Leipzig, 1909.

Fröbel, Julius. *Die deutsche Auswanderung und ihre kulturhistorische Bedeutung*. Leipzig, 1858.

Gad, Johannes. *Die Betriebsverhältnisse der Farmen des mittleren Hererolandes*. Hamburg, 1915.

German Colonial Society. *Die Deutsche Kolonialgesellschaft*. Berlin, 1908.

_____. "Die Deutsche Kolonialgesellschaft." Berlin, 1910.

_____. *Jahresbericht*. Berlin, 1894–98.

_____. *Satzungen der Deutschen Kolonialgesellschaft*. Berlin, 1908.

_____. *Verhandlungen des Deutschen Kolonialkongresses 1902*. Berlin, 1903.

_____. *Verhandlungen des Deutschen Kolonialkongresses 1905*. Berlin, 1906.

_____. *Verhandlungen des Deutschen Kolonialkongresses 1910*. Berlin, 1910.

Götzen, G. A. Graf von. *Deutsch-Ostafrika in Aufstand 1905–6*. Berlin, 1909.

Gunzert, E. Th. "Native Communities and Native Participation in the Government of German East Africa." Mimeograph, distributed by *Die Deutsche Gesellschaft für Eingeborenekunde*, no date.

Hansen, Joseph, ed., *Rheinische Briefe und Akten zur Geschichte der politischen Bewegung, 1830–1850*. 2 vols. Osnabrück, 1967.

Hasse, Ernst. *Deutsche Politik*. Munich, 1905.

Helferrich, Karl. *Zur Reform der kolonialen Verwaltungs-Organisation*. Berlin, 1905.

Heyder, Franz. *Beiträge zur Frage der Auswanderung und Kolonisation*. Heidelberg, 1894.

Hintze, Otto, et al., eds., *Deutschland und der Weltkrieg*. Berlin, 1915.
Hobohm, Martin, and Rohrbach, Paul. *Die Alldeutschen*. Berlin, 1919.
Hoffmann, Karl. *Das Ende des kolonialpolitischen Zeitalters*. Leipzig, 1917.
Hoffmann, Max. *Der Krieg der versäumten Gelegenheiten*. Munich, 1923.
Hübbe-Schleiden, Wilhelm. *Deutsche Colonisation*. Hamburg, 1881.
―――. '*Überseeische Politik, eine culturwissenschaftliche Studie*. Hamburg, 1881.
Hundeshagen, Friedrich. *Die deutsche Auswanderung als Nationalsache*. Frankfurt am Main, 1849.
Jacob, Ernst Gebhard, ed. *Deutsche Kolonialpolitik in Dokumenten*. Leipzig, 1938.
Jäckh, Ernst. *Der goldene Pflug: Lebensernte eines Weltburgers*. Stuttgart, 1954.
Kapp, Friedrich. *European Emigration to the United States*. New York, 1869.
―――. *Über Auswanderung*. Berlin, 1871.
―――. *Über Colonisation und Auswanderung*. Berlin, 1880.
―――. *Vom radikalen Frühsozialisten des Vormärz zum liberalen Parteipolitiker des Bismarckzeit: Briefe 1843–1884*. Edited by Hans-Ulrich Wehler. Frankfurt am Main, 1969.
Kardorff, Wilhelm von. *Bebel oder Peters: Die Amtstätigkeit des Kaiserlichen Kommissars Dr. Karl Peters am Kilimanjaro*. Berlin, 1907.
Karstedt, Oskar. *Deutschlands koloniale Not*. Berlin, 1917.
Kölner, Otto. *Einführung in die Kolonialpolitik*. Jena, 1908.
Kurtze, Bruno. *Die Deutsch-Ostafrikanische Gesellschaft: Ein Beitrag zum Problem der Schutzbriefgesellschaften und zur Geschichte Ostafrikas*. Jena, 1913.
Lehmann, Emil. *Die deutsche Auswanderung*. Berlin, 1861.
Lepsius, Johannes, Mendelssohn-Bartholdy, Albrecht, and Thimme, Friedrich, eds. *Die Grosse Politik der europäischen Kabinette, 1871–1914: Sammlung der diplomatischen Akten des Auswärtigen Amtes*. 40 vols. Berlin, 1922–27.
Lettow-Vorbeck, Paul Emil von. *Mein Leben*. Biberach, 1957.
―――. *Meine Erinnerungen aus Ostafrika*. Leipzig, 1920.
Leutwein, Paul, ed. *Dreissig Jahre deutscher Kolonialpolitik*. Berlin, 1914.
―――. *Mitteleuropa-Mittelafrika*. Dresden, 1917.
Leutwein, Theodor. *Elf Jahre Gouverneur in Deutsch-Südwestafrika*. Berlin, 1908.
Liebert, Eduard von. *Aus einem bewegten Leben: Erinnerungen*. Munich, 1925.
List, Friedrich. *Das nationale System der politischen Ökonomie*. Edited by Artur Sommer. Berlin, 1930.
Lüderitz, C. A., ed. *Die Erschliessung von Deutsch-Südwest-Afrika*. Oldenburg, 1945.

Michaelis, H., Schraepler, E., and Scheel, G., eds. *Ursachen und Folgen vom deutschen Zusammenbruch 1918 und 1945 bis zur staatlichen Neuordnung Deutschlands in der Gegenwart*. Vols. 1 and 2. Berlin, 1958.

Mohl, Robert von. "Über Auswanderung." *Zeitschrift für die gesammte Staatswissenschaft* 4 (1847): 320–49.

Moszkowski, Walter. *Bernhard Dernburg*. Berlin, 1908.

Naumann, Friedrich. *Mitteleuropa*. Berlin, 1915.

Noske, Gustav. *Kolonialpolitik und Sozialdemokratie*. Stuttgart, 1914.

Obst, Erich. *Die Vernichtung des deutschen Kolonialreichs in Afrika*. Berlin, 1921.

Pan-German League. *Zwanzig Jahre alldeutscher Arbeit und Kämpfe*. Berlin, 1910.

Peters, Carl. *Gesammelte Schriften*. Edited by Walter Frank. 3 vols. Munich, 1943.

————. *Die Gründung von Deutsch-Ostafrika*. Berlin, 1906.

————. *Zur Weltpolitik*. Berlin, 1912.

Pfeil und Klein-Ellguth, Joachim Friedrich, Graf von. *Die Erwerbung von Deutsch-Ostafrika: Ein Beitrag zur Kolonial-Geschichte*. Berlin, 1907.

Philippovich, Eugen von, ed. *Auswanderung und Auswanderungspolitik in Deutschland*. Leipzig, 1892.

Protokallischer Bericht über den am 16. Okt 1848 zu Frankfurt a. M. abgehaltenen Congress der Vereine für deutsche Auswanderung und Ansiedlung. Frankfurt am Main, 1848.

Puttkamer, Jesko von. *Gouverneursjahre in Kamerun*. Berlin, 1912.

Radlauer, Ernst Ludwig. *Die lokale Selbstverwaltung der kolonialen Finanzen*. Breslau, 1909.

Rathenau, Walther. *Die neue Gesellschaft*. Berlin, 1919.

————. *Die neue Wirtschaft*. Berlin, 1919.

————. *Tagebuch 1907–1922*. Edited by Hartmut Pogge von Strandmann. Düsseldorf, 1967.

Ratzel, Friedrich. *Wider die Reichsnörgler: Ein Wort zur Kolonialfrage aus Wählerkreisen*. Munich, 1884.

Rechenberg, Freiherr Albrecht von. "Kriegs- und Friedensziele." *Nord und Süd* 41 (1917): 131–43.

Rohrbach, Paul. *Dernburg und die Südwestafrikaner*. Berlin, 1911.

————. *Der deutsche Gedanke in der Welt*. Düsseldorf and Leipzig, 1912.

————. *Deutsche Kolonialwirtschaft: kulturpolitische Grundsätze für die Rassen- und Missionsfrage*. Berlin, 1909.

————. *Koloniale Siedlung und Wirtschaft der führenden Kolonialvölker*. Cologne, 1934.

————. *Die Kolonie*. Frankfurt am Main, 1907.

————. "Das Kriegsziel in Schützengraben." *Deutsche Politik*, 4 February 1916, pp. 241–48.

————. "Ostafrikanische Studien." *Preussische Jahrbücher* 135 (1909): 82–107, 276–317.

————. *Um des Teufels Handschrift: Zwei Menschenalter erlebter Weltgeschichte.* Hamburg, 1953.

————. *Wie machen wir unsere Kolonien rentabel?* Halle, 1907.

Roscher, Wilhelm, and Jannasch, Robert. *Kolonien, Kolonialpolitik und Auswanderung.* Leipzig, 1885.

SPD German Social Democratic Party. *Die deutsche Kolonialpolitik.* Berlin, 1907.

Samassa, Paul. *Die Besiedlung Deutsch-Ostafrikas.* Berlin, 1909.

Sander, Ludwig. *Geschichte der deutschen Kolonialgesellschaft für Südwest-Afrika von ihrere Gründung bis zum Jahre 1910.* 2 vols. Berlin, 1912.

Schäfer, Dietrich. *Kolonialgeschichte.* 2 vols. Berlin, 1921.

————. *Mein Leben.* Berlin, 1926.

Scharlach, Julius. *Koloniale und politische Aufsätze und Reden.* Berlin, no date.

Schmidt, Geo. A. *Das Kolonial-Wirtschaftliche Komitee.* Berlin, 1934.

Schmidt, Rochus. *Deutschlands Kolonien: ihre Gestaltung, Entwicklung und Hilfsquellen.* 2 vols. Berlin, 1895.

Schnee, Heinrich. *Als letzter Gouverneur in Deutsch-Ostafrika: Erinnerungen.* Heidelberg, 1964.

————. *Die deutschen Kolonien vor, in und nach dem Weltkrieg.* Leipzig, 1935.

————. ed. *Deutsches Kolonial-Lexikon.* 3 vols. Leipzig, 1920.

Schroeder-Poggelow, Wilhelm. *Unsere Afrika-politik in den letzten zwei Jahren.* Berlin, 1890.

Schütze, Woldemar. *Schwarz gegen Weiss: Die Eingeborenefrage als Kernpunkt unserer Kolonialpolitik in Afrika.* Berlin, 1908.

Schwabe, Kurd. *Der Krieg in Deutsch-Südwestafrika, 1904–1906.* Berlin, 1907.

Schwerin, Friedrich von. *Kriegersansiedlung vergangener Zeiten.* Leipzig, 1917.

Seidel, August. *Deutsch-Kamerun.* Berlin, 1906.

Seitz, Theodor. *Vom Aufstieg und Niederbruch deutscher Kolonialmacht.* 3 vols. Karlsruhe, 1929.

Sering, Max. *Die innere Kolonisation in östlichen Deutschland.* Leipzig, 1893.

————., ed. *Westrussland in seiner Bedeutung für die Entwicklung Mitteleuropas.* Leipzig, 1917.

Solf, Wilhelm H. *Germany's Right to Recover Her Colonies.* Berlin, 1919.

————. *Kolonialpolitik: Mein politisches Vermächtnis.* Berlin, 1919.

————. *Die Lehren des Weltkrieges für unsere Kolonialpolitik.* Stuttgart and Berlin, 1916.

Tesch, Johannes. *Die Laufbahn der deutschen Kolonialbeamter.* Berlin, 1902.

Treitschke, Heinrich von. *Politics.* Translated by B. Dugdale and T. de Bille. 2 vols. London, 1916.

Trierenberg, Georg. *Togo: Die Aufrichtung der deutschen Schutzherrschaft und die Erschliessung des Landes.* Berlin, 1914.

Vietor, J. K. von. *Wirtschaftliche und kulturelle Entwicklung unserer Schutzgebiete.* Berlin, 1913.

Virchow, Rudolf. *Sozialismus und Reaktion.* Berlin, 1878.

Walthemath, Kuno. "Vergesst die Kolonien nicht!" *Preussische Jahrbücher* 161 (1916):26–48.

Weber, Ernst von. *Die Erweiterung des deutschen Wirtschaftsgebiets und die Grundlegung zu überseeischen deutschen Staaten.* Leipzig, 1879.

Weber, Hans Siegfried. *Ansiedlung von Kriegsinvaliden.* Berlin, 1916.

_____. *Rucksi edlung Auslanddeutscher nach dem Deutschen Reich.* Jena, 1915.

Werner, C. von. *Antrag des Abgeordneten v. Werner, die Bildung eines Emigrations- und Colonisations-Verein betreffend.* No place, no date (c. 1840).

Wirth, Moritz, ed. *Kleine Schriften von Dr. Carl Rodbertus-Jagetzow.* Berlin, 1890.

Wohltmann, F. *Die nationale und ethische Bedeutung unserer Kolonien.* Berlin, 1908.

Zimmermann, Adolf. *Mit Dernburg nach Ostafrika.* Berlin, 1908.

Zimmermann, Alfred. *Geschichte der Deutschen Kolonialpolitik.* Berlin, 1914.

Zimmermann, Emil. *Die Bedeutung Afrikas für die deutsche Weltpolitik.* Berlin, 1917.

_____. *Die deutsche Kaiserreich Mittelafrikas als Grundlag einer neuen deutschen Weltpolitik.* Berlin, 1917.

_____. *Kann uns Mesopotamien eigene Kolonien ersetzen?* Berlin, 1917.

_____. *Neu-Kamerun: Reiseerlebnisse und wirtschaftspolitische Untersuchungen.* Berlin, 1913.

IV. SECONDARY SOURCES

Anderson, Pauline Relyea. *The Background of Anti-English Feeling in Germany, 1890–1902.* Washington, 1939.

Austen, Ralph A. *Northwest Tanzania under German and British Rule: Colonial Policy and Tribal Politics, 1889–1939.* New Haven, Ct., 1968.

Aydelotte, William O. *Bismarck and British Colonial Policy; The Problem of South West Africa, 1883–1885.* Philadelphia, 1937.

Bald, Detlef. *Deutsch-Ostafrika, 1900–1914.* Munich, 1970.

Barkin, Kenneth D. *The Controversy over German Industrialization, 1890–1902*. Chicago, 1970.

Basler, Werner. *Deutschlands Annexionspolitik in Polen und im Baltikum, 1914–1918*. Berlin, 1962.

Bley, Helmut. *South-West Africa under German Rule, 1894–1914*. Translated by Hugh Ridley. Evanston, Ill., 1971. Original German edition, 1968.

Böhm, Hermann. *Carl Peters, der Begründer von Deutsch Ostafrika*. Leipzig, 1939.

Böhme, Helmut. "Big Business, Pressure Groups, and Bismarck's Turn to Protectionism, 1873–1879." *Historial Journal* 10 (1967): 224–35.

————. *Deutschlands Weg zur Grossmacht: Studien zum Verhältnis von Wirtschaft und Staat während der Reichsgründungszeit, 1848–1881*. Cologne, 1966.

Bridgman, Jon, and Clarke, David E. *German Africa: A Select Annotated Bibliography*. Stanford, Calif., 1965.

Brunschwig, Henri. *L'expansion allemande outre-mer du xve siècle à nos jours*. Paris, 1957.

Cecil, Lamar. *Albert Ballin: Business and Politics in Imperial Germany*. Princeton, N.J., 1967.

Chéradame, André. *La colonisation et les colonies allemandes*. Paris, 1905.

Collins, Robert O. "Origins of the Nile Struggle: Anglo-German Negotiations and the Mackinnon Agreement of 1890." In *Britain and Germany in Africa: Imperial Rivalry and Colonial Rule*, edited by Prosser Gifford and Wm. Roger Louis, pp. 119–51. New Haven and London, 1967.

Conze, Werner. *Polnische Nation und deutsche Politik im ersten Weltkrieg*. Cologne, 1958.

Cornevin, Robert. "The Germans in Africa before 1918." In *Colonialism in Africa, 1870–1960*, edited by L. H. Gann and Peter Duignan. Vol. 1, *The History and Politics of Colonialism, 1870–1914*, pp. 383–419. Cambridge, 1964.

————. *Histoire du Togo*. 3d ed. Paris, 1969.

Coupland, Reginald. *The Exploitation of East Africa, 1856–1890: The Slave Trade and the Scramble*. Evanston, Ill., 1967.

Craig, Gordon A. *The Politics of the Prussian Army*. New York, 1964.

Crothers, George Dunlop. *The German Elections of 1907*. New York, 1941.

Crowe, Sybil Eyre. *The Berlin West African Conference, 1884–1885*. London, 1942.

Dahrendorf, Ralf. *Society and Democracy in Germany*. Garden City, N.Y., 1969.

Decharme, Pierre. *Compagnies et sociétés coloniales allemandes*. Paris, 1903.

Drechsler, Horst. "Jacob Morenga: A New Kind of Southwest African Leader." In *Études africaines. African Studies. Afrika-Studien*, edited by Walter Markov, pp. 95–105. Leipzig, 1967.

———. *Südwestafrika unter deutscher Kolonialherrschaft*. Berlin, 1966.

Epstein, Klaus W. *Matthias Erzberger and the Dilemma of German Democracy*. Princeton, N.J., 1959.

Esterhuyse, J. H. *South West Africa, 1880–94: The Establishment of German Authority in South West Africa*. Cape Town, 1968.

Firth, S. G. "The New Guinea Company, 1885–1899: A Case of Unprofitable Imperialism." *Historical Studies* 15 (1972): 361–77.

Fischer, Fritz. *Germany's Aims in the First World War*. New York, 1967. Original German edition, 1961.

———. *Krieg der Illusionen: Die deutsche Politik von 1911 bis 1914*. Düsseldorf, 1969.

Full, August. *Fünfzig Jahre Togo*. Berlin, 1935.

Funke, Alfred. *Carl Peters: Der Mann, der Deutschland ein Imperium schaffen wollte*. Berlin, 1937.

Geiss, Imanuel. *Der polnische Grenzstreifen, 1914–1918*. Lübeck, 1960.

Gifford, Prosser, and Louis, Wm. Roger, eds. *Britain and Germany in Africa: Imperial Rivalry and Colonial Rule*. New Haven, Ct., and London, 1967.

Gilson, R. P. *Samoa, 1830 to 1900: The Politics of a Multi-Cultural Community*. Melbourne, 1970.

Gordon, Michael R. "Domestic Conflict and the Origins of the First World War: The British and German Cases." *The Journal of Modern History* 46 (1974): 191–226.

Hagemann, Walter. *Die Revisionen der Kolonialmethoden in Afrika*. Münster, 1929.

Hagen, Maximilian von. *Bismarcks Kolonialpolitik*. Stuttgart, 1923.

Hallgarten, George W. F. *Imperialismus vor 1914*. 2 vols. Munich, 1951.

Hamerow, Theodore S. *Restoration, Revolution, Reaction: Economics and Politics in Germany, 1815–1871*. Princeton, N.J., 1958.

———. *The Social Foundations of German Unification, 1858–1871*. 2 vols. Princeton, N.J., 1969, 1972.

Hansen, Marcus L. *German Schemes of Colonization before 1860*. Northampton, Mass., 1923–24.

Hargreaves, John D. *Prelude to the Partition of West Africa*. London, 1963.

Hausen, Karin. *Deutsche Kolonialherrschaft in Afrika: Wirtschaftsinteressen und Kolonialverwaltung in Kamerun vor 1914*. Zurich, 1970.

Heffter, Heinrich. *Die deutsche Selbstverwaltung im 19. Jahrhundert*. Stuttgart, 1950.

Henderson, W. O. "German East Africa 1884–1918." In *History of East Africa*, edited by Vincent Harlow and E. M. Chilver, vols. 2. Oxford, 1965.

———. *Studies in German Colonial History*. Chicago, 1962.

Hildebrand, Klaus. *Vom Reich zum Weltreich. NSDAP und koloniale Frage 1919–1945*. Munich, 1969.

Hirsch, Helmut, ed. *August Bebel: Sein Leben in Dokumenten, Reden und Schriften*. Cologne, 1968.

Hollborn, Hajo. *A History of Modern Germany, 1840–1945*. New York, 1969.

Holst, Meno. *Lüderitz emkämpft Südwest*. Berlin, 1941.

Iliffe, John. *Tanganyika under German Rule, 1905–1912*. Cambridge, 1969.

Jäckh, Ernst, ed. *Kiderlen Wächter der Staatsmann und Mensch*. 2 vols. Stuttgart, 1924.

Jaeger, Hans. *Unternehmer in der deutsche Politik, 1890–1918*. Bonn, 1967.

Jarausch, Konrad H. *The Enigmatic Chancellor: Bethmann Hollweg and the Hubris of Imperial Germany*. New Haven, Ct., and London, 1973.

Kaeble, Hartmut. *Industrelle Interessenpolitik in der wilhelmischen Gesellschaft. Centralverband deutscher Industrieller, 1885–1914*. Berlin, 1967.

Kehr, Eckart. *Schlachtflottenbau und Parteipolitik, 1894–1901*. Berlin, 1930.

Kennedy, Paul M. *The Samoan Tangle: A Study in Anglo-German-American Relations, 1878–1900*. New York, 1974.

Kienitz, Ernst. *Zeittafel zur deutschen Kolonialgeschichte*. Munich, 1941.

Klamper, Erich zu. *Carl Peters, ein deutsches Schicksal um Ostafrika*. Berlin, 1938.

Klemperer, Klemens von. *Germany's New Conservatism*. Princeton, N.J., 1957.

Knoll, Arthur Joseph. "Taxation in the Gold Coast Colony and Togo: A Study in Early Administration." In *Britain and Germany in Africa: Imperial Rivalry and Colonial Rule*, edited by Prosser Gifford and Wm. Roger Louis, pp. 417–53. New Haven, Ct., and London, 1967.

———. "Togo under German Administration, 1884–1910." Ph.D. dissertation, Yale University, 1964.

Krätschell, Hermann. *Carl Peters, 1856–1918: Ein Beitrag zur Publizistik des imperialistischen Nationalismus in Deutschland*. Berlin, 1959.

Krieger, Leonard. *The German Idea of Freedom: History of a Political Tradition*. Boston, 1957.

Kruck, Alfred. *Geschichte des alldeutschen Verbandes*. Wiesbaden, 1954.

Lebovics, Hermann. *Social Conservatism and the Middle Classes in Germany, 1914–1933*. Princeton, N.J., 1969.

Leutwein, Paul. *Karl Peters*. Lübeck, 1943.

Loth, Heinrich. *Griff nach Ostafrika: Politik des deutschen Imperialismus und antikolonialer Kampf, Legende und Wirklichkeit*. Berlin, 1968.

Louis, Wm. Roger. *Ruanda-Urundi, 1884–1919*. Oxford, 1963.

Lütge, Friedrich. *Deutsche Sozial- und Wirtschaftsgeschichte*. Berlin, 1952.

Markov, Walter, ed. *Études africaines. African Studies. Afrika-Studien*. Leipzig, 1967.

Metzger, O. F. *Unsere alte Kolonie Togo*. Neudamm, 1941.

Meyer, Henry Cord. *Mitteleuropa in German Thought and Action, 1815–1945*. The Hague, 1955.

Mosse, George L. *The Crisis of German Ideology: Intellectual Origins of the Third Reich*. New York, 1964.

Müller, Fritz Ferdinand. *Deutschland-Zanzibar-Ostafrika: Geschichte einer deutschen Kolonialeroberung*. Berlin, 1959.

––––––., ed. *Kolonien unter der Peitsche*. Berlin, 1962.

Nahmer-Köln, Ernst von der. "Deutsche Kolonisationspläne in der Türkei vor 1870." *Jahrbuch für Gesetzgebung, Verwaltung und Volkswirtschaft im Deutschen Reich* 40 (1916): 387–448.

Newbury, Colin. "Partition, Development, Trusteeship: Colonial Secretary Wilhelm Solf's West African Journey, 1913." In *Britain and Germany in Africa: Imperial Rivalry and Colonial Rule*, edited by Prosser Gifford and Wm. Roger Louis, pp. 455–77. New Haven, Ct., and London, 1967.

––––––. *The Western Slave Coast and its Rulers*. Oxford, 1961.

Nussbaum, Manfred. *Togo–eine Musterkolonie?* Berlin, 1962.

––––––. *Vom "Kolonialenthusiasmus" zur Kolonialpolitik der Monopole: Zur deutschen Kolonialpolitik unter Bismarck, Caprivi, Hohenlohe*. Berlin, 1962.

Oelhafen von Schöllenbach, Hans. *Die Besiedlung Deutschsüdwestafrikasbos zi, Weltkriege*. Berlin, 1926.

Oliver, Roland. *The Missionary Factor in East Africa*. London, 1952.

Pehl, Hans. *Die deutsche Kolonialpolitik und das Zentrum, 1884–1914*. Lemburg, 1934.

Pierard, Richard Victor. "The German Colonial Society, 1882–1914." Ph.D. dissertation, State University of Iowa, 1964.

Pogge von Strandmann, Hartmut J. "Domestic Origins of Germany's Colonial Expansion under Bismarck." *Past and Present* 42 (1969): 140–59.

––––––. "The German Colonial Office and its Foreign Politics in the Dernburg Era, 1907–1910." Mimeograph, no date.

––––––. "The German Role in Africa and German Imperialism: A Review Article." *African Affairs* 69 (1970): 381–89.

––––––. "A Place in the Sun." *Twentieth Century History* 12 (1968): 332–36.

––––––. and Smith, Alison. "The German Empire in Africa and British Perspectives: A Historiographical Essay." In *Britain and Germany in Africa: Imperial Rivalry and Colonial Rule*, edited by Prosser Gifford and Wm. Roger Louis, pp. 709–95. New Haven, Ct., and London, 1967.

Puhle, Hans-Jürgen. *Agarische Interessenpolitik und preussischer Konservatismus*. Hannover, 1966.

Ringer, Fritz. *The Decline of the German Mandarins: The German Academic Community, 1890–1933*. Cambridge, Mass., 1969.

Robinson, Ronald, and Gallagher, John. *Africa and the Victorians*. London, 1961.

Röhl, J. C. G. "The Disintegration of the *Kartell* and the Politics of Bismarck's Fall from Power, 1887–90." *Historical Journal* 9 (1966): 60–89.

————. *Germany without Bismarck: The Crisis of Government in the Second Reich, 1890–1900*. Berkeley and Los Angeles, 1967.

Rohr, Donald G. *The Origins of Social Liberalism in Germany*. Chicago, 1963.

Rosenberg, Hans. *Grosse Depression und Bismarckzeit: Wirtschaftsablauf, Gesellschaft und Politik in Mitteleuropa*. Berlin, 1967.

Rotberg, Robert I. "Resistance and Rebellion in British Nyasaland and German East Africa, 1888–1915: A Tentative Comparison." In *Britain and Germany in Africa: Imperial Rivalry and Colonial Rule*, edited by Prosser Gifford and Wm. Roger Louis, pp. 667–90. New Haven, Ct., and London, 1967.

Rudin, Harry R. *Germans in the Cameroons, 1884–1914: A Case Study in Modern Imperialism*. New Haven, Ct., 1938.

Schieffel, Werner. *Bernhard Dernburg, 1865–1937: Kolonialpolitiker und Bankier in wilhelmischen Deutschland*. Zurich and Freiburg, 1974.

Schmidt, Rochus. *Hermann von Wissmann und Deutschlands koloniales Wirken*. Berlin, 1925.

Schmokel, Wolfe W. *Dream of Empire: German Colonialism, 1919–1945*. New Haven, Ct., 1964.

Schramm, Percy Ernst. *Deutschland und Übersee*. Brunswick, 1950.

————. *Hamburg, Deutschland, und die Welt*. Munich, 1943.

Schrecker, John E. *Imperialism and Chinese Nationalism: Germany in Shantung*. Cambridge, Mass., 1971.

Schröder, Hans-Christoph. *Sozialismus und Imperialismus: Die Auseinandersetzung der deutschen Sozialdemokratie mit dem Imperialismusproblem und "der Weltpolitik" vor 1914*. Hannover, 1968.

Schüssler, Wilhelm. *Adolf Lüderitz: Ein deutscher Kampf um Südafrika, 1883–86*. Bremen, 1936.

Schwarze, Fritz. *Das deutsch-englische Abkommen über die portuguiesischen Kolonien vom 30. August 1898*. Göttingen, 1931.

Sevin, Ludwig. "Die Entwicklung von Friedrich Lists kolonial- und weltpolitischen Ideen bis zum Pläne einer englischen Allianz 1846." *Jahrbuch für Gesetzgebung* 31 (1909): 1673–1715.

Sieveking, Heinrich. *Karl Sieveking, 1787–1847*. Hamburg, 1928.

Smith, Woodruff D. "The Ideology of German Colonialism, 1840–1906," *Journal of Modern History* 46 (1974): 641–62.

Spellmeyer, Hans. *Deutsche Kolonialpolitik im Reichstag*. Stuttgart, 1931.

Spidle, Jake Wilton, Jr. "Colonial Studies in Imperial Germany." *History of Education Quarterly* 13 (1973): 231–47.

————. "The German Colonial Service: Organization, Selection, and Training." Ph.D. dissertation, Stanford University, 1972.

Spiethoff, Arthur. *Die wirtschaftlichen Wechsellagen: Aufschwung, Krise, Stockung*. 2 vols. Tübingen and Zurich, 1955.

Steinberg, Jonathan. *Yesterday's Deterrent: Tirpitz and the Birth of the German Battle Fleet*. New York, 1965.

Stern, Fritz. *Gold and Iron: Bismarck, Bleichröder, and the Building of the German Empire*. New York, 1977.

————. *The Politics of Cultural Despair*. New York, 1965.

————. *The Failure of Illiberalism*. New York, 1972.

Stillich, Oskar. *Die politische Parteien in Deutschland*. Vol. 2, *Der Liberalismus*. Leipzig, 1911.

Stoecker, Helmuth. *Deutschland und China im 19. Jahrhundert*. Berlin, 1958.

————. "The Expansionist Policy of Imperialist Germany in Africa South of the Sahara, 1908–1918." In *Etudes africaines. African Studies. Afrika-Studien*, edited by Walter Markov. Leipzig, 1967.

————, ed. *Kamerun unter deutscher Kolonialherrschaft*. 2 vols. Berlin, 1960, 1968.

Stolper, Gustav. *The German Economy, 1870–1940*. New York, 1940.

Taylor, A. J. P. *Germany's First Bid for Colonies, 1884–1885*. London, 1938.

Tetzlaff, Rainer. *Koloniale Entwicklung und Ausbeutung: Wirtschafts- und Sozialgeschichte Deutsch-Ostafrikas, 1885–1914*. Berlin, 1970.

Townsend, Mary E. *The Origins of Modern German Colonialism, 1871–1885*. New York, 1921.

————. *The Rise and Fall of Germany's Colonial Empire, 1884–1918*. New York, 1930.

Turner, Henry Ashby, Jr. "Bismarck's Imperialist Venture: Anti-British in Origin?" In *Britain and Germany in Africa: Imperial Rivalry and Colonial Rule*, edited by Prosser Gifford and Wm. Roger Louis. New Haven, Ct., and London, 1967.

Vedder, Heinrich. *South West Africa in Early Times*. Oxford, 1938.

Vietsch, Eberhard von. *Wilhelm Solf: Botschafter zwischen den Zeiten*. Tübingen, 1961.

Walker, Mack. *Germany and the Emigration, 1816–1885*. Cambridge, Mass., 1964.

Washausen, Helmut. *Hamburg und die Kolonialpolitik des Deutschen Reiches, 1880 bis 1890*. Hamburg, 1968.

Wehler, Hans-Ulrich. *Bismarck und der Imperialismus*. Cologne, 1969.

Wehner, Siegfried. *Der alldeutsche Verband und die deutsche Kolonialpolitik der Vorkriegszeit.* Berlin-Steglitz, 1935.

Wernecke, Klaus. *Der Wille zur Weltgeltung: Aussenpolitik und Offentlichkeit im Kaiserreich am Vorabend des ersten Weltkrieg.* Düsseldorf, 1970.

Wertheimer, Mildred S. *The Pan-German League, 1890–1914.* New York, 1924.

Wheeler-Bennett, J. W. *Brest-Litovsk: The Forgotten Peace.* London, 1938.

Willequet, Jacques. *Le Congo belge et la Weltpolitik.* Brussells, 1962.

Wingenroth, Carl G. *Deutscher und englischer "Imperialismus" vor dem Weltkrieg.* Bottrop, 1934.

Wirz, Albert. *Vom Sklavenhandel zum kolonialen Handel: Wirtschaftsräume und Wirtschaftsformen in Kamerun vor 1914.* Zurich and Freiburg, 1972.

Wright, Marcia. *German Missions in Tanganyika, 1891–1941: Lutherans and Moravians in the Southern Highlands.* Oxford, 1971.

―――. "Local Roots of Policy in German East Africa." *Journal of African History* 9 (1968): 621–30.

V. PERIODICALS

Alldeutsche Blätter. Mitteilungen des Alldeutschen Verbandes.

Deutsche Kolonialzeitung.

Deutsche Politik.

Deutsches Kolonialblatt.

Koloniale Rundschau.

Nord und Süd.

Norddeutsche Allgemeine Zeitung.

Preussische Jarbücher.

Der Tropenpflanzer.

Index